POLICE AND POLICING
An Introduction

Richard J. Lundman
The Ohio State University

HOLT, RINEHART AND WINSTON
*New York   Chicago   San Francisco   Dallas   Montreal   Toronto   London
Sydney*

To
Jean, Bobby, and Julie Lundman and
John P. Clark and Richard E. Sykes

Library of Congress Cataloging in Publication Data

Lundman, Richard J 1944–
  Police and policing.

  Includes index.
  1. Police. I. Title.
HV7921.L86   363.2   70–20124
ISBN 0–03–042551–4

ACKNOWLEDGMENTS

Grateful acknowledgment is made for the following material:
1. Table on p. 129 is reprinted from Donald Black, "Production of Crime Rates," *American Sociological Review, 35* (August 1970), p. 748. Copyright © 1970 by The American Sociological Association. Reprinted with permission of author and publisher.
2. Table on p. 128 is reprinted from Donald Black and Albert J. Reiss, Jr., "Police Control of Juveniles," *American Sociological Review, 35* (February 1970), p. 75. Copyright © 1970 by The American Sociological Association. Reprinted with permission of authors and publishers.
3. Table on p. 92 is reprinted by permission of the *Journal of Police Science and Administration,* copyright 1977 by the International Association of Chiefs of Police, Inc., Vol. 5, No. 4, p. 459.
4. Tables on pp. 115 and 129 are from Richard J. Lundman, "Routine Police Arrest Practices: A Commonweal Perspective," *Social Problems, 22* (Fall 1974), p. 135. Copyright © 1974 by The Society for the Study of Social Problems. Reprinted with permission of author and publisher.
5. Table on p. 130 from "Organizational Norms and Police Discretion: An Observational Study of Police Work with Traffic Law Violators," by Richard J. Lundman is reprinted from *Criminology,* Vol. 17, No. 2 (August 1979) by permission of the publisher, Sage Publications, Inc.
6. Table on p. 130 is from Richard J. Lundman, Richard E. Sykes, and John P. Clark, "Police Control of Juveniles: A Replication," *Journal of Research in Crime and Delinquency, 15* (January 1978), p. 86. Copyright © 1978 by the National Council on Crime and Delinquency. Reprinted by permission of authors and publisher.
7. Quotes by William Ker Muir on pp. 80–81, 98, 119, 120–21, 138, and 194–195 are from William Ker Muir, *Police: Streetcorner Politicians.* Chicago: The University of Chicago Press, 1977. Copyright © 1977 by The University of Chicago Press. Reprinted by permission of author and publisher.
8. Table on p. 128 is from Irving Piliavin and Scott Briar, "Police Encounters with Juveniles," *American Journal of Sociology, 70* (September 1964), p. 210. Copyright © 1970 by The University of Chicago Press. Reprinted by permission of first author and publisher.
9. Tables on pp. 120 and 121 are from Albert J. Reiss, Jr., *The Police and the Public.* New Haven: Yale University Press, 1971, p. 50. Copyright © 1971 by the Yale University Press. Adapted and reprinted with permission of author and publisher.
10. Quotes by James F. Richardson on pp. 14, 20, 23, 24, 25, 29, 31, and 33 are from James F. Richardson, *The New York Police: Colonial Times to 1901.* New York: Oxford University Press, 1970. Copyright © 1970 by Oxford University Press. Reprinted with permission of publisher.
11. Selections from *City Police* by Jonathan Rubinstein (on pp. 28, 43–44, 53, 60, 62, 83, and 159) are reprinted with the permission of Farrar, Straus and Giroux, Inc., and International Creative Management. Copyright © 1973 by Jonathan Rubinstein.

12. Table on p. 123 is from Richard E. Sykes and John P. Clark, "Deference Exchange in Police–Civilian Encounters," *American Journal of Sociology, 81* (November 1975), p. 593. Copyright © 1975 by The University of Chicago Press. Reprinted with permission of authors and publisher.
13. Table on p. 129 is from *The Ambivalent Force: Perspectives on Police* by Arthur Niederhoffer and Abraham Blumberg. Copyright © 1976 by The Dryden Press, a division of Holt, Rinehart and Winston. Reprinted by permission of Holt, Rinehart and Winston.
14. Table on p. 158 is reprinted from *Violence and the Police* by William A. Westley, p. 122, by permission of The MIT Press, Cambridge, Massachusetts, and the author. Copyright © 1970 by The MIT Press.
15. Table on p. 117 is from Mary Glenn Wiley and Terry L. Hudik, "Police–Citizen Encounters: A Field Test of Exchange Theory," *Social Problems, 22* (October 1974), p. 124. Copyright © 1974 by The Society for the Study of Social Problems. Reprinted with permission of authors and publisher.

PREFACE

This book is an introduction to police and policing, one which is comprehensive rather than parochial. It stresses that many social science disciplines share an ability to free persons from inaccurate or narrow images about police and policing. It emphasizes that sociology gathers additional strength as it utilizes the ideas and information sets of the other social science disciplines concerned with police and policing, principally criminal justice, political science, criminology, public administration, psychology, and history. It also stresses that sociology offers a rich and continuous conceptual and empirical resource for the study of police and policing. This book is a sociological introduction which seeks synthesis rather than exclusion.

The chapters of the book reflect this synthesizing or multidisciplinary approach. They include a general introduction, the history of the police idea, structural analysis of police organizations, social-psychological explanation of police socialization, and conceptually guided analyses of routine policing, police misconduct, and control of police and policing. Each chapter combines the ideas and information sets of a number of social science disciplines.

My reasons for writing the book are both academic and personal. The academic motivation derives from a belief that we as social scientists know a great deal more about police and policing than we did just a short time ago. This growth in knowledge has occurred in a variety of social science fields. No one discipline has anything near a monopoly on knowledge about police and policing. But we often write and sometimes teach as if that were the case. This book seeks to demonstrate that we can write more accurately and comprehensively if we move across rather than within disciplines.

The personal motivation stems from the thousands of hours I have spent observing, questioning, and teaching police officers. Almost always as a social scientist and occasionally as a friend, I have observed and interviewed in squad cars, precinct stations, and over beer after a shift. I have taught at universities and at police academies. This book seeks to present what I learned during those many hours, the compassion and sometimes the brutality, in a responsible and generalizable manner.

The book is intended for several audiences. Instructors in criminal justice, sociology, political science, and criminology departments should find the book useful. Most of these departments offer courses devoted exclusively or in large part to police and policing. It is believed that this book, because of its multidisciplinary approach, will prove helpful.

Most of the same departments, as well as others such as public administration and history, offer courses which include police and policing as one of several topics. I believe that this book, because of its comprehensiveness and length, will be a valuable supplement.

The book also is directed at social scientists and police administrators. For social scientists, the book has been extensively researched and documented. It also advances a perspective on police and policing which can stimulate and guide research. For police administrators, it provides a comprehensive description of contemporary policing and analysis of opportunities for change.

The debts I incurred in writing this book are extensive. Jean Planty Lundman provided intellectual stimulation as well as a needed sense of perspective. Our children, Bobby and Julie, also helped and for a while gave me more than I gave them. John P. Clark and Richard E. Sykes aroused my interest in police and policing some ten years ago. At that time they were kind mentors and are now good friends. I continue to learn from them. Frank Graham, my editor, expressed confidence throughout the writing process, something I needed very much. Randall Walker and M. David Ermann read the earliest version of the manuscript and pointed me in the right direction. William Sanders, Gary Holton, Richard Farmer, and Hugh Barlow read later versions and insisted that they be academically sound and readable. Professors Sanders and Barlow were especially helpful in this latter respect. Kenneth Eckhardt read the penultimate draft of the final chapter and, as he has done so often in the past, provided invaluable assistance. The typists in the sociology department at Ohio State, especially Marsha Nicol, Laurie Taress, Inez Brown, and Cindy Brown, typed and retyped, patiently, professionally, and sympathetically. Robin Gross provided needed editorial assistance and helped see the book into print. Students in my university and police academy classes heard and criticized nearly all of the ideas presented in this book. Hundreds of police officers gave of their time and insight as they allowed me to observe and ask about their work. I thank all of you very much.

Richard J. Lundman

Worthington, Ohio
September 1979

CONTENTS

CHAPTER 1

Police and Policing

INTRODUCTION

Police patrol officers are a familiar sight in contemporary society. They patrol in easily identified cars, direct traffic at downtown intersections, answer our requests to restore order, and respond to our more urgent calls as victims of criminal incidents. They also appear out of nowhere to stop us for traffic law violations.

The entertainment industry has helped contribute to the seeming familiarity of the police patrol officer. Popular novels such as Joseph Wambaugh's *The Blue Knight* and *The Choirboys* provide accounts of the work and recreation of the patrol officer.[1] And the television and motion picture industries have produced a host of police and police-related programs and movies.

This familiarity, however, may be misleading in presenting incomplete and inaccurate images of police and policing. Consider the nature of police patrol work and some of the ways in which our own experiences may be deceptive. For many of us, contact with a police patrol officer has been limited to our being stopped for a traffic law violation. Our embarrassment at being stopped, along with our belief that the police officer's time could be better spent "fighting crime," generally produces feelings of resentment and antagonism.

It is possible that we would feel differently if we were to observe some of the other things police patrol officers do. It is possible that our feelings of resentment might be less if we were to observe a patrol officer frantically attempt to breath life into the body of a dying child and then watch the officer's silent tears as the child died. Perhaps we would be more sympathetic if we watched as a patrol officer helped pack a "ripe" DOA into a coroner's rubber bag. Few of us have been able to observe these other activities.

The entertainment industry has done little to improve our images of police and policing. Based upon their portrayals, it seems reasonable to conclude that crime-related chases, fights, and use of weapons are frequent activities for patrol officers. These things happen, but not very often.[2] Far more frequent than chases is the refereeing of disputes between husbands and wives, landlords and tenants, and customers and proprietors. More often than fighting are the responses to our requests to quiet the parties, televisions, radios, stereos, and barking dogs of neighbors. Instead of using weapons, police officers spend more hours gently helping the locked-out, the sick or injured, and the scared. Because these more ordinary activities have less commercial appeal, the entertainment industry devotes little attention to them.

It is wrong to base our images of police or policing on personal experiences or entertainment industry portrayals. Our personal experiences are sketchy and entertainment industry versions are biased. We must look elsewhere for complete and accurate views of police and policing.

The purpose of this book is to provide a sociological introduction to police and policing. It utilizes the ideas and informational resources of sociology and related disciplines to generate realistic images of this occupation. In this first chapter, we will describe the nature of sociology and preview the chapters which follow.

NATURE OF SOCIOLOGY

Sociology is but one of many social science disciplines whose members have studied and written about police and policing. Other fields concerned with law enforcement are criminal justice,[3] organizational psychology,[4] criminology,[5] psychology,[6] political science,[7] and anthropology.[8] What, then, are the advantages of developing a sociological introduction to police and policing?

Sociology as "Imagination"

Sociology shares with these other disciplines the ability to enlighten persons as to the real nature of police and policing. It discourages the retention of narrow preconceptions or firm convictions based upon limited personal experiences or misleading movies and television shows. Sociology stimulates determined search for general principles that can be supported by available evidence.

We will call this shared ability a "sociological imagination." C. Wright Mills has described several of the benefits of developing and applying a sociological imagination:

The sociological imagination is the most fruitful form of . . . self-conscious-
ness. By its use . . . (people) . . . whose mentalities have swept only a series of
limited orbits often come to feel as if suddenly awakened in a house which
they had only supposed themselves to be familiar. Correctly or incorrectly,
they often come to feel that they can now provide themselves with adequate
summations, cohesive assessments, comprehensive orientations. Older decisions that once appeared sound now seem to them products of a mind unac-
countably dense. Their capacity for astonishment is made lively again. They
acquire a new way of thinking, they experience a transvaluation of values:
in a word, by their reflection and by their sensibility, they realize the cultural
meaning of the social sciences.[9]

A sociological imagination is thus a promise. It promises alternatives to
fragmentary personal experiences and mass media portrayals. *This book
seeks to arouse a sociological imagination and it promises development of
complete and accurate images of police and policing.*

Sociology as Method

In addition to describing the promise of a sociological imagination,
Mills also was quick to describe its multidisciplinary method. He argued
that fundamental to the development of a sociological imagination is "the
capacity to shift from one perspective to another."[10] Mills specifically
stated that three general types of analysis must be undertaken: historical,
structural, and social psychological.[11]

Historical analysis seeks discovery of the ways in which a particular
aspect of reality has been shaped by earlier forces and events. In the
context of police and policing, we look for descriptions of the ways in
which the police function was fulfilled prior to the emergence of distinctly modern police organizations. We also are obligated to define the
forces which gave rise to police and policing as we know them.

Structural analysis sensitizes us to the ways in which general social
forces shape police organizations. We must discover the normative setting
of policing and describe the ways in which these expectations guide police
organizations. We also must consider the ways in which community
resources shape policing. Within police organizations, we must examine
the positive and negative consequences of bureaucratic structure on police
and policing.

Social psychological analysis directs our attention to the persons who
enact the contemporary police role. It seeks to determine how police
officers are "selected and formed, liberated and repressed, made sensitive
and blunted"[12] by their training and their work. In our study of police and
policing, we investigate the ways police departments select and socialize
new members. We must be sensitive to the ways in which selection,
socialization, and actual policing shape the "working personality"[13] char-

acteristic of the patrol officer. We also must be aware of changes in police socialization practices.

The sociological method is of necessity multidisciplinary. Historians, for instance, have devoted a great deal of careful attention to the origins of the police idea.[14] Political scientists have described and analyzed the social forces which shape police and policing.[15] Representatives of disciplines such as criminal justice and organizational psychology have examined and traced the effects of police socialization practices.[16]

This book recognizes and incorporates the ideas and informational resources of the other social science fields concerned with police and policing. It acknowledges and takes advantage of the concepts and data of disciplines such as history, political science, criminal justice, psychology, criminology, and urban anthropology. It also utilizes the contributions of persons in professions such as public administration and law.[17] *This book recognizes that development of integrated views of police and policing requires that sociology's method be multidisciplinary.*

Sociology as Resource

Sociology is not entirely dependent upon the ideas and informational resources of other disciplines. Sociologists also have studied police and policing and they have generated distinctly sociological concepts and informational resources. The results of these efforts are concentrated in three areas—routine policing, police misconduct, and control of police and policing.

Sociologists have devoted considerable attention to the study of routine policing.[18] And many of their findings are contrary to what might be expected. For instance, personal experiences and movie portrayals combine to suggest that police–citizen contacts frequently involve acts of violence, displays of temper, and impolite verbal exchanges. Sociological research results make it clear that police–citizen contacts are primarily polite and free of displays of anger and violence.[19] Sociology offers a rich and provocative resource for the study of routine policing.

Sociologists also have been attentive to the problem of police misconduct, principally corruption and unnecessary police force. Their explanations for these actions run contrary to those typically advanced. Most people blame immoral or sadistic officers—"bad apples"—for police corruption and brutality.[20] Recent sociological explanations emphasize the organizational origins of these actions; sociologists speak of corrupt departments rather than corrupt officers.[21] Sociology thus offers an alternative to existing images of the causes of improper police actions.

As a result of their research, sociologists have offered a variety of strategies for controlling police and policing. A number of researchers have emphasized the importance of making police accountable to civilians.[22]

Others have suggested the entry of persons with nonpolice backgrounds into administrative positions and the training of recruits in civilian settings.[23] Still other sociologists have stressed that revelations of scandal by the media are fundamental to effective reform.[24] These proposals for control are detailed and generally well supported. Sociology thus offers an important resource for addressing the problem of regulating police and policing.

However, sociologists have not limited themselves to the study of routine police work, police misbehavior, and control of police and policing. They have also devoted their attention to the analysis of the origins of the police idea,[25] as well as considering the social forces which shape police and policing.[26] And they have described and examined police socialization practices.[27] Sociological concepts and informational resources complement and enrich the ideas and findings of persons in disciplines such as history, political science, and psychology.

Sociology is not entirely dependent upon the insights and information of other disciplines. Specific sociological ideas and data are available and they constitute a rich resource. *This book demonstrates that sociology offers a rich and continuous resource for the study of police and policing.*

The advantages of developing a sociological introduction to police and policing are several. Sociology promises the development of a thorough understanding of police and policing. Sociology's method is multidisciplinary; it recognizes and incorporates the ideas and informational resources of other disciplines. Sociology offers a rich and continuous resource for the study of police and policing.

PREVIEW OF THE CHAPTERS

Having described sociology as imagination, method, and resource, it is entirely appropriate to ask whether these promises can be kept. Can sociology stimulate the full understanding of police and policing? Can sociology shift perspectives by combining the ideas and informational resources of a variety of social science disciplines? These are but two of the questions which arise from the preceding description of the nature of sociology. In the remainder of this chapter, sociology as imagination, method, and resource is illustrated by previewing the topics of the chapters which follow.

Historical Analysis: Origins of the Police Idea

The first modern police force was created by Sir Robert Peel in London in 1829.[28] In the United States, New York City went without a formal, police organization until 1845,[29] while Washington, D.C.'s police force was not created until 1861.[30] In Boston, full-time police were not appointed until 1838.[31] As compared to the more mundane agencies of municipal government which preceded police in many jurisdictions, including public health departments, animal control boards, and even firewood inspectors, police organizations are of relatively recent origin.

Historical analysis reveals several reasons for the relatively recent emergence of the modern police department. First, not all societies require a full-time police force accountable to a central government authority. In preindustrial societies, common attitudes and life experiences make it possible for citizens to share the police function. Second, even as the sharing of the police responsibility proved difficult in the wake of industrialization and increased crime, and as the possible need for full-time police was recognized, citizens resisted their creation. People were fearful of government and fearful of the "capacity for awareness" represented by organized police. The police idea was resisted long after the need for modern police was recognized.

Therefore, central to the emergence of a modern police force was the power to overcome the reluctance of a fearful citizenry. Powerful elites played a deciding role in the establishment of modern police:

> The history of social control in the United States is the history of transition from "constabulary to police society" . . . which . . . was not essentially for the protection of the " general welfare" of society but was for the protection of the interests and life-styles of but one segment of society—those holding positions of wealth, "respectability," and power.[32]

Structural Analysis: The Police Organization

Structural analysis reveals that police departments share three important characteristics with other large-scale organizations: a complex and contradictory normative environment, a variable clientele and resource base, and a bureaucratic structure. All have a profound influence on policing.

Sociologist Jerome Skolnick has ably described one aspect of the environment which surrounds police organizations. He notes that police are expected to maintain order, but they are expected to do so under the rule of law. Police must protect society against crime and other threats to civility while at the same time extending procedural safeguards to the persons responsible for crime and disorder. These contradictory expectations place "an unceasing burden upon the police as a social institution."[33]

Political scientist James Q. Wilson has identified the ways in which a community's resources influence styles of policing.[34] He states that in some communities, residents share a common life style, set of values, and level of affluence. In such a community policing is generally "service"-oriented, emphasizing counseling and referral rather than arrest. Residents in other communities do not share much in common with each other. In these communities, policing is either "watch" or "legalistic" in orientation, depending upon the orientation of top-level municipal and police administrators. In cities where these officials are part of a political machine, policing tends to be watch-oriented and emphasizes informal "street justice." In cities where governmental leaders are reform-oriented, law enforcement is legalistically oriented, stressing formal processing of nearly all criminal incidents.

The effects of bureaucratic structure also are profound. Bureaucracies represent a highly rational and efficient type of organization.[35] They feature official functions according to written rules, a clear division of labor, and hierarchical configuration. Bureaucratic structure facilitates routine policing, principally by linking needy citizens with available officers as mediated by the dispatch room. But it also hinders routine policing, forcing officers to lie in an effort to give an appearance of being efficient.

Social Psychological Analysis: Police Socialization

Police socialization is the process whereby new police officers learn the values, attitudes, and actions characteristic of their work group. Although it is a continuous process, it can be broken down into three general stages: selection, academy training, and early street experiences.

The single most important feature of contemporary police socialization is slow and uneven change. In the past, discriminatory selection procedures meant that nearly all police recruits were white and male.[36] Recruits also were high-school-educated because few colleges or universities offered criminal justice or police science programs. Recent congressional and court actions, along with the emergence of criminal justice and police science college programs, have brought demographic diversity to urban recruit classes. Currently, police recruits are female as well as male, black as well as white, and college as well as high school graduates.[37]

This same rate of change is characteristic of academy training and early street experiences. Until very recently, training was a quasi-military or stress experience featuring inflexible rules and harsh sanctions.[38] Currently, academy training is generally less stressful, with fewer rules and more counseling regarding their infraction.[39] And, in departments which offer nonstress training, early street experiences frequently represent an extension of the academy experience.[40]

Sociology as Resource: Routine Policing

Police patrol officers routinely deal with a wide variety of problems. Most are identified by citizens who use the telephone to call the police. The incidents range from barking dogs to silent alarms at grocery stores, most of which are of the former type.

Police patrol officers also encounter many different types of citizens. Some are scared, others are lost, many have been victimized, and some represent a serious danger to the well-being of the officer and other citizens who may be present. The majority are of the scared, lost, and victimized variety.

Police patrol officers engage in numerous actions and make a large number of decisions. They reassure the scared, help the lost, listen to the victimized, and confront the dangerous. Most actions and decisions are of the reassuring, helping, and listening kind.

In an effort to safely sort out problems, citizens, and decisions, police patrol officers develop and apply "typifications" and "recipes for action" in their work.[41] Typifications are general classifications of problems and citizens. Police patrol officers see themselves as handling two types of problems, and two types of citizens. Problems of the barking-dog variety are seen as part of a large, residual category of policing occasionally labelled "bullshit."[42] Silent-alarm incidents are placed in much a smaller class of events known as "real policing."

Citizens are placed by reference to a typification known as "attitude."[43] There are two types of attitude and thus two types of citizens. Citizens who are polite and respectful of police authority are said to have a "good attitude." Those who are impolite or indifferent to the police are characterized as having a "bad attitude."

Recipes for action are guidelines for behavior and they follow from these typifications. Police patrol officers respond slowly to calls not involving real policing with the hope that the problem will somehow disappear on its own.[44] Perhaps the barking dog will grow hoarse or the complainant deaf. Silent alarms and the other calls involving "real policing" are responded to quickly with emergency speed, signal lights, and siren.

Citizens' attitudes also shape police reactions. Those people having a good attitude are treated politely, and if they have violated the law in some minor way, they tend to be treated leniently. Those with a bad attitude are treated cautiously, impolitely, and formally.[45]

Sociology as Resource: Police Misconduct

Police patrol work is rich in opportunities for misconduct.[46] A small but important proportion of police time is spent attempting to enforce laws intended to define and control public morality—gambling, prostitution, and drug use. Because community sentiment regarding these actions is mixed, some citizens are willing to corrupt their police by offering individual police officers money or other favors in exchange for ignoring selected law violations. Additionally, patrol work occasionally requires the use of physical force to subdue a citizen or to make an arrest. But supervision of patrol officers is minimal and the citizens against whom force is used frequently are relatively powerless. An officer who is so inclined finds it both easy and safe to use unnecessary force. In both of these forms of misconduct—corruption and unnecessary force—it is clear that individual officers are involved, and the initial tendency is to focus on the characteristics of these persons.

There is, however, a great deal more to police misbehavior than individual pathology or immorality. William A. Westley was one of the first to encounter the extraindividualistic dimensions of police misconduct. In his early study of unnecessary police force, Westley had difficulty making sense of the fact that "decent, humble, urban men, usually with wives, children and small homes"[47] who expressed personal misgivings about excessive force to him were the *same* people who engaged in unnecessarily forceful activities out on the street—or were at least willing to remain silent about the needlessly violent actions of their colleagues. More recently, the attorneys who investigated police corruption in Chicago observed that even officers who were extensively involved were " . . . not bad . . . evil, or vicious . . . they'll buy you a beer, tell a joke, and offer to take your kid fishing."[48] It does not appear sufficient to attempt to explain police misconduct solely in terms of the characteristics of individual officers.

Sociological research reveals that extraindividualistic or social forces are operative in the context of police wrongdoing. Specifically, community and departmental characteristics, police training procedures, patterns of subcultural solidarity, and administrative attitudes must all be examined in order to fully understand police immorality. As police officer Thomas Barker and sociologist Julian Roebuck observe:

> Police . . . (misconduct) . . . is best understood, not as the exclusive deviant behavior of individual officers, but as group behavior guided by contradictory norms linked to the organization to which the erring individuals belong.[49]

Sociology as Resource: Controlling Police and Policing

Police organizations are a central feature of contemporary society. Patrol officers, as the primary representative of municipal police organizations, provide services not available or not constantly available from other agencies. Officers also respond to our requests to restore order as, for example, when we use the telephone to call the police about "rowdy" juveniles. And, police officers react to our more urgent requests as victims of criminal incidents. Much routine policing is thus effectively under the control of the citizenry whom a department is normatively mandated to serve.

This is generally not true of police misdeeds. Actions ranging from the "little lies" involved in the alteration of crime statistics to those such as police brutality escape direct citizen control. In the past, attempts at controlling police and policing have almost exclusively been individualistically oriented.[50] The search has been for the "bad apples' thought responsible for police misconduct. These strategies have not been successful. In New York,[51] Chicago, [52] and elsewhere,[53] misconduct and police have been synonymous for over a century despite repeated attempts to eradicate police deviance.

This dismal record of failure suggests the need for alternative solutions to the regulation of police and policing. One such possibility is clear recognition that many of the sources of police misconduct are external to police organizations. A potential solution, therefore, is to focus attention on controlling the external opportunities for impropriety.

SUMMARY

The chapters which follow provide a sociological introduction to police and policing. In each, sociology as imagination, method, and resource is illustrated. The search is for "adequate summations, cohesive assessments, comprehensive orientations."[54] We begin with a historical analysis of the origins of the police idea.

A Word About the Illustrations

Starting in the third chapter, you will note that certain points are illustrated using the actions and experiences of patrol officers in a number of cities. These observations have been drawn from my research experiences with police officers in seven different cities across the last eleven years. They are episodes I witnessed while riding with patrol officers as an unarmed, nonuniformed social science researcher. My research and writing interests were fully known to all the officers observed. At no time did I act as a police officer.

All of the officers and departments were promised anonymity and confidentiality. This promise is kept throughout the book, just as it has been kept in the past.[55] In order to help insure generalizability, illustrations are advanced only when other researchers have reported similar experiences.

Notes

1. Joseph Wambaugh, *The Blue Knight* (Boston: Atlantic Little, Brown, 1972) and *The Choirboys* (New York: Delacourt, 1975).

2. For a general discussion of the nature of police patrol work, see Joseph Livermore, "Policing," *Minnesota Law Review, 55* (1971): 651–665.

3. For example, Louis A. Radelet, *The Police and the Community,* 2nd ed. (Encino, Calif.:Glencoe Press, 1977).

4. For example, John Van Maanen, "Rookie Cops and Rookie Managers," *The Wharton Magazine* (Fall 1976): 1–7.

5. For example, George Kirkham, *Signal Zero* (New York: Ballantine, 1976).

6. For example, Jesse G. Rubin, "Police Identity and the Police Role," in Jack Goldsmith and Sharon S. Goldsmith (eds.), *The Police Community* (Pacific Palisades, Calif.: Palisades Publishers, 1974), pp. 122–153.

7. For example, William K. Muir, *Police: Streetcorner Politicians* (Chicago: University of Chicago Press, 1977).

8. For example, James P. Spradley, *You Owe Yourself a Drunk* (Boston: Little, Brown, 1970).

9. C. Wright Mills, *The Sociological Imagination* (New York: Oxford University Press, 1959), pp. 7–8.

10. Mills, *The Sociological Imagination,* p. 7.

11. Mills, *The Sociological Imagination,* pp. 6–7.

12. Mills, *The Sociological Imagination,* p. 7.

13. Jerome Skolnick, *Justice Without Trial* (New York: Wiley, 1966), pp. 42–70.

14. For example, James F. Richardson, *The New York Police: Colonial Times to 1901* (New York: Oxford University Press, 1970).

15. For example, James Q. Wilson, *Varieties of Police Behavior* (Cambridge, Mass.: Harvard University Press, 1968).

16. For example, John J. Broderick, *Police in a Time of Change* (Morristown, N.J.: General Learning Press, 1977), pp. 179–186; and John Van Maanen, "Rookie Cops."

17. For example, Herman Goldstein, *Policing in a Free Society* (Cambridge, Mass.: Ballinger, 1977); and Herbert Beigel and Allan Beigel, *Beneath the Badge: A Story of Police Corruption* (New York: Harper & Row, 1977).

18. For example, Albert J. Reis, Jr., *The Police and the Public* (New Haven, Conn.: Yale University Press, 1971).

19. See Richard J. Lundman, "Routine Police Arrest Practices: A Commonweal Perspective," *Social Problems, 22* (October 1974): 127–141; and Paul A. Pastor, Jr., "Mobilization in Public Drunkenness Control: A Comparison of Legal and Medical Approaches," *Social Problems, 25* (April 1978): 373–384.

20. For a description of this approach, see Ellwyn R. Stoddard, "The Informal 'Code' of Police Deviancy: A Group Approach to 'Blue-Coat' Crime," in Lawrence W. Sherman (ed.), *Police Corruption: A Sociological Perspective* (Garden City, N.Y.: Doubleday Anchor Books, 1974), pp. 278–280.

21. Lawrence W. Sherman, *Scandal and Reform: Controlling Police Corruption* (Berkeley, Calif.: University of California Press, 1978), pp. 3–29 and passim. Also see Stoddard, "The Informal 'Code.'"

22. Reiss, *The Police,* pp. 173–221.

23. Rodney Stark, *Police Riots* (Belmont, Calif.: Wadsworth, 1972), pp. 226–239.

24. Sherman, *Scandal and Reform,* pp. 59–91.

25. For example, Allan Silver, "The Demand for Order in Civil Society," in David J. Bordua (ed.), *The Police: Six Sociological Essays* (New York: Wiley, 1967), pp. 1–24.

26. For example, Peter K. Manning, *Police Work: The Social Organization of Policing* (Cambridge, Mass.: The M.I.T. Press, 1977), pp. 208–254 and passim.

27. Richard Harris, *The Police Academy: An Inside View* (New York: Wiley, 1973).

28. T.A. Critchley, *A History of Police in England and Wales, 900–1966* (London: Constable, 1967), pp. 47–57.

29. Richardson, *The New York Police.*

30. Kenneth G. Alfers, *The Washington Police: A History, 1800–1886* (unpublished Ph.D. dissertation, George Washington University, 1975).

31. Roger Lane, *Policing the City: Boston, 1822–1885* (Cambridge, Mass.: Harvard University Press, 1967).

32. Evelyn L. Parks, "From Constabulary to Police Society," *Catalyst, 5* (1970): 76.

33. Skolnick, *Justice Without Trial,* p. 9.

34. Wilson, *Varieties of Police Behavior.*

35. For a general discussion of bureaucracy, see Hans Gerth and C. Wright Mills (trans.), *From Max Weber: Essays in Sociology* (New York: Oxford University Press, 1946), pp. 329–341.

36. Stark, *Police Riots,* pp. 119–124.

37. Goldstein, *Policing,* pp. 267–268.

38. See Harris, *The Police Academy.*

39. Earle H. Howard, *Police Recruit Training: Stress vs. Non-Stress, A Revolution in Law Enforcement* (Springfield, Ill.: Charles C Thomas, 1973).

40. Muir, *Police,* p. 57.

41. For discussion of typifications and recipes for action, see David Sudnow, "Normal Crimes: Sociological Features of the Penal Code in a Public Defenders Office," in Richard Quinney (ed.), *Crime and Justice in Society* (Boston: Little, Brown, 1969), pp. 308–335.

42. For example, John Van Maanen, "Kinsmen in Repose: Occupational Perspectives of Patrolmen," in Peter K. Manning and John Van Maanen (eds.), *Policing: A View from the Streets* (Santa Monica, Calif.: Goodyear, 1978), p. 118.

43. Stark, *Police Riots,* pp. 61–62.

44. For example, Richard J. Lundman, "Domestic Police–Citizen Encounters," *Journal of Police Science and Administration, 2* (March 1974): 25.

45. Stark, *Police Riots,* pp. 61–62.

46. For a general discussion, see Thomas Barker and Julian Roebuck, *Police Corruption: A Study in Organizational Deviance* (Springfield, Ill.: Charles C Thomas, 1973).

47. William A. Westley, *Violence and the Police* (Cambridge, Mass.: The M.I.T. Press, 1970), p. x.

48. Beigel and Beigel, *Beneath the Badge,* p.x.

49. Barker and Roebuck, *Police Corruption,* p. 10. Also see Sherman, *Scandal and Reform;* and Stoddard, "The Informal 'Code.'"

50. For a discussion of this approach, see Gene H. Carte and Elaine H. Carte, *Police Reform in the United States: The Era of August Vollmer, 1905–1932* (Berkeley, Calif.: University of California Press, 1975).

51. See *The Knapp Commission Report on Police Corruption* (New York: Braziller, 1973), pp. 61–62.

52. See Mike Royko, *Boss: Richard J. Daley of Chicago* (New York: Signet, 1971), pp. 107–132; and Beigel and Beigel, *Beneath the Badge.*

53. See Sherman, *Scandal and Reform.*

54. Mills, *The Sociological Imagination,* p. 8.

55. See Richard J. Lundman and James C. Fox, "Maintaining Research Access in Police Organizations," *Criminology, 16* (May 1978): 87–98.

2

Origins of the
Police Idea

INTRODUCTION

Each year the Federal Bureau of Investigation publishes the *Uniform Crime Reports.* It contains counts of serious offenses known to and reported by local police authorities. Although it generally underestimates the actual volume of crime—by half in the case of most serious crimes against property[1]—reading it is an informative experience. In 1977, for instance, there were over 19,000 homicides reported, over a half million aggravated assaults, and almost 6 million larcenies.[2] The *Uniform Crime Reports* also contains a "crime clock" and it tells us that in 1977 there was a murder every 27 minutes, a rape every 8 minutes, an aggravated assault every 60 seconds, a robbery every 78 seconds, a burglary every 10 seconds, a larceny every five seconds, and an auto theft every 33 seconds. In the time it took you to read this paragraph, approximately three burglaries, six larcenies, and one auto theft occurred. If you took time to glance out the window, you can add a robbery and an aggravated assault to your list.

As large as these figures are, there is clear evidence that eighteenth-and nineteenth-century residents of London confronted even higher rates of criminality. Historian Gilbert Armitage describes the level of criminal activity prevalent in London in the early 1700s:

London ... enjoyed a melancholy pre-eminence in crime probably unequalled by any town in earlier or subsequent history.... Sneak-thieves, pickpockets, shoplifters, and armed footpads [robbers] swarmed in filthy and unlighted streets; and for twenty or so miles into the country the main roads approaching the metropolis were infested with highwaymen, some of whom ... had grown so bold as to hold up coaches openly ... in broad daylight.[3]

The situation was essentially similar in the United States. Historian James Richardson cites an 1842 description of crime in New York City:

> The property of citizens is pilfered, almost before his eyes. Dwellings and warehouses are entered with an ease and apparent coolness of detection which shows that none are safe. Thronged as our city is, men are robbed in the street ... and the defenseless and the beautiful are ravished and murdered in the daytime, and no trace of the criminals is found. The man of business, in his lawful calling, at the most public corner of our city, is slaughtered in the Sunshine and packed up and sent away ... and suspicion is hardly excited.[4]

It was partly in response to rising levels of criminality that modern police organizations first arose. In London, the first police department was created by Sir Robert Peel in 1829.[5] In the United States, New York City established a modern police force in 1845,[6] while Boston's police emerged in 1838.[7] In Washington, D.C., full-time police were appointed in 1861.[8] A rising level of criminality is thus one of the conditions associated with the establishment of police departments.

Other factors also were important. First, changes in patterns of social solidarity are related to changes in types of policing. In primitive, mechanically solidary societies there exists a common or jointly shared set of values and life style. This "collective conscience" allows primitive societies to engage in informal or community policing. But, as societies modernized and became organically solidary, informal policing proved increasingly ineffective. Urbanization and industrialization created large cities wherein systems of mutal citizen responsibility for crime control became unacceptable. Alternatives to informal policing began to emerge, and eventually separate police forces were created. The movement from mechanical to organic solidarity is another of the conditions associated with the foundation of organized police.

But, even as crime increased, people resisted the police idea. Many preferred the relative liberty and informality of community police rather than risk the perceived threat to democracy associated with modern police. Increasing crime played an important role in overcoming this historic reluctance to place more power in the hands of the state. Three other factors also were important: public riots, public drunkenness, and the emergence of a "dangerous classes" imagery of the persons responsible for crime, disturbances, and public intoxication.

But these factors are not sufficient in themselves to account for the origination of modern policing. Public intoxication had become a serious nuisance in London as early as 1700 and for a week in the summer of 1780, London was controlled by mobs during the Gordon Riots. In 1785 a bill was introduced into Parliament to create a modern police force. It was rejected as "a dangerous innovation and an encroachment on the rights and security of the people."[9] Not until 1829 did a police bill successfully pass the Parliament.

The final factor responsible for the formal organization of municipal police was elite interest and involvement. Persons of power, wealth, and prestige overcame the historic reluctance surrounding the police idea. Their motivation was purely economic—elites used their influence to create police who would protect and promote their vested interests.

Purpose of the Chapter

The purpose of this chapter is to describe and illustrate the ways in which *changes* in these three factors—patterns of social solidarity, rates/images of crime, and elite interests—gave rise to organized police forces. The overall argument to be presented can be diagramatically represented as follows:

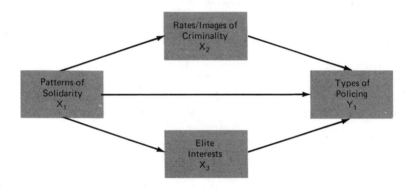

Before turning to this argument, however, it is necessary to provide some definitions for certain terms we will be using.

TYPES OF POLICING: SOME DEFINITIONS

In this chapter, three types or systems of policing will be identified: informal, transitional, and modern. We will begin by providing brief working definitions for each type of policing.

Informal Policing

Informal policing refers to a system where community members are jointly responsible for the maintenance of order. Absent are persons whose sole responsibility is policing. One example of informal policing is the *frankpledge* system of medieval England. Under this system, every family joined with nine others to form a *tything.* The tything consisted of a mutual pledge of good behavior and a jointly accepted responsibility to alert others to crime by raising the "hue and cry." Tything members then joined to apprehend violators; if that was unsuccessful, the members had a mutual obligation to reimburse victims. W. L. Melville Lee describes the operation of the tything:

> When a crime was committed, information had to be at once given to the ... tythingmen of the district, and it was their duty to pursue, arrest, and bring to justice all peace-breakers. In the event of the non-appearance of a culprit ... his nine fellow-pledges were allowed one month in which to produce him, when, if he was not forthcoming, a fine was exacted the liability falling ... on any property of the fugitive ... [and] in the second place on the tything.[10]

This informal system, with constant modification, existed in England for the 800 years preceeding creation of modern police in 1829.

Transitional Policing

Transitional policing was characteristic of the systems which emerged in response to the breakdown of informal police networks such as the frankpledge. These systems of policing anticipated modern police departments in office and procedure. But they lacked continuity and they were not accountable to a central governmental authority.

The absence of continuity in office and procedure is illustrated by the transitional systems of policing in the city of New York between 1697 and 1783.[11] From 1697 to 1731 bellmen, people who made regular rounds calling out the time and ringing their bells, provided police services. In 1731, they were replaced by a permanent citizen's watch wherein residents took turns patrolling the city's streets. This "permanent" watch was replaced by a group of paid constables in 1734. From 1735 until the end of the Revolutionary War in 1783, the police function was alternately performed by the state militia, a paid watch, and yet another permanent citizen's watch. It was not until 1845 that professional, fulltime police were appointed in New York.

The transitional systems of policing characteristic of eighteenth-century London illustrate the absence of accountability to a central governmental authority. In 1748, Sir Henry Fielding became Chief Magistrate (a combination of judge and prosecutor) of the Bow Street district of London. Under his leadership and authority, a group of "thief takers," known as the Bow Street Runners, was formed. These thief takers attempted to apprehend criminals and they clearly performed a police function. But they reported to Fielding and, when he died, to his brother John.[12] Similarly, in 1798, English merchant and police reformer Patrick Colquhoun established a "River Police" to protect merchants along the River Thames. Although they also performed a police function, they were restricted to the river area and reported to merchants rather than government officials.[13]

Modern Policing

Modern policing has four distinctive characteristics: persons generally recognized as having full-time police responsibilities, continuity in office, continuity in procedure, and accountability to a central governmental authority. Following the turmoil and uncertainty of transitional policing in Washington, D.C., for example, Congress passed a bill in 1861 which reorganized District police and gave them modern features. Full-time police officers were hired, issued uniforms and revolvers, and assigned to districts and shifts so as to provide complete and continuous police protection to all areas of the District of Columbia. The bill also merged Washington, Georgetown, and Washington County police into a single "Metropolitan Police District" administered by a central five-member police commission.[14] Policing has been continuous in Washington, D.C., since 1861.

In the sections which follow, we will be concerned with the forces and events which prompt change in these three types of policing. We begin by examining the relations between patterns of social solidarity and types of policing.

PATTERNS OF SOLIDARITY AND TYPES OF POLICING

Among the lessons to be learnt from the life of rude tribes is how society can go on without the police ... to keep order.[15]

French sociologist Emile Durkheim (1855–1917) made a number of important contributions to sociology. One was an overgeneralized but useful distinction between the types of social solidarity, or "affective glue," which hold persons in a society together. Durkheim suggested that societies could be classified according to two general types of social solidarity: mechanical and organic.[16]

Patterns of Social Solidarity

Mechanically solidary societies are characterized by a low division of labor, internal population homogeneity, and a simple technology. In these "primitive" societies, there exists a common or "collective conscience" reflective of an undifferentiated and repetitive life experience. Values, beliefs, and sentiments are jointly held in such a society because tasks and experiences for all persons are similar. In a mechanically solidary society almost everyone is his or her own farmer, waste disposer, food preparer, prophet, and physician.

A high division of labor, internal population heterogeneity, and an advanced technology are features of organically solidary societies. In these "developed" societies, a collective conscience is only weakly developed because of a differentiated life experience. Values, beliefs, and sentiments are not universal in such a society because the tasks, experiences, and interests of its members are varied. In an organically solidary society people are generally dependent upon others for the provision of necessities such as food, waste disposal, prophesizing, and medical attention.

Types of Policing

One method for determining the type of social solidarity characteristic of a society is to examine its law enforcement mechanisms. In mechanically solidary societies, law enforcement is an undifferentiated and unelaborated responsibility which is jointly shared by the members of the collectivity. Bound by feelings of appreciation for one another and for their society by a collective conscience, members of mechanically solidary societies respond unthinkingly and automatically to law violations. Every person is a police officer because "the police are the public and the public are the police."[17] *Informal systems of policing are characteristic of mechanically solidary societies.*

The *frankpledge* system described earlier is an example of the relatively informal systems of policing possible in such communities. British historian T. A. Critchley describes the frankpledge system and emphasizes that it rested upon the existence of a collective conscience:

> From very early times ... the primary responsibility for maintaining ... peace fell upon each locality under a well-understood principle of social obligation, or *collective* security.... Every male person, unless excused through high social position or property, was enrolled for police purposes in a group of about ten families known as a tything.... If any member of the group committed a crime, the others had to produce him for trial.... *In essence ... the system relied on the principle that all members of a community accepted an obligation for the good behavior of each other.*[18]

As societies move towards organic solidarity, informal systems of policing become less effective. The essential reason for this is the slow extinction of the one cultural feature central to both mechanical solidarity and informal policing: a collective conscience. A collective conscience is possible only when life experiences are similar for nearly all members of a society. As people's experiences become dissimilar, a collective conscience is slowly eliminated.

The movement toward organic solidarity brings diversity to a society. As technology and the division of labor increase, one source of similarity, the work experience, declines. People become involved in different productive activities. With the growth of cities, several additional common features disappear. A jointly shared rural experience and lifestyle is slowly replaced by rural–urban differences and by differences in intraurban lifestyles. Urbanization also generally implies immigration and migration and both are productive of diversity.

Divergence rather than similarity begins to dominate the society moving towards organic solidarity. Previously taken-for-granted matters such as work, religion, and family structure, as well as more mundane matters such as food and style of dress, become variable and subject to change. The individual and group consciences characteristic of an organically solidary society slowly replace the collective conscience found in a mechanically solidary society.

One major consequence of the transition from mechanical to organic types of social solidarity is the emergence of persons and organizations which anticipate, in certain of their features, modern police and police organizations. Between 1200 and 1500 in England, for instance, the offices of constable and justice of the peace were introduced.[19] In London, nightly watch systems were established in an attempt to deal with the increase in criminality rates.[20] Essentially similar procedures arose in large cities in the United States. In New York, Boston, and Washington, D.C., a variety of different day police and night police, as well as formal citizen watch systems, replaced informal systems of policing.[21] Therefore, *as societies experience movement from mechanical to organic systems of solidarity there emerge transitional systems of policing with offices and procedures which are prototypes of more modern organizations.*

There remain, however, several important differences between these transitional systems and actual organized police. First, during periods of change there is frequent elimination and replacement of transitional police systems. In Boston, the county sheriff provided police services from 1692 to 1802. From 1802 until 1838 appointed constables, a night watch, and a city marshall alternately served as law-enforcement authorities.[22]

A second characteristic of transitional policing is reliance upon other than full-time police officers. Typically, the individuals involved in citizen watch systems had other full-time occupations. They were bakers or other laborers during the day and, when it was their turn, members of the watch at night. Exceptions to this were members of the elite. Although all males were supposed to serve on the watch, elites generally paid small sums to the unemployed or elderly to take their place. The overall consequence was inept watchmen. They were either tired from working all day or less than committed to firm action because they were paid very little by the upper class. In 1812, an angry citizen of London offered the following sarcastic observation regarding the quality of the individuals serving as watchmen:

> Wanted, a hundred thousand men for London watchmen. None apply for this lucrative situation without being the age of sixty, seventy, eighty, or ninety years; blind with one eye or seeing very little with the other; crippled in one arm or both legs; deaf as a post; with an asthmatical cough that tears them to pieces; whose speed will keep pace with a snail, and the strength of whose arm will not be able to arrest an old washer-woman of fourscore returned from a hard day's fag at the washtub; whose constitution is worn out in hard service, either in the army or navy, some unhealthy business, or from the effects of a gay and profligate life; and that such will neither see or hear what belongs to their duty, or what does not, unless well palmed or garnished for the same.[23]

A resident of the city of New York expressed a similar opinion, albeit more succinctly: "While the city sleeps, the watchmen do too."[24]

A final important feature of transitional policing is the absence of accountability to a central governmental authority. In Denver, Colorado, for example, a city marshall was appointed in 1859, only to resign in 1860 in the face of uncontrolled lawlessness. Night police briefly appeared in 1860 but they too proved ineffective. By the summer of 1860, "respectable" town members had organized a "vigilance committee" which apprehended law violators, and a "people's court" which passed sentence. Death sentences were frequently handed down by the people's court, although neither the vigilance committee or the court were under the control of city government—it "had completely collapsed and no longer even pretended to operate."[25] It was not until October of 1860 that a permanent city marshall accountable to a Mayor was appointed in Denver. Similar to Fielding's Bow Street Runners and Colquhoun's River Police, Denver's transitional police in the summer and early fall of 1860 were closer to contemporary private than public police.

It is only when the transition from mechanical to organic solidarity is nearly complete that police organizations are formed. One sign of the emergence of an organically solidary society is the proliferation of governmental agencies intended to administer the many interdependent agencies of an industrializing society. Activities formerly structured in terms of a collective conscience now require external administration and integration. Police organizations, along with health boards, zoning committees, and the other administrative and enforcement agencies characteristic of contemporary municipal government, function organically to sustain a society. What was formerly accomplished by a society as a collectivity (mechanically) is now assigned and accomplished organically.

Police organizations are simply one indication of the functional interdependence characteristic of an organically solidary society.

The London police created in 1829[26] were important not only because they were the first organization of its kind but also because they served as a model for police forces in the United States. In New York City, the law which created modern police (on May 23, 1845) was modelled after the London police.[27] Additionally, police departments in Philadelphia, Baltimore, Washington, D.C., Boston, and most other large cities in the United States used Peel's police as an example.[28] We will examine the London police in order to establish the features of modern police departments.

The London Police

The London police was created by the Metropolitan Police Act of 1829. The organization displayed the four characteristics of modern police departments. Selection criteria and standards of dress were immediately established by Peel. Officers had to be under thirty-five, healthy, at least five feet seven inches in height, literate, and of "good character."[29] Officers were clothed in a long "blue-tailed coat, blue trousers . . . and a glazed black top-hat . . . with a leather crown."[30] They were to be unarmed save for short batons which were to be discreetly hidden under the long tails of their coats. Officers were full-time and easily recognizable in their distinctive uniforms.

The basic mission of the new police was to prevent crime and disorder.[31] Towards that end, London was divided into seventeen police districts, each with its own station house.[32] Approximately 165 officers were assigned to each district for a total of nearly 3000 "new police." Each district was headed by the equivalent of a contemporary captain and four lieutenants. The actual supervision of constables (patrol officers) was the responsibility of sergeants. It was they who assigned patrol officers to particular beats so that all areas of the district received continuous police attention.

The administrative personnel in each district reported through a chain of command to a representative of central government: a police commissioner.[33] The first commissioner, Charles Rowan, was a retired army colonel, and he established and enforced a system of discipline reflective of his military experiences. Rowan made the new police into a quasi-military organization with numerous rules and severe punishments for even minor violations. Policemen were dismissed altogether for serious rule violations, such as drinking while on duty. During the early years of the department, approximately one-third of the force was discharged each year.

The new police were thus the first to display the characteristics of contemporary police organizations. Officers were full-time and recognizable in their special uniforms. Their mission was to prevent crime, and they were territorially organized with patrol officers providing basic police services. The organization was under the control of central government and quasi-military in structure. Police in the United States modelled themselves after London's new police, and contemporary police departments continue to display these same attributes.

Patterns of social solidarity therefore relate to styles of policing. Mechanical solidary societies utilize informal systems of policing based upon mutual citizen responsibility. However, as societies move from mechanical to organic solidarity, transitional systems of policing emerge. A modern police force is a feature of the functional interdependence characteristic of an organically solidary society.

Other factors, however, also played a role in the development of modern police. Two of the most important—elimination of the apprehension about the police idea and an elite motivated to protect and promote its own interests—occupy our attention in the sections which follow.

LIBERTY VERSUS CIVILITY: THE TENSION SURROUNDING THE POLICE IDEA

The police occupy an especially sensitive position in all modern societies. They represent a full-time capacity for learning of legal infractions and other forms of misconduct. This centrally coordinated "capacity for awareness"[34] contains a fundamental threat to individual liberty, as Jerome Skolnick and J. Richard Woodworth state:

> As one observes such a process in action, one becomes increasingly aware of the totalitarian potential.... Totalitarianism implies tight socialization. Its conception of man is relatively fixed and inflexible, and its symmetry and conventionalism imply a mandate for developing instrumentalities of conformity. We are not referring here only to such totalitarian social orders as Hitlerism or Stalinism. We are discussing the idea of a totalitarian potential inherent in any society, even the most constitutionally protected and democratic, as, bit by bit, legal definitions increasingly standardize the conception of moral man and as the apparatus for social control becomes increasingly refined.[35]

Modern systems of policing thus pose a fundamental threat to individual liberty.

However, crime is sometimes an equally worrisome issue. This is especially the case when citizens in a transitionally policed society experience or perceive a significant increase in crime. They are fearful and alter their behavior out of a sense of fear. A citizen of Denver wrote of the crime problem and its impact in the fall of 1859:

There are people here from Mexico, from South America, from Europe, and from almost every state in the Union, yet a majority of the decidedly bad men hail from Missouri, daring, desperate and lawless characters; having no fear of God or man; genuine specimens of border ruffianism ... and woe to the individual who opposes their freaks when under the influence of rum.[36]

Crime thus poses a fundamental threat to civility.

This tension between liberty and civility is central to any understanding of the process whereby modern police organizations were founded. Specifically, the relatively late emergence of police departments is partially attributable to recurrent decisions to protect liberty over and against civility. In London, for example, citizens faced a level of criminality perhaps unparalleled in contemporary society. From 1500 to 1829 there were recurrent calls for the establishment of modern police. Yet, it was not until 1829 that a police force was introduced. Once created, London newspapers called for their elimination, arguing that the threat to personal liberty outweighed the civilizing potential of the police.[37]

Such controversy also arose in the United States and was responsible for the delayed initiation of American police forces. James Richardson describes the situation:

Even with the widely known deficiencies of the police and the watch, it was still difficult to achieve a more highly organized and efficient police. In the pre–Civil War period many Americans feared the spread of governmental power. They believed in public action that enhanced citizens' opportunities to make money, but they objected to any activity that interfered with personal liberty. In short, they did not want to be policed.[38]

One way for us to understand the historic reluctance surrounding the creation of organized police is to briefly consider a contemporary example of this same issue. In the United States, it is periodically suggested that some type of "national identity card" system be established. Proponents of the notion argue that the benefits would include: 1) reduction of paperwork by substituting a single identifying number for all persons; 2) instant voter registration; 3) development of central, computerized dossiers on all citizens; and 4) identification of the one million illegal aliens currently employed in the United States. But, like the residents of London or New York in the eighteenth century, many citizens perceive a threat to liberty in a national identity card system. Opponents argue that such a system would: 1) increase paperwork during the transition to a single identifying number; 2) encourage and facilitate attempts to buy votes during elections; 3) increase governmental surveillance and coercion; and 4) undermine an historic commitment to reach out to the disadvantaged of other nations.

The current debate about the creation of a national identity card system closely resembles the historic tension surrounding the police idea. Residents of London and large cities in the United States in the eighteenth and nineteenth centuries could see the advantages of modern police who were charged with the task of maintaining civility. They also could perceive the threat to liberty associated with the creation of such an organization.

The question thus becomes: what factors tipped the historic balance in favor of the establishment of police departments? Study of the circumstances surrounding the emergence of modern police in London and the United States suggests that four factors were important: 1) rising levels of crime; 2) public riots; 3) public intoxication; and 4) the conception of a "dangerous class" of persons responsible for crime, public disturbances and drunkenness.

Rising Levels of Crime

There is clear evidence that citizens in London and in most large cities in the United States believed that crime was increasing in the period immediately preceding the rise of organized police forces. T. A. Critchley observes that in London:

> The extent of criminality . . . at the end of the seventeenth century and during the first half of the eighteenth, defies description. . . . Whole districts were regarded . . . as sanctuaries in which thieves enjoyed complete immunity. To Henry Fielding the vast growth of London, with its lanes, alleys and courts . . . appeared "as a vast wood or forest, in which a thief may harbour with as great security as wild beasts do in the deserts of Africa or Arabia."[39]

Although it is difficult to determine with any precision that actual rates of criminality were increasing, the public *perceived* that crime was increasing dramatically in London.

Public perception appears to have been essentially similar in many American cities. In the 1830s the citizens of New York despaired at the rising levels of criminality:

> Destructive rascality stalks at large in our streets and public places, at all times of the day and night, with none to make it afraid; mobs assemble deliberately . . . in a word, lawless violence and fury have full dominion over us whenever it pleases them to rage.[40]

The situation was the same in Washington, D.C. In May 1837, a local newspaper observed:

> If the robberies, burglaries, fires, and outrages which have frequently occurred in the city . . . do not call forth on the part of our citizens, some prompt

and active measures of prevention ... it will almost be dangerous to go about our streets, either by day or night.[41]

One result of these beliefs was the suggestion that municipal police forces be created. Representative of this opinion was a House of Representatives Committee for the District of Columbia Report on the police of Washington City in 1842:

It is well known that persons of ill-fame congregate in this city, during the sittings of Congress, with a view to depredate upon those assembled here at such times. Members of Congress, their constituents having business at the seat of Government, executive officers, the representatives of foreign powers located here, and resident citizens, are liable to suffer from the crimes of thieves, incendiaries, and burglars. *The Committee are of the opinion that the safety of all may be secured, in a very great degree, by establishing a police for the city.*[42]

The first factor responsible for reducing the tension associated with the police idea was a felt increase in criminality rates. In London, New York, Washington, D.C., and elsewhere, citizens began to see crime as being at least as great a threat to liberty as professional police.

Public Riot

There also is clear evidence that the perceived seriousness and possibly the incidence of public riot increased in the years immediately preceding the founding of police departments. Riots were common in London in the early years of the nineteenth century. Gilbert Armitage provides one description of the nature of public riot in London:

From time to time some real or fancied grievance, some wave of ignorant prejudice or enthusiasm, would animate the low and brutal inhabitants of the poorer quarters, and the whole town would be at the mercy of a destructive and ferocious mob, who fired buildings, smashed windows, broke into and rifled shops, private houses, and even places of religious worship....[43]

Public uprisings were also common in New York. James Richardson notes:

As much as moralists objected to commercialized vice ... their most serious fears arose from the threat riots posed to property and public order. And riots were frequent.... There were so many in 1834 alone that it was long remembered in New York history as the year of riots.[44]

A police force emerged in Boston in 1837 following three major riots, two of which were ethnically and religiously based. The first, on August 11, 1834, involved an attack and burning of an Irish-Catholic school for girls by several thousand anti-Irish (Protestant) nativists.[45] The second, on June 22, 1837, resulted from a clash between Protestant volunteer firefighters and members of an Irish funeral procession. Roger Lane describes what happened:

> The Irish had at first the advantage of numbers, [but] more fire companies were summoned and they were followed by others with grievances against the immigrants. It was Sunday, few men were at work, and residents of the Irish tenements all along the street were driven out and beaten by a mob eventually estimated at fifteen thousand, more than one-sixth of the city's population.... No one was killed, but large numbers were badly injured, and property damage amounted to several thousand dollars.[46]

Riots were also frequent in Washington, D.C. in the years preceding the creation of the "Metropolitan Police."[47] In 1841, President John Tyler vetoed an important bank measure. A drunken crowd formed and occupied the White House for two hours. During the 1850s, racial tensions increased and the night police were frequently called upon to deal with groups of white rioters who launched attacks on white abolitionists. In 1857, nativist "Know-Nothings" attacked naturalized citizens attempting to vote in a local election. Washington's transitional police force was unable to cope with the disorder and United States Marines were called in. During the gunfights which ensued, eight people were killed and 21 wounded.

The establishment of professional police came to be seen as a possible solution to the problem of public disorder. Transitional police proved ineffective in the face of riots and the military was frequently called in to suppress them. These latter actions, however, had serious political connotations and citizens looked to agencies other than the military for help. Representative of support for a police force was Mayor Samuel Elliot of Boston. Following the riots of 1837, Mayor Elliot called in the city council for the:

> ... creation of a new class of officers. Citing the "spirit of violence abroad," he pointed out that the danger from "the incendiary, burglar, and the lawlessly violent" was "increasing at a ratio faster than that of the population." The criminal ... was "guilty of treason against the constitution of his country." And it was necessary to take strong measures appropriate to Boston's metropolitan standing: "The police of this city has hitherto consisted of a small number of constables, and is rather adapted to circumstances as they were half a century ago."[48]

The second factor in favor of the idea of organized police was the impression that public riots had increased. In London and most large cities in the United States, citizens saw public commotion as potentially more threatening to freedom than modern police. This was especially so since the alternative—use of the military—was seen as an even graver menace to independence.

Public Intoxication

Prior to 1690 in England, hard liquor was imported from France and it was heavily taxed.[49] Because it was so expensive, only the well-to-do could afford liquor and the drunkenness its consumption could produce. Alcohol facilitated fights, and homicides were largely restricted to the affluent members of English society, where they apparently were quite frequent.[50]

For the poorer segments of English society, the consumption of alcoholic beverages was restricted to wine and beer. Most of their drinking took place in the home with meals. Since drinking was done on a smaller scale, there was less alcoholism and therefore fewer disturbances caused by intoxication. And, because there were few commercial establishments devoted exclusively to drinking, *public* drunkenness by members of the less advantaged segments of society was extremely infrequent.[51]

In 1690, England placed an even higher tax on French liquor and granted permission to distill gin using surplus English corn. As a result, hard liquor became extremely inexpensive, and dram shops and "flash houses" were quickly opened. London residents availed themselves of a beverage which had heretofore been available only to the elite. There is general consensus that the effects were devastating. Gin "democratized drunkenness"[52] as drinking, especially by young males, shifted from a meal-related and home-based activity to commercial settings. Gin also created an entirely new social problem: public drunkenness. Smollet describes the process and effects of the consumption of gin by persons accustomed to drinking small amounts of beer or wine with their meals:

> The retailers of this poisonous compound set up painted boards in public inviting people to be drunk for the small expense of one penny and assuring them they might be dead drunk for twopence.... As his guests get intoxicated they are laid together promiscuously, men, women, and children, till they recover their senses, when they proceed to get drunk, or having spent all they had, go out to find wherewithall to return to the same dreadful pursuit....[53]

Similar changes and problems occurred in the American colonies. Prior to about 1750, the only alcoholic beverages routinely available were the wines and beers consumed at home during meals.[54] However, the marketing advantages of hard liquor—less spoilage and easier shipment—stimulated its manufacture and sale. By 1800, nearly all of the alcohol that

United States citizens consumed was in the form of hard liquor.[55] Drinking patterns changed from a family-and meal-related custom to an individual practice. Young unmarried men took advantage of easier access to hard liquor and frequented newly opened public drinking places. The effects appear to have been troublesome as persons changed their drinking habits.[56] And, as in England, public intoxication began to become a problem.

The affluent generally viewed the drinking and public drunkenness of the lower classes with alarm. In England there was agreement that the poor resorted to crime to acquire money to purchase hard liquor.[57] There also was agreement that consumption of hard liquor facilitated public riot and that it had a particularly disastrous effect on members of the dangerous classes. In 1751, the Chief Magistrate of Bow Street, Henry Fielding, observed:

> A new kind of drunkenness, unknown to our ancestors, is lately sprung up amongst us, and which if not put a stop to, will infallibly destroy a great part of the inferior people.[58]

Elite opinion was similar in the United States. A poll revealed that Boston physicians, prosecutors, and judges believed that three-quarters of all criminal offenses were alcohol related.[59] Drinking and public drunkenness were believed to cause other problems.[60] Alcohol consumption was seen as one cause of public riot. Under the influence of drink, passion and frustrations otherwise suppressed were released during mob violence. Members of the "dangerous class" were thought to be especially sensitive to alcohol and to react violently upon drinking it. We will turn to this issue momentarily.

The proposed responses to the problems posed by public intoxication were several, prohibition among them. For our purposes, the most important of these responses was the suggestion that police forces be created. Jonathan Rubinstein describes the way in which this suggestion emerged:

> There was growing demand for protection, and private societies for the enforcement of the law flourished.... At mid-century [1750], Henry Fielding ... proposed that the watch-and-ward system be centralized and constables organized to patrol the streets. For a brief time he organized a mounted patrol.... It languished when he died, but for the first time the idea of a mobile police had been advanced.[61]

The third factor supporting the creation of professional police was the fear of public intoxication. In London and most large cities in the United States, affluent citizens saw public intoxication, and the crime and public riot it doubtless facilitated, as potentially more sinister to freedom than modern police. They were especially alarmed by the effects of alcohol on members of the dangerous classes.

The "Dangerous Classes"

In the years preceding the rise of police departments in London and cities in the United States, middle-class and elite members of society attributed crime, riot, and public drunkenness to the members of the "dangerous classes." The image was that of a convulsively and possibly biologically criminal, riotous, and intemperate group of persons located at the base of society. Their actions were seen as destroying the very fabric of society. The variation within this overall imagery was in the types of persons thought to make up the dangerous classes.

In London, the dangerous classes were understood to consist of immigrants and the intemperate poor. Allan Silver describes the commonly held view:

> In the London ... of the late eighteenth and early nineteenth centuries, people often saw themselves as threatened by agglomerations of the criminal, vicious, and violent—the rapidly multiplying poor of cities whose size had no precedent in Western history. It was much more than a question of annoyance, indignation, or personal insecurity: the social order itself was threatened by an entity whose characteristic name reflects the fears of the time— the 'dangerous classes.' The phrase occurs repeatedly.... But even where the term is not explicitly invoked, the image persists—one of an unmanageable, volatile, and convulsively criminal class at the base of society.[62]

Residents of New York, Boston, and Washington, D.C., also were familiar with the dangerous classes idea. By this they meant the immigrant poor, and the criminal, riotous, and intemperate. Added, however, was a distinctly American contribution: black citizens as a component of the dangerous classes. James Richardson writes of the vision of the dangerous classes maintained by middle-and upper-class residents of New York:

> From the 1740s on, New Yorkers thought themselves engulfed in a rising tide of crime and disorder. The simplest explanation ... was that foreigners and Negroes were responsible. Immigration from non-English sources did rise rapidly in mid-century, and to contemporaries this accounted for the difficulties.... Negro slaves, a despised and degraded group ... were an unstable and unruly element often treated with great brutality.[63]

Residents of Boston maintained a similar idea, one that included black Americans as a component of the dangerous classes. In the eyes of Boston's largely Protestant elite, however, the primary threat was seen as Boston's Irish-Catholic population. An example from rather late in the period—the Boston Police Debates of 1863—suggests the view held by Boston's Protestant elite:

> In cities there are large bodies who are amongst us, but not of us, whose sentiments and principles do not harmonize with those of the State; who have influence, though they not have rightful influence; or, if citizens, have not the same influence as the great body of citizens—a foreign, floating population—those controlled by extraneous, alien influences, trade, criminal, or other. You have amongst you those elements of society called . . . the dangerous classes. . . .[64]

In Washington, D.C., the problems of crime and public riot were seen as largely a black problem. In the ten years following the start of the Civil War, the black population grew by 203 percent and by 1870, 30 percent of Washington residents were black. Most lived in squalid poverty, and white District residents saw black citizens as *the* dangerous class. An editorial in *The Washington Post* declared that black residents were responsible for a "reign of terror" brought on by "an organized system of lawlessness on the part of blacks."[65]

The dangerous classes notion was an all-encompassing idea, a summary and justification for modern police. Not only were crime, riot, and public intoxication problems in themselves, but the persons responsible for these actions constituted a fundamental threat to society. Present but not part of society, this compulsively criminal group was seen as threatening the very fabric of society. Only organized police forces could deal effectively with the dangerous classes.

Thus, four factors were responsible for tipping the balance in favor of modern police: increased crime, public riot, public intoxication, and the factor which summarized the other three: the dangerous classes. Each of these factors was *necessary* for the creation of city-wide police departments. They helped overcome the apprehension about the notion of police, providing convincing evidence why modern police were needed. However, alone or in combination, these factors do not constitute a *sufficient* explanation for the establishment of police organizations. A sufficient explanation requires that we attend to the role of elites in the creation of professional police.

THE ROLE OF ELITES IN THE CREATION OF MODERN POLICE

The above four factors do not in themselves explain the rise of modern police departments. Rising levels of criminality were characteristic of

London, New York, and Washington, D.C., for many years preceding professional police. Peel's professional police did not begin to patrol London until late in 1829, yet in 1752 Henry Walpole wrote that "one is forced to travel, even at noon, as if one were going to battle."[66] Modern police did not arise in New York until 1846, yet "from the 1740s on, New Yorkers thought themselves engulfed in a rising tide of crime and disorder."[67] Rising levels of criminality were a justification for modern police. However, increased crime did not automatically or even quickly result in the creation of police forces.

The same is true of the impact of public riot, public intoxication, and the dangerous classes notion. None either automatically or even quickly resulted in the founding of organized police. In the summer of 1780, London was controlled by mobs during the Gordon Riots; professional police did not appear for another forty-nine years. Public drunkenness was a serious nuisance in Boston as early as 1775, yet professional police did not materialize until 1838. And the existence of the dangerous classes was widely acknowledged well before the dawn of professional police.

Elite Power in Organically Solidary Societies

The power to bring about meaningful change in an organically solidary society is not uniformly distributed across all social class levels. Instead, power is concentrated in the hands of a relatively small number of elites, persons of power, wealth, and prestige. In certain situations in which elite power is exercised, elite interests overlap with those of the less powerful and their actions have uniformly beneficial consequences. In other situations, elites undertake actions which have purely class-related benefits. This is especially the case in the context of elite actions focusing on the law-making and enforcement machinery of the state. Sociologist Richard Quinney has argued that "definitions of crime are composed of behaviors that conflict with the interests of the dominant class."[68] Elites take control of the law creation and enforcement machinery of the state when the actions of the powerless threaten the position of elites. By making certain actions illegal and by creating law enforcement agencies, the powerless are brought under the control of the state.

The available evidence suggests that a sufficient explanation of the establishment of police forces must recognize that police were created by and for elites. In the words of Evelyn L. Parks:

> The history of social control in the United States is the history of transition from "constabulary" to "police society" ... which ... was not essentially for the protection of the "general welfare" of society but was for the protection of the interests and life-styles of but one segment of society—those holding positions of wealth, "respectability," and power.[69]

Elite Power and the London Police

Allan Silver has examined the issue of elite involvement in the creation of a police department in London. In his frequently cited essay on the topic, Silver provides strong evidence that London police were created by and for elites.[70]

He begins his essay by noting that as the transition from mechanical to organic solidarity neared completion, English elites increasingly benefited from the "tightly woven political and market" structure of English society. Crime, riot, intoxication, and the members of the dangerous classes thought responsible for these actions were seen as a threat to English society as a whole and to the position of elites within that society. Elites acted to produce a police force in London to protect and promote elite interests.

Modern police functioned to protect elite interests in several ways. They buffered contacts between elites and members of the dangerous classes. Modern police gave the appearance of serving societal rather than class interests, and they proved more effective and less threatening than the military in the prevention and suppression of public riots. They could be more quickly and reliably assembled. Additionally, modern police relieved ordinary citizens of the burdensome and time-consuming duties of the watch. Productive energy was thus released for the economic activities which ultimately benefited elites. Police officers also penetrated the dangerous and lower classes on a regular basis and brought a "civilizing" middle-class and elite conception of morality. The police mission was not only against crime but also against "vices" such as public intoxication and profanity. Lastly, violations of the law and decorum now came to the attention of central government through the police. A centralized "capacity for awareness" became a reality. For these reasons, Silver argues that elites were actively involved in and benefitted from the organized police force in London.

Elite Power and Police in the United States

New York. The history of elite interest in and control of New York City revolves around a single major issue: labor. It was essentially an economic issue, and elite actions illustrate the extent to which New York City police were created by and for elites.

In the sixty years between 1810 and 1870, the number of factory workers in the United States increased from about 75,000 to about 2.5 million.[71] In New York City as elsewhere, these workers had few rights and their working and living conditions were depressing and frequently debilitating: "This early industrial work force was subject to harsh exploitation in the factories and grim living conditions in the growing slums of the industrial cities."[72]

One response by workers was to organize in an effort to protect and better their collective interests. In New York City, public meetings were held in an effort to generate support for public work for the unemployed and strikes became more frequent. Elite-controlled police responded to these actions in a violent manner. On January 12, 1874, thousands of men, women, and children rallied for public work for the unemployed. Without warning or provocation, New York City police charged into the crowd, dispersing it in what was described as an "orgy of brutality."[73] During strikes, "police invariably supported the employers' efforts to hire strike-breakers and hampered picketing workmen and assembled labor groups."[74]

In doing these things, police clearly acted to protect and promote the interests of an economic elite. Elites saw labor as a commodity whose wages and hence living conditions were a function of the laws of supply and demand. As immigrants flooded into New York City, labor's supply exceeded the demand and became cheap. Any effort to alter or overturn these processes was viewed as threatening not only elites but the society as a whole. Such efforts, in the eyes of elites (and, increasingly, the police which they controlled) smacked of communism and radicalism. James Richardson describes the perceived threat of "radicalism" and the responses of elite-controlled police:

> Freedom was a highly placed value, as long as the poor were not going to use that freedom to bring about basic social change. The police with their clubs were the agency charged with the defense of the status quo when more subtle means were insufficient.[75]

Boston. Prior to the establishment of a police force in 1838, Boston was controlled and governed by an aristocratic, native-born elite. Boston's mayors, Josiah Quincy (1823–1829) and Harrison Grey Otis (1830–1832) were part of this elite and shared a common conception of the city. For elites, Boston was a source of pride for both residents and visitors. It was a major port, financial capital, and place of business. For elites it was a refined and profitable city.[76]

Boston was, of course, other things. It was rich in crime, public intoxication, public riot, poverty, disease, and intense conflict between nativists and Irish-Catholics. Yet, these other aspects of Boston rarely affected elites. As Roger Lane observes:

> The aimless brawls ... were dangerous largely to the participants, and not to those who governed the community.... A certain degree of disorder was endemic, even traditional, and tolerated accordingly.[77]

These other aspects of Boston were tolerated by elites because they did not alter the flow of benefits to elites.

The public riots of 1834, and 1837 *did* threaten to disturb the flow of benefits to elites. The riot of 1834 (the attack and burning of an Irish-Catholic school for girls by anti-Irish, Protestant nativists) was different from the "aimless brawls . . . dangerous largely to participants." The riot of 1834 revealed to elites that their position was vulnerable—a mob could gain control of the city because there was nothing to stop it from doing so. The riot of 1837 (which started as a fight between Protestant volunteer fire companies and members of an Irish funeral procession) had the same effect on elites, revealing their vulnerable position.[78]

The elite response was to create a London-style police organization in Boston in 1838. The police mission was to discover incidents before they had time to grow to the point where they threatened the stability of the city. Public riot did not cause the organization of a police force in Boston; elite *fear* of public riot did.

Police in Other Cities.   Examination of the events preceeding the establishment of police departments in other cities in the United States provides additional support for the argument that police were created by and for elites. In Washington, D.C., for instance, professional police emerged in the wake of recurrent tensions between black and white citizens.[79] The tensions were seen as threatening not only the stability of the District but the seat of federal government as well. Members of Congress created a "Metropolitan Police" to deal with these perceived threats.

Essentially similar portraits of elite interest and involvement are available in analyses of the origins of police forces in Denver, Colorado,[80] Buffalo, New York,[81] and (state police in) Texas.[82] Sociologists David Bordua and Albert J. Reiss, Jr., summarize these studies as well as the basic point advanced in this section:

> The paramilitary form of early police bureaucracy was a response not only, or even primarily, to crime *per se,* but to the possibility of riotous disorder. Not crime and danger but the "criminal" and "dangerous classes" as part of the urban social structure led to the formation of uniformed and military organized police. *Such organizations intervened between the propertied elites and the propertyless masses who were regarded as politically dangerous as a class.*[83]

SUMMARY

The essential purpose of this second chapter was to describe and illustrate the ways in which changes in three social subsystems—patterns of solidarity, rates/images of rates of criminality, and elite interests—relate to changes in a fourth subsystem—types of policing.

The overall argument presented can be diagrammatically represented as follows:

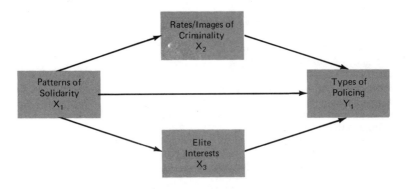

The available data suggest that as patterns of social solidarity shift from the mechanical to the organic they cause direct changes in rates/images of criminality, elite interests, and styles of policing. Changes in patterns of solidarity also have indirect effects on styles of policing via their effects on the rates/images of criminality and elite interests. Of the three variables or factors which relate to types of policing, elite interests are of singular importance. In an organically solidary society, only elites have the power and resources to bring about change.

Notes

1. See, for instance, *Crimes and Victims: A Report on the Dayton–San Jose Pilot Survey of Victimization* (Washington, D.C.: U.S. Department of Justice, June 1974).

2. *Uniform Crime Reports, 1977* (Washington, D.C.: U.S. Government Printing Office, 1978), pp. 6–10.

3. Gilbert Armitage, *The History of the Bow Street Runners, 1729–1829* (London: Wishart, 1935), pp. 10–11.

4. James F. Richardson, *The New York Police: Colonial Times to 1901* (New York Oxford University Press, 1970), p. 26.

5. T. A. Critchley, *A History of Police in England and Wales, 900–1966* (London: Constable, 1967).

6. Richardson, *The New York Police.*

7. Roger Lane, *Policing the City: Boston, 1822–1885* (Cambridge, Mass.: Harvard University Press, 1967).

8. Kenneth G. Alfers, *The Washington Police: A History, 1800–1886* (Unpublished Ph.D. dissertation, George Washington University, 1975).

9. Critchley, *A History*, p. 37.

10. See W. L. Melville Lee, *A History of Police in England* (London: Methuen, 1901), p. 10.

11. Richardson, *The New York Police*, pp. 3–22.

12. Armitage, *Bow Street Runners.*

13. Critchley, *A History*, pp. 42 ff.

14. Alfers, *The Washington Police.*

15. E. B. Tylor, *Anthropology*, Vol. II (London, 1946), p. 134, in Stanley Diamond, "The Rule of Law Versus the Order of Custom," *Social Research, 38* (1971): 45.

16. Emile Durkheim, *The Division of Labor in Society*, trans. by George Simpson (New York: Free Press, 1964), pp. 70–132.

17. Louis A. Radelet, *The Police and the Community*, 2d ed. (Encino, Calif.: Glencoe Press, 1977), p. 5.

18. Critchley, *A History*, p. 2, emphasis added.

19. Critchley, *A History*, pp. 1–27.

20. Critchley, *A History*, pp. 29–46.

21. See Alfers, *The Washington Police*.

22. Lane, *Policing the City*, pp. 2–38.

23. Leon Radzinowicz, *A History of English Criminal Law and its Administration from 1750*, Volume 3 (New York: Macmillan, 1957), p. 326.

24. Richardson, *New York Police*, p. 35.

25. Eugene Rider, *The Denver Police Department: An Administrative, Organizational, and Operational History, 1858–1905* (unpublished Ph.D. dissertation, University of Denver, 1971, p. 14).

26. Critchley, *A History*, pp. 47–50.

27. Richardson, *New York Police*, p. 49.

28. Lane, *Policing the City*, p. 1; and Radelet, *The Police*, p. 5.

29. Critchley, *A History*, p. 52.

30. Critchley, *A History*, p. 51.

31. Radelet, *The Police*, p. 4.

32. Critchley, *A History*, p. 52.

33. Jonathan Rubinstein, *City Police* (New York: Ballantine, 1973), p. 11. All of the information in this paragraph is based upon this source.

34. Jerome H. Skolnick and J. Richard Woodworth, "Bureaucracy, Information, and Social Control," in David J. Bordua (ed.), *The Police: Six Sociological Essays* (New York: Wiley, 1967), p. 101.

35. Skolnick and Woodworth, "Bureaucracy," p. 101.

36. Rider, *The Denver Police*, p. 8.

37. Critchley, *A History*, p. 34.

38. Richardson, *New York Police*, p. 36.

39. Critchley, *A History*, p. 21.

40. Richardson, *New York Police*, p. 26.

41. Alfers, *The Washington Police*, p. 44.

42. Alfers, *The Washington Police*, p. 50, emphasis added.

43. Armitage, *Bow Street Runners*, pp. 17–18.

44. Richardson, *New York Police*, p. 27.

45. Lane, *Policing the City*, pp. 29–30.

46. Lane, *Policing the City*, p. 33.

47. See Alfers, *The Washington Police*, passim.

48. Lane, *Policing the City*, p. 34.

49. Evelyn L. Parks, "From Constabulary to Police Society: Implications for Social Control," in William J. Chambliss and Milton Mankoff (eds.), *Whose Law? What Order? A Conflict Approach to Criminality* (New York: Wiley, 1976), p. 134.

50. Rubinstein, *City Police*, p. 5.

51. Parks, "From Constabulary"; and Rubinstein, *City Police*, pp. 5–7.

52. Rubinstein, *City Police*, p. 5.

53. Cited in Armitage, *Bow Street Runners*, pp. 17–18.

54. Parks, "From Constabulary," p. 134.

55. Parks, "From Constabulary," p. 134.

56. Parks, "From Constabulary," p. 134.

57. Armitage, *Bow Street Runners*, p. 18.

58. Cited in Rubinstein, *City Police*, p. 6.

59. Lane, *Policing the City*, p. 41.

60. Lane, *Policing the City*, pp. 41ff.

61. Rubinstein, *City Police*, p. 9.

62. Allan Silver, "The Demand for Order in Civil Society," in David J. Bordua (ed.), *The Police: Six Sociological Essays* (New York: Wiley, 1965), p. 3.

63. Richardson, *New York Police*, pp. 4–5.

64. *The Argument of Charles M. Ellis, Esq., in Favor of the Metropolitan Police Bill*, Wednesday, March 18, 1863 (Boston: Wright and Potter Printers, 1863), p. 7. Reprinted in *Boston Police Debates: Selected Arguments* (New York: Arno Press and The New York Times, 1971).

65. Alfers, *The Washington Police*, p. 148.

66. Cited in Critchley, *A History*, p. 21.

67. Richardson, *New York Police*, p. 4

68. Richard Quinney, *Criminology* (Boston: Little, Brown, 1975), p. 38.

69. Parks, "From Constabulary," p. 129.

70. Silver, "The Demand for Order."

71. Center for Research on Criminal Justice, *The Iron Fist and The Velvet Glove* (Berkeley, Calif.: Center for Research on Criminal Justice, 1975), p. 17.

72. Center for Research, *The Iron Fist*, p. 16.

73. Richardson, *New York Police*, p. 196.

74. Richardson, *New York Police*, p. 199.

75. Richardson, *New York Police*, p. 198.

76. Lane, *Policing the City*, pp. 26–27.

77. Lane, *Policing the City*, p. 29.

78. Lane, *Policing the City*, p. 30.

79. Alfers, *The Washington Police*, passim.

80. Rider, *The Denver Police*.

81. Mark S. Hubbell, *Our Police and Our City: A Study of the Official History of the Buffalo Police Department* (Buffalo, N.Y.: Bensler and Wesley, 1893).

82. Center for Research, *The Iron Fist*, p. 17.

83. David Bordua and Albert J. Reiss, Jr., "Law Enforcement," in Paul F. Lazarsfeld and others (eds.), *The Uses of Sociology* (New York: Basic Books, 1967), p. 282, emphasis added.

CHAPTER 3

The Police Organization

INTRODUCTION

Most social organizations and some bureaucracies emerge as a consequence of naturally occurring processes. They represent an accumulation of frequent interactions between persons across time. The structure and relations of small children in play groups generally develop in a spontaneous and unplanned manner.

Other social organizations are deliberately created for an explicit purpose. When an organization is purposefully created it is a *formal* organization.[1] Since police departments were originally created by and for elites, they are a type of formal organization. Because police departments are formal organizations they share three structural characteristics with other large organizations: a complex and contradictory normative environment, a particular community context, and bureaucratic structure. All have a profound influence on police and policing.

Purpose of the Chapter

The purpose of this chapter is to analyze and illustrate the ways in which these structural characteristics influence police and policing. First, attention will be directed towards the nature and consequences of normative environment of police organizations. Then, we will examine the varying styles of policing according to community context. Third, the bureaucratic nature of contemporary policing will be described and illustrated. Last, the positive and negative consequences of bureaucratic structure will be assessed.

THE CONTRADICTORY NORMATIVE ENVIRONMENT OF POLICE ORGANIZATIONS

As is true of all formal organizations, police departments are typified by complex and contradictory normative environments. To develop and illustrate this point, we turn to the ideas of sociologists Peter Blau and W. Richard Scott.[2]

A Typology of Formal Organizations

Blau and Scott have suggested a typology of formal organizations which is useful in the identification of the contradictory expectations which surround police organizations. They begin by observing that four basic categories of persons are in contact with all formal organizations: 1) members or rank-and-file participants; 2) the owners of the organization, 3) clients or other persons in direct contact with the organization; and 4) the members of the society in which the organization exists.

Having identified these four categories, Blau and Scott propose that formal organizations be classfied according to a *cui bono* or who benefits criterion.[3] They ask: which of these four types of persons is supposed to benefit from the existence of any particular formal organization?

If we ask this question about police organizations in a democratic society, it is clear that they no longer are expected to benefit only elites. Instead, democratic norms emphasize the public serving obligations of police organizations. In a democratic society, police departments are expected to be *commonweal* organizations serving the general public welfare. This commonweal obligation is what distinguishes police departments from other types of formal organizations.[4]

However, all formal organizations have debts to persons other than prime beneficiaries. Police departments have responsibilities toward the other categories of persons identified by Blau and Scott: members, owners, and clients. *Analysis of the obligations due these "secondary beneficiaries" reveals the complex and contradictory normative environment of police organizations.*

The members of police organizations (patrol officers, detectives, and administrators) expect to benefit from membership in their departments. Police organizations are obligated to provide members an adequate salary, effective training, reliable equipment, and reasonable health and retirement benefits. Contradictions occur when these secondary obligations interfere with (or are perceived as interfering with) the commonweal obligation of police organizations.

Police organizations also have obligations to their "owners"—the municipal governments which fund them. Municipal funding authorities control local police and expect efficient policing and budget accountability. Police organizations seek independence and flexibility in attempting to prevent and control crime.

Perhaps the greatest contradiction surrounding contemporary police organizations is the conflict between a police department's primary obligation and the obligations due the citizens in contact with the police organization. Police officers are expected to enforce the law by apprehending citizens alleged to have violated it. But they are expected to do so under the rule of law.

The Contradictions Illustrated

Labor Negotiations.   Many police officers believe that because their work is difficult and occasionally dangerous, they deserve above-average compensation. In their salary negotiations with municipal administrators, one traditionally effective weapon of labor—the strike—generally has been denied to police because of their commonweal obligations.

In 1919, however, Boston police abandoned their commonweal duties.[5] Protracted negotiations over low pay and poor working conditions had prompted only token improvements. A newly formed police union reluctantly called for a strike. Over three-quarters of Boston's police answered their union's strike call. For three days mobs controlled large portions of Boston, eight people were killed, and there was considerable looting and property damage. Order was restored when state military forces were called into Boston by Governor Calvin Coolidge. The Boston police strike was widely condemned in the local and national press, and a number of states passed laws prohibiting police from joining unions.

The Boston police strike had a profound effect on the police union movement. It is generally credited with having eliminated police unions for nearly forty years.[6] Police officers formed fraternal and benevolent societies largely concerned with attempting to meet the welfare and social needs of members. In some states, even fraternal and benevolent societies were banned.

Since about 1960, however, the police union movement has grown stronger and bolder. But it continues to be constrained by the contradictions surrounding labor negotiations involving police. Formal police unions and fraternal orders acting as unions routinely use techniques which allow them to make their grievances and demands known while simultaneously giving the appearance of not having completely abandoned their primary obligation to the public-at-large. The ticket blizzard —issuing traffic citations to anything or anybody that moves—is one alternative. It permits police to make their demands known without abandoning their commonweal obligations. The work slowdown involving a refusal to budge save for the most serious of incidents has the same communicative effect. The "blue flu," where large numbers of officers are suddenly taken ill, is a more serious work action, one which closely resembles a strike. But attacks of the blue flu do not involve an overt repudiation of the primary obligation of the police.

Recently, however, outright strikes by police have become somewhat common. This suggests that police are becoming more willing to see their interests as equal in importance to their obligations to the public. What is interesting is that when police do strike, commonweal interests are not greatly damaged.

Across the last seven years there has been a total of four police strikes in major United States cities.[7] In Baltimore, Maryland, police went on strike for five days starting July 11, 1974.[8] Police in Cleveland, Ohio, struck for three days on December 15, 1977.[9] On August 10, 1978, police in Memphis, Tennessee, began a strike which lasted nearly two weeks.[10] And, on February 8, 1979, police in New Orleans, Louisiana, began a strike which lasted three weeks.[11] With the partial exception of the New Orleans strike, police went out over wage disputes. They were lured in by court orders, improved contract offers, and promises of amnesty. The New Orleans police went on strike when city officials refused to recognize a Teamster's local as the bargaining agent for police. They returned in the face of stiff opposition to union recognition by city officials.

An interesting result is that unlike the Boston police strike, commonweal interests do not appear to have been greatly damaged by these recent police strikes. In Baltimore, during the first full day of the strike two people died and there was some looting. State police patrols kept Baltimore peaceful during the remainder of the strike. In Cleveland, police administrators and detectives donned uniforms and worked twelve-hour patrol shifts. There was no increase in reported crime and no deaths, mob violence, or looting. In Memphis and New Orleans National Guard Patrols kept order.

There are several reasons that police strikes do not greatly disrupt the peace. Contrary to the 1919 Boston police strike, where three days elapsed before striking police were replaced by state military forces, the police function is quickly filled when police go on strike. City officials routinely request and receive National Guard assistance as soon as police go on strike. State police units also provide help during strikes. Finally, administrative and nonuniformed personnel are assigned patrol duty. These actions give every appearance of keeping the peace when police strike.

But it would be a serious mistake to assume that the general absence of disorder is simply a function of quicker responses by city officials. National Guard troops and state police personnel are not trained to police our cities. Administrative and nonuniformed police personnel are more comfortable shuffling papers than settling domestic quarrels. Untrained and uncomfortable people police our cities during strikes and yet nothing much happens. Why?

The reason is that strikes help reveal what police otherwise feel obli-

gated to obfuscate: contemporary police organizations can do little to prevent or control crime. Since we will consider the issue in detail later in
the chapter, a brief observation by Herman Goldstein will suffice: "In the
case of crime, factors like the birth rate, unemployment, the sense of
community that exists in a given neighborhood, and even the weather
probably have much more to do with the incidence of crime than do the
police."[12] Nothing much happens during police strikes because police can
do little to prevent or control crime.

Traditionally, then, labor negotiations involving police have been
different from other types of labor negotiations. This has been the case
because police organizations confront a set of contradictory obligations:
they are obligated to protect commonweal and member interests. Ticket
blizzards, work slowdowns, and attacks of the blue flu all reflect attempts
to advance member interests without repudiating commonweal responsibilities. Recent police strikes suggest that in certain situations some police
are willing to place member interests ahead of their commonweal obligations. In doing so, however, they reveal that police do little to prevent or
control crime.

Crime Statistics.   Police organizations have obligations to their owners,
the municipal governments which fund them. Municipal funding authorities control local police and expect efficient policing. Police departments
seek independence and autonomy in attempting to meet their commonweal obligations. This contradiction generates tension and, occasionally,
improper police actions.

Most local police departments provide the FBI with counts of offenses
in their jurisdictions. These crime statistics appear in the annual *Uniform
Crime Reports,* which is represented as an indicator of the crime problem
in the United States. For municipal administrators, local crime statistics
serve a different purpose: they suggest whether local police are efficiently
utilizing scarce municipal resources. The police are therefore in a delicate
a position vis-à-vis their crime statistics: too much crime suggests that
resources are not being used efficiently while too little may suggest that
additional funding is not necessary.[13]

The solution for local police organizations is to alter their crime statistics so as to arrive at crime rates municipal administrators will consider
proper. A proper crime rate is one that neither suggests inefficiency by
unduly frightening municipal administrators nor leaves them compla-
cent. In 1971, for instance, Albuquerque police frightened municipal authorities by reporting the highest crime rate of any large city in the
United States. Albuquerque's chief of police explained his mistake: "We're
a victim of honest statistics. Many other cities are less than candid in their
reporting."[14] By 1977, Albuquerque police had corrected their mistake and

slipped into a more comfortable sixth position among large cities in rates of crime reported in the *Uniform Crime Reports.*[15]

Problems with crime statistics have not been limited to Albuquerque. The available evidence suggests that many police organizations alter their crime statistics so as to create a favorable image in the eyes of municipal authorities and other outsiders.[16] The extent of such alteration is suggested by the FBI, the recipient and publisher of the crime statistics reported by local police departments. It is cautious, to say the least, in its endorsements of the accuracy of these figures:

> Regardless of the extent of the statistical editing processes used by the FBI, the accuracy of the data assembled under this Program depends primarily on the adherence of each contributor to the established standards of reporting. For this reason, the FBI is not in a position to vouch for the validity of individual agency reports.[17]

The important point is not that local police departments alter crime statistics. Rather, it is important that they do so because of a tension between their primary obligation to the general public and a secondary obligation to their municipal owners.

Due Process Protections. Perhaps the greatest contradiction surrounding contemporary police organizations is the conflict between a department's primary obligation and those due citizens who allegedly have violated the law. Police officers are expected to protect the public against crime while at the same time extending due process protections to those supposedly responsible for crime. Louis Radelet describes the nature and impact of this secondary obligation:

> Some recent decisions of criminal and appellate courts defining the limits of interrogation, search of the person and property and the seizure of evidence, and of the use of force have been seen by both the police and the courts as limiting discretionary latitude. The clear implication of such court rulings is that the police must be subject to the authority of law, the prosecutor, and the courts....[18]

Many police officers believe that due process protections make it more difficult for police to effectively control crime and they have complained publicly about them.[19] Police officers also have proven very resourceful in overcoming or ignoring court decisions and other legal guidelines. Jonathan Rubinstein provides an extreme example of such actions:

> There are police willing to farm anyone they believe cannot resist them or whose protests will not be acknowledged because of their reputation or previous record. There are many more ... who hold these colleagues in contempt but are willing, nonetheless, to plant evidence on a person whom they regard

as guilty. They defend their patently illegal behavior in terms of the need to get activity (arrests) and the guilt of the suspect. They implicitly argue for the morality of their actions in comparison with the immorality of those who frame the innocent along with the guilty. This pathetic effort to maintain their dignity and honor is something only ... police ... can understand.[20]

It is very important to understand why police officers farm and engage in other illegal actions intended to secure convictions. Generally speaking, it is not because the officers involved are immoral or vicious.[21] On the contrary, they frequently are among the hardest working and most competent officers in a department.[22] They are vitally concerned with protecting the public against crime and criminals and their actions reflect this concern. But in attempting to protect us from crime they deny criminals basic due process protections.

It also is very important to understand that police officers are not alone in their support for these actions. Contrary to Rubinstein's assertion that only police can understand these actions, many citizens are sympathetic and even supportive. Many people continue to work with what is essentially a "dangerous classes" imagery of the persons responsible for crime and disorder. They see little reason for extending or protecting the rights of persons who threaten the fabric of society. A prominent political scientist, Edward Banfield, is such a person.[23] Banfield has argued that it is proper and necessary to minimize due process protections so as to maximize the crime prevention and control capacities of police. Citizens and not just police believe that crime must be controlled, even at the expense of certain due process protections.[24]

Other citizens and quite a number of police hold a contrary view. They emphasize that in a democratic society police must abide by these secondary obligations. They argue that to do otherwise is to invite emergence of a police state. They also argue that an uncontrolled capacity for awareness ultimately will destroy democratic institutions. For these people, all citizens are entitled to basic procedural safeguards. This applies to persons who have allegedly violated the law since "civil liberties must be guarded even at some cost in crime."[25]

To sum the analysis to this point: police departments are a special type of formal organization. They are commonweal organizations with a primary mission to protect and promote the best interests of the general community. As is true of all formal organizations, they also have secondary obligations to three other categories of persons: members, owners, and public-in-contact. These secondary obligations create many of the contradictions which surround contemporary policing. Labor actions such as ticket blizzards, alteration of crime statistics, and denial or minimization of due process protections result from the conflicts between these contradictory norms. Two additional points deserve brief mention.

First, these contradictory norms are probably not resolvable. Police officers do have commonweal obligations but they also have the right to protect their own interests. Attacks of the blue flu and perhaps outright strikes are likely to be part of the urban landscape for the foreseeable future. Municipal funding authorities do have evaluative responsibilities, but police organizations do require some degree of independence. As compared to rigid accountability, perhaps the "little lies"[26] associated with alteration of crime statistics are a minor problem. Court and appellate decisions do make it somewhat more difficult to control crime. But elimination or reduction of civil liberties invites creation of the police state that English and United States citizens feared in the nineteenth century. To paraphrase Jerome Skolnick, these dilemmas can never be resolved because they contain built-in contradictions.[27]

The preceding discussion should also alert us to some of the ways in which forces and organizations outside police departments affect policing. Court and appellate decisions influence the searches and arrests made by police officers. Municipal authorities have an impact on the methods used to assemble and disseminate crime statistics. Policing is thus structured by forces and organizations external to police departments. But the effects of external forces and organizations are not limited to those just identified. The types of communities and citizens patrolled by a police organization also have a profound effect on styles of policing.

STYLES OF POLICING AND COMMUNITY CONTEXT

Political scientist James Q. Wilson has identified three styles of policing: 1) watch, 2) legalistic, and 3) service.[28] Additionally, he provides evidence to suggest that these differences result from differences in the communities and citizens served by a police department.

The Watch Style of Policing

Watch departments tend to be located in older cities with high concentrations of poor and minority citizens. Machine politics are also characteristic of these cities. Chicago, under the leadership of the late Richard J. Daley,[29] and Philadelphia, under Mayor Frank Rizzo,[30] are two cities with high concentrations of poor and minority citizens, machine politics, and a watch style of policing.

In such cities, police officers minimize the law enforcement aspect of their role by acting primarily as reluctant maintainers of order. *Avoidance is the dominant characteristic of the work of the patrol officer.*[31] Police ignore many minor problems such as traffic violations and juvenile rowdiness. Problems involving minority and poor citizens also tend to be ignored. Gambling and other crimes with willing victims are seen as something the community—at least its powerful members—wish to tolerate, if not encourage. Consequently, these actions are generally ignored by police. Misdemeanors and other problems such as domestics (husband–wife disputes) are seen as private matters. Police officers are encouraged to follow paths of least resistance. They are tough in serious situations but render curbstone "justice" in others. Officers are generally poorly trained and little emphasis is placed upon the appearance of police officers or standardized procedures. And watch departments rarely have anything more than token planning, research, and community relations divisions.

The consequences of the watch style of policing are several. There is generally evidence of discriminatory arrests by patrol officers. Certain citizens—black, poor, young, and defiant—are special targets of police action. Crimes with willing victims are ignored, generally because police are paid to ignore these actions. Organized police corruption is frequent in watch departments. Unnecessary police violence also is frequent. The boundaries and expectations for police use of force are poorly defined and personal force is used to impose one's will or to render street justice.

The Legalistic Style of Policing

Legalistic departments also may be characteristic of older cities with relatively high numbers of poor and minority citizens. When such is the case, it is generally because a previous political machine and watch-style police administrator were both replaced by reformers. Los Angeles, under its former chief of police Edward Davis[32] and New Haven, Connecticut, under its former chief James Ahern,[33] were both examples of watch-style departments made legalistic by reform administrators.

Legalistic departments also are located in newer and relatively affluent cities administered by city managers. When such is the case, citizens in these communities want professional but unobstrusive policing. Oakland, California,[34] and Highland Park, Illinois,[35] are examples of legalistic departments located in affluent areas.

In such cities, police officers maximize the law enforcement aspect of their role. *Enforcement is the dominant characteristic of the work of the patrol officer.*[36] Common problems such as traffic law violations, public drunkenness, gambling, and other vices are all seen as situations requiring formal intervention. Juvenile rowdiness and domestic problems are handled as law-enforcement problems, with citizens sometimes arrested "for their own good." Officers in legalistic departments therefore generate large numbers of arrests and traffic citations. Police officers are rewarded for proceeding according to the book. Great emphasis is placed upon the personal appearance of police officers, with overweight officers encouraged to diet. Legalistic departments have functioning planning, research, and community relations divisions, and they use them to enhance the law-enforcement mission of the department. Community-relations officers may visit local merchants and encourage them to report all instances of shoplifting to the police.

The consequences of the legalistic style of policing are different from those of the watch style. Legalistic departments do not discriminate against minority, poor, or young citizens. The reason is quite straight forward: almost all misdemeanants and felons are arrested, almost all traffic law violators receive citations. Crimes with willing victims are vigorously investigated and organized police corruption is infrequent. Unnecessary police force also is infrequent since justice and punishment are seen as belonging to the courts and prisons, not the police.

The Service Style of Policing

Service departments are generally located in the affluent suburbs which surround many large cities. These suburbs generally contain white, middle- and upper-class citizens. Lakewood, Colorado,[37] Nassau (County), New York,[38] and Burnsville, Minnesota,[39] are three examples of affluent suburbs policed by service-oriented departments.

Service departments take all requests for police presence seriously. They also tend to be more proactive, initiating relatively large numbers of contacts. Although police intervention is frequent, it is rarely formal. The pace of work remains leisurely and is generally not troublesome. *Leniency is the dominant characteristic of the work of the patrol officer.*[40] Juveniles, traffic law violators, and citizens who are publicly drunk are warned rather than arrested or ticketed. Domestics are seen as opportunities to provide counsel or suggest referrals. Service departments generally have a sincere community-relations orientation and it may be located in a specific division. However, community relations also is the job of every officer, and special efforts, including team police, neighborhood police, and school liaisons are made to accomplish these ends. Officer Dick or Jane speaks to first graders about crossing streets safely, to fourth graders on bicycle safety, and to teenagers about "rational" approaches to drug and alcohol use. Officers receive a high salary and long training. In a minority of service departments, they wear blazers instead of uniforms.

In most respects, the consequences of a service orientation parallel those of the legalistic approach. There is little evidence of discrimination because nearly all citizens are counseled and released. Organized police corruption is infrequent since citizens can take advantage of opportunities available in nearby urban areas. Unnecessary police force also is infrequent since the usual precipitants—defiant or deviant citizens—are rarely present.

The Styles Illustrated

Perhaps the best way to illustrate these differences in styles of policing is to briefly consider typical reactions to two common problems: domestics (husband–wife disputes) and traffic law violations.[41] As can be seen in Table 3–1, there are clear differences in the ways officers in watch-, legalistic-, and service-oriented departments respond to domestics. In the watch department, officers treat the domestic as a private matter. At the very most, and then only after an extremely leisurely journey to the scene of a domestic, the watch-oriented officer will suggest that the combatants separate. The watch officer also is likely to warn the participants not to call again.

The legalistically oriented officer views the domestic as an arena potentially productive of serious criminality (an assault) and hence responds quickly. Unlike the watch officer, the legalistic officer views the domestic as a situation in which law enforcement in the form of arrest may become necessary. This is especially the case when the participants are disturbing the peace of persons other than themselves or when arrest appears to be in the best interests of those involved.

The officer in the service-oriented department views the domestic as an opportunity to exercise and polish the counselling and referral skills acquired during academy and in-service training programs. Occasionally dressed in a blazer, and having the time to do so because of the leisurely pace of work, the officer engages in "crisis intervention." If a neighborhood police system is in effect, the officer may stop by or discretely chat in a store to determine whether the problem has been resolved or whether suggested agencies have been contacted.

Similar differences exist in responses to traffic law violations. For officers located in watch departments, minor traffic law violations are something to be ignored. If they can't be ignored, the officer may gather the attention of the offending motorist by using the squad car's horn, pulling alongside, and yelling a warning out the window. Traffic stops are made

TABLE 3–1. Typical Police Responses by Type of Department and Problem

Type of Department	Problem and Typical Police Responses	
	Domestic	Traffic
Watch	Ignore/ minimize/ separate and warn not to call again	Ignore/honk horn and yell out window/ opportunity for money
Legalistic	Potentially productive of serious criminality/ law enforcement problem/arrest possible	Traffic citation
Service	Opportunity to counsel and refer citizen/"crisis intervention"	Counsel and advise

only when the violation is serious, when other motorists saw the officer witness the violation or, most frequently, when both conditions are present.

The exception to the tendency of officers in watch-oriented departments to ignore or minimize traffic law violations is when they represent a regularized source of (improper) income for officers. Chicago newspaper journalist Mike Royko describes the Chicago police early in the 1960s:

> ... On the Outer Drive, two policemen in a squad car spotted a speeder. They flipped on their red light and one of them played the spotlight on the car's rear window. The motorist pulled onto the shoulder, stopped, took out his license, folded a ten-dollar bill around it, and handed it to one of the policemen. The policeman put the ten dollars in his pocket, cautioned the man against speeding, returned the license, and they parted. The motorist was the kind the policeman liked. If he had been shy, or dense, the policeman would have had to stand there, hemming and hawing, trying to get the message across. That failing, he would have sighed and written a ticket.[42]

Most Chicago residents knew what was expected of them in traffic stop encounters and were prepared for them. They *kept* a five- or ten-dollar bill wrapped around their licenses, as James Q. Wilson reports:

> When I lived in Chicago during the late 1950s, police corruption was so pervasive and so readily evident as to be a source of nightclub humor. When Mort Sahl said the city's thoroughfares were "the last outpost of free enterprise," everyone laughed—nobody had to explain that traffic officers regularly solicited bribes from the motorists they stopped. When a friend of mine who was teaching at a local university asked the students in his class to open their wallets, he found that well over half had a $5 or $10 bill tucked into the plastic envelopes that held their driver's licenses.[43]

For officers in legalistic- or service-oriented departments, the traffic stop is a more perfunctory event. For the legally oriented officer it is simply an occasion for a traffic citation. For the service officer, it is an opportunity to advise and counsel the offending motorist about safe driving or the necessity of checking equipment such as brake lights or turn signals.

Sources of Variation in Styles of Policing

As evidenced by the differing approaches to domestics and traffic law violations, there exists considerable variation in styles of policing. The sources or determinants of this variation appear to be several.

First, a department's style of policing results from the interplay of the contradictory external norms examined earlier. In watch departments, primary emphasis is given the norms supportive of member interests.

Citizens are served, but only the most affluent or only in the most serious of situations. In the mundane flow of minor problems of which most police work is made, avoidance is the dominant concern. Avoidance minimizes the amount of effort put forth by officers so that paths of least opposition are followed. If organized patterns of corruption are present (and in many watch-style departments they are), then the interests of members, as well as those who do the corrupting, are again being served.

In legalistic departments, primary stress is given to the norms supportive of the interests of the persons in contact with the organization. Procedural and due process protections are rigidly followed during contacts with citizens. Commonweal obligations are acknowledged via an inflexible policy of arrest for nearly all who violate the law.

It is only in the service-oriented department that we find some evidence that commonweal interests are directly served. In this type of department, sincere effort is made to identify and then respond to the needs of community members. Police are responsible to and under the control of the community. In certain respects, the service department represents the ideal: a democratically controlled institution serving public interests.

The second important source of variation in styles of policing are the social and monetary resources of a community. Service-oriented departments are able to serve commonweal interests because they are given the time, money, and officers fundamental to democratic policing. The citizens policed also share similar lifestyles and values.

Watch departments are typically located in significantly less affluent areas. Resources are limited and relatively fixed or caste-like boundaries exist between community groups. These boundaries both represent and occasion the mutual suspicion and hostility often characteristic of intergroup contacts. People in one group share only one thing with people in other groups: a mistrust of one another.

The political orientation of elected officials in the communities served by watch departments contributes to this style of policing. In these communities, elected officials often represent privatized or special interests. The interests of the community's elite are almost always represented, but frequently the interests of those who provide illegal but widely demanded services—gambling, prostitution, drugs, and pornographic materials—are among those considered important by elected officials. Often this is the case because elected officials are illegally paid to represent these interests.[44] A police department in such a community generally has little choice but to offer a watch style of policing, one that ignores the criminal actions of persons protected by elected officials. If a legalistic department replaces a corrupt watch-style department, limited resources when combined with caste and class lines permit but one solution: rigid law enforcement with little or no effort at assistance or change.

In addition to the contradictory norms which define police departments, policing is shaped by other structural forces. The social and monetary resources of a community are reflected in its style of policing. However, independent of the community context of a department, all styles of policing are bureaucratically situated. And bureaucracy imposes its own structural requirements on police and policing.

THE POLICE BUREAUCRACY

Almost all formal organizations are bureaucratically structured. A bureaucratic organization has an administrative staff charged with the task of maintaining and increasing organizational efficiency. This is generally accomplished by coordinating and integrating member activities. In addition to an administrative staff, the late German sociologist Max Weber (1864–1920) suggested that an ideal or complete bureaucracy displays nine other characteristics.[45] We will examine these characteristics as we establish the bureaucratic structure of contemporary police organizations.

Clearly Defined Duties and Responsibilities

This first characteristic essentially refers to a division of labor and responsibility within the organization. Nearly all large police organizations and many smaller departments display a relatively fixed division of labor. The organizational structure of the Columbus, Ohio, Police Department is typical of departments of intermediate size (see Illustration 1).[46]

As can be seen in the illustration, the various responsibilities of the department are located within specific subdivisions. There is an administrative subdivision charged with the task of maintaining the organization by coordinating the other units of the department. An executive officer, with responsibilities to the chief, directs the administrative subdivision and the other three basic departmental subdivisions—service, uniformed, and investigative. These subdivisions are further divided into bureaus, each with specific responsibilities. The uniformed subdivision, the largest in all municipal police departments, contains the patrol, traffic, helicopter, and marine–park bureaus. The department also is hierarchically organized. Officers at each level report to persons at a higher level. All ultimately report to the Chief of Police.

Activities Guided by Rules and Regulations

Police organizations attempt to guide and control the actions of officers. Thick operations manuals full of rules and regulations are typical of nearly all police departments. In New York City, the current rule book is almost one foot thick.[47] Officers are told when they can legitimately fire their weapons (clear and present danger of injury to an officer or citizen, no warning shots, and never from a moving car), how to fill out reports (in black ink with no erasures), and how to deal with citizens

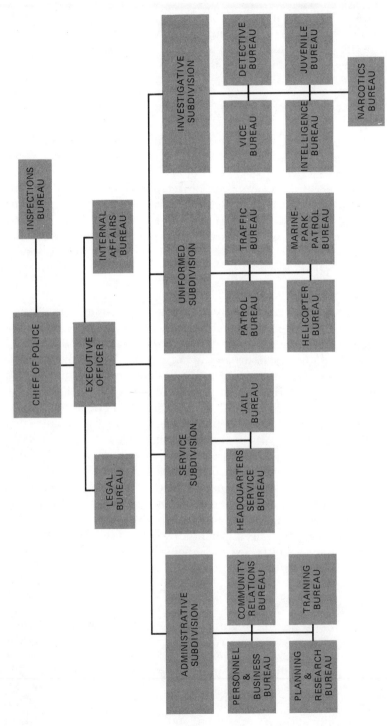

ILLUSTRATION 1. Organization Chart, Division of Police, Columbus, Ohio
Source: Columbus, Ohio, Division of Police, Police History (Columbus, Ohio: Police Athletic League, 1974), p. 54. Reprinted by permission.

(politely, impartially, and uniformly.) Rules also exist for more mundane activities:

> Even going to the toilet ... the rules dictate the formula by which ... (an officer) ... must request permission from a superior officer to leave post for "personal necessity." Any substantial departure from this will probably bring a complaint and fine.[48]

One important thing to know about these rules is that they are essentially useless.[49] Policing is an enormously complex task and even situations which appear similar vary in important ways. Some husbands involved in domestic disputes with their wives are drunk while others are sober; others are unemployed and drunk; and some are unemployed, drunk, and angry. No single rule or admonition can possibly cover all these contingencies. What exists is vague sermonizing as to what should be done. What actually is done depends on the nuances of the situation and the officer's skill in interpreting these signs. Politeness, impartiality, and uniformity hardly tell an officer how to handle the many different problems confronted during a working shift.

In addition to being useless, rules and regulations tend to be unenforceable. Police organizations are somewhat unique in that the lowest level members, street-level patrol officers, possess a great deal of latitude in their work.[50] To a great extent, the work of the patrol officer is unsupervised, and to a lesser extent it is unsupervisable. For most of the eight hours a patrol officer is out on the street, police supervisors have no reliable method for determining what the officer is doing. Police command is therefore precarious since most supervisors are not in a position to determine whether regulations are being followed.

One solution for the police administrator is to exercise strategic leniency. Administrators routinely ignore the minor violations of departmental regulations in exchange for adherence to a few important rules and a modicum of organizational loyalty. Jonathan Rubinstein provides a description of an instance of strategic leniency:

> Although nobody questions a supervisor's right to punish his men ... he will exhaust every available alternative before exercising his formal authority. For example, the operations room occasionally fills up with men who come in to drop off their reports and hang around to drink a cup of coffee.... The supervisors, even when they are annoyed, rarely tell the men in a direct fashion to get back on the street.... One day a captain from outside the district was about to enter the operations room when he noticed how many policemen were standing inside. He quickly turned away and walked over to the drinking fountain, where he took a long drink. Their sergeant, who had been urging the men to move ... said only, "I think he wants to come in here, but he does not want to embarrass anyone so he is waiting for you to leave."[51]

Decisions on the Bases of Technical Knowledge

Over the past decade, policing seemingly has become a more technical enterprise. Police departments have their own computers and they have access to national computerized information. When the computers are operating they speed warrant and identification checks. Patrol cars also have more equipment and this too is sometimes useful. It now is possible to produce an incredible variety of presumably altering sounds with the new electronic sirens. Additionally, police officers receive more extensive forensic training with the hope that they will make better arrests.

This equipment and training has little to do with routine policing and almost nothing to do with police decision making. Computers add information but they are not frequently used since most patrol time is spent providing services and engaging in administrative tasks such as report writing.[52] Most calls do not require quick police responses and thus do not require sirens that warble as well as wail.[53] Most arrest decisions do not reflect forensic knowledge.[54] Generally speaking, officers without forensic training make the same decisions as officers with it. Contemporary policing is thus situated in a more technical environment. But few instances of policing and almost no police decisions are based upon technical knowledge.

Written Documents and Permanent Files

Written documents preserved in permanent files are dominant characteristics of contemporary police organizations. Because police supervision is precarious, written documents are used by administrators as a clue to what patrol officers have been doing with their time. Additionally, because others are dependent upon reports of criminal incidents for their work (for instance, detectives charged with the apprehension of violators and prosecutors), written reports are part of the work of the patrol officer.

One way to think of the uniformed, motorized patrol officer is as a clerk/stenographer in a moving, cramped, and sometimes untidy office.[55] First, there are the patrol logs kept by all officers detailing when they went on duty, the weather conditions, the radio calls they were assigned, the pedestrian and traffic stops they initiated, and the total number of miles they drove during their watch. Sergeants use the mileage information to satisfy themselves that at least part of the squad's assigned district was patrolled during the eight hours officers are not under direct supervisory control. Next are the reports of the criminal and other incidents handled—the theft, burglary, damage to property, and accident reports. If an arrest is made, there are arrest reports; some are very short as in public drunkenness arrests, and some very long, such as robbery situations. If an officer is unlucky enough to hit another car, drive into a fixed object such as a fireplug, be required to use force to subdue a citizen, or discharge a gun, there are special report forms for each of these incidents. All of these and other forms are preserved in permanent files where they are accessible to supervisors, detectives, prosecutors, and other members of the criminal justice system.

Impersonal Relations Among Role Incumbents

Intensely *personal* relations are characteristic of the ties between patrol officers and to a lesser extent between patrol officers and their immediate superiors, sergeants. Most students of policing have commented on extent to which police officers display a sense of in-group solidarity. Whether it be attributed to the concerns with danger, authority, and efficiency said to be uniformly characteristic of the working personalities of police officers,[56] the occasionally dirty nature of police work,[57] or the simple facts of rotating hours and days off,[58] police officers display an exceptional degree of cohesiveness. This cohesiveness also apparently extends to off-duty relationships—patrol officers report frequent socialization with one another.[59]

Once above the level of the patrol officer's immediate supervisor, relations do tend to be somewhat impersonal. Above the sergeant are lieutenants and a precinct or district captain, and uniformed majors, colonels, and inspectors in charge of entire subdivisions. As is true of all large organizations, relations between high-level administrators and rank-and-file members are fleeting, impersonal, and frequently ceremonial.

However, the degree of impersonality between subordinates and superiors in police organizations is blunted by two features of police organizations—promotion from within and a shared sense of defensiveness. Almost without exception, the persons who occupy administrative positions within police departments began their police careers as patrol officers. Street experience is literally required since most departments do not allow patrol officers to take the sergeant's exam without first having spent a fixed amount of time—three to five years is not unusual—as a patrol officer.[60] Similar requirements exist for each additional step within the department. This common street experience reduces what would otherwise be entirely impersonal relations between supervisors and patrol officers.

This experience also produces a sense of defensiveness, which exists at all levels of the organization.[61] It consists of suspicion of persons not connected with policing and a feeling that outsiders cannot be trusted. The defensive feeling motivates officers of all levels to turn inward, thereby creating common ties between superiors and patrol officers. This collective isolation further reduces the impersonality of relations within police organizations.

Selection by Fixed Criteria of Merit

One of the characteristics of police forces is the existence of fixed criteria for the selection of new members. The "new police" who began their
work in London in 1829 had to be "under thirty-five, of good physique, at
least five feet seven in height, literate, and of good character."[62] In Washington, D.C., the "Metropolitan Police" who began their work in 1861 had
to meet the following requirements:

1. read and write the English language
2. United States citizenship
3. no criminal record
4. 5'6" height
5. 25–45 years old
6. local residence for at least two years
7. good health
8. good moral character[63]

In the century and a half since the development of modern police departments, selection criteria have changed very little. Until very recently
in New York, police recruits had to be at least five feet seven in height,
aged 21–35, in good health, of good character, and "literate," as evidenced
by possession of a high school diploma or its equivalent.[64] In Oakland,
California, recruits had to be United States citizens, at least 21 years of age,
free of felony convictions and emotional problems, five feet seven in
height and 150 pounds, of good moral character, and literate as indicated
by a high school diploma or its equivalent.[65]

What has changed over the last one hundred and fifty years is the way
police organizations screen potential recruits.[66] In addition to measuring
and weighing applicants, moral character is assessed via an extensive
background investigation, paper and pencil "personality tests" such as the
Minnesota Multiphasic Personality Inventory (MMPI) and, in some departments, polygraph checks and oral interviews. In addition to a high
school diploma or its equivalent, applicants take a civil service examination and the probability of selection increases with one's score. In addition
to signs of good physical health, departments require physical examinations by a police physician for all applicants and a physical agility test.

However, some of the "fixed" criteria are changing. For many years in
cities which contained sizeable minority populations and where, roughly
speaking, half of the residents were female, only one type of person occupied the police role: the white male. Deliberate policies of discrimination
and fixed selection criteria functioned to exclude minority citizens and
women.[67]

In 1972, Congress amended Title VII of the 1964 Civil Rights Act to
include state and local governmental agencies. Race and gender could no

longer be used as informal or formal selection criteria.[68] For those selection criteria which do remain, as in physical agility testing, a department now must prove that they are job-related. Additionally, court decisions are forcing police departments to increase the proportion of minority police. In Chicago, New York, Columbus, Cleveland, St. Paul, Tucson, Detroit, and elsewhere, departments are under court order to bring the proportion of minority police in the department up to the level of minority citizens in the city's population.[69] Currently in most large cities, selection criteria now include a modified physical agility test, civil service examination results, and minority group status.

Fixed criteria of selection have long been characteristic of modern police organizations. For too long, however, these criteria also functioned to discriminate against women and members of minority groups. Recent court decisions and congressional actions are beginning to alter selection criteria which had remained unchanged for one hundred and fifty years.

Impartial Evaluation and Discipline

The seventh characteristic of bureaucracies, "evaluation on the basis of proficiency and impartial disciplinary procedures," is only partially met by police organizations. Evaluative criteria generally are well known. They include the number of felony arrests and involvement in dramatic and visible situations such as fights. Evaluation also reflects the extent to which a patrol officer manages to stay out of trouble, helps sergeants by writing the required traffic and parking citations, and by doing the other things which help keep more distant administrators distant.

The problem with these evaluative criteria is that they do not measure proficiency. Most felony arrests are a matter of assignment, the nature of the offense (a crime against person involves a victim who may be able to point an accusing finger while a crime against property generally involves a victim who does not have a clue about the identity of the criminal), and colleagues willing to share felony arrests with other patrol officers. Visibility also is an inadequate evaluative criteria. As Egon Bittner notes: "Every officer knows that he will never receive a citation for avoiding a fight but only for prevailing in a fight at the risk of his own personal safety."[70] Since the criteria generally apply to all patrol officers, they can be described as impartial. It can hardly be said that they measure proficiency.

Discipline also is problematic within most police organizations. As noted, police command is precarious and strategic leniency is the norm. Patrol officers who violate departmental rules and regulations or who abuse their privileges generally are protected by their colleagues. Administrators share with patrol officers a sense of collective isolation and they tend to react defensively to charges of misconduct. What develops is a kind of double standard.[71] To outsiders, top-level administrators generally seek to give an appearance of impartial discipline. To insiders generally, and patrol officers specifically, police administrators protect their subordinates. An officer whose actions have proven somewhat troublesome may be assigned to a desk, hidden in the communications room or the city hall, or sent to police the squirrels, ducks, and occasional people that populate the department's outlying districts. If, however, there is a *significant and sustained public* outcry about the improper actions of an officer, the officer is alone; formal rules emphasize and force impartial disciplinary action and internal understandings emphasizing protection and defense cannot be acknowledged. Discipline, therefore, tends to be infrequent, but when it occurs formally it is impartial.

Work as a Sole or Primary Occupation

Prior to the rise of police forces, the people who served on the watch were engaged in full-time, nonpolice occupations during the day. At night, when it was their turn, they became part-time police officers.

Currently, policing is the major occupation of the urban police officer. Many officers, however, moonlight in a variety of police-related jobs such as security guard or bouncer. Others work part-time directing traffic at construction sites and in front of banks on Friday evenings. But policing remains their primary occupation.

Job Security

Job security, in the form of salaries, tenure, and retirement benefits, is characteristic of contemporary police departments. Until recently, police salaries were relatively low—averaging $5,300 for starting patrol officers in large cities in 1966. By the summer of 1977, salary levels had improved dramatically.[73] Police patrol officers start at $12,000 in Denver and Seattle, at $13,000 in New York, and at $14,000 in Los Angeles. Officers with three to five years' experience average between $17,000 and $20,000 in most large cities. The salaries of the urban patrol officers' immediate superiors, sergeants and lieutenants, range from $20,000 to $30,000. Salaries for starting and experienced officers thus compare favorably with those of public school teachers, solo practice attorneys and, for that matter, young college professors, occupations which require more than a high school education to enter but are generally less dangerous.

The tenure provisions for police officers also compare quite favorably with those of other occupations, including inexperienced college professors. Police officers must complete their academy training and a year as a probationary officer before receiving job security in the form of tenure.

Civil service and due process safeguards then serve to protect an officer against dismissal save for the most extraordinary of infractions. Most college professors, by contrast, start as assistant professors and generally serve five untenured years. At the end of that time, they are reviewed for *possible* promotion and tenure.

Retirement benefits are among the reasons that people choose to become police officers. Although considerable variation exists from city to city, half pay after 20 years if the officer retires before age 50, and three-quarters pay after 20 years if an officer retires after age 50, are not unusual provisions. Policing does take its toll after twenty or more years of sometimes tense and dangerous work. But many retired police officers are full-time employees bringing in a considerable "retirement" income.

In summary: we compared the characteristics of the idealized bureaucracy with those of contemporary police departments. We found that in most respects contemporary police organizations are bureaucratic, with a division of labor and responsibility, formal rules and procedures, written records preserved in permanent files, selection by reference to fixed criteria, work as a primary occupation, and job security. Other characteristics of a complete bureaucracy—decisions on the basis of technical knowledge, impersonal relations among role incumbents, and impartial evaluation and discipline—were found to be only partially characteristic of contemporary police forces. However, there exists sufficient agreement with the criteria laid down by Weber to confidently label police organizations bureaucracies.

THE POLICE BUREAUCRACY IN OPERATION

Bureaucratic structure is intended to permit the efficient attainment of organizational goals. For police departments, these goals include the prevention of crime, the apprehension of violators, and the maintenance of order. When bureaucratic structure facilitates goal attainment, its effects are positive. When it hinders or distorts goal attainment, the effects of bureaucratic structure are negative.

Positive Consequences of Bureaucratic Structure

In most respects, bureaucratic structure is well suited to the demands placed upon contemporary police organizations. For instance, the operational center of all urban police bureaucracies is the telephone center and dispatch room. In this room, telephone consoles must be constantly attended to and police dispatchers available to direct radio-equipped patrol cars to the scenes of incidents reported by citizens. Jonathan Rubinstein describes the division of labor and procedural rules of the dispatch room:

The dispatcher's major responsibilities are to interpret incoming calls and to dispatch assignments to the cars on his network. When one of the phones at the console rings, the "phone man" makes out a card containing the address of the caller and the nature of the complaint. The card is handed to the dispatcher, who sits before a lighted panel marked with the numbers of all the cars and wagons assigned to his division and a detailed map with district and sector boundaries clearly marked. He punches the card on a time clock and assigns the "job" to a car. He then files the card in a slot above the lighted panel reserved for that particular car and flips a switch turning off the light under the car's number on the panel. When the officer reports back to the dispatcher that he has completed the assignment, the card is again time-punched and the light turned on.[74]

Bureaucratic structure also permits the officers in the patrol subdivision to efficiently respond to the calls put out by dispatchers. The patrol subdivision puts a minimum of three shifts of officers on the street each day. Typically, the shifts run from 8:00 a.m. to 4:00 p.m. ("day watch"), 4:00 p.m. to midnight ("middle watch"), and midnight to 8:00 a.m. ("dog watch" or "last out"). In many police jurisdictions, and in most large cities, there is also a fourth or back-up shift which is on the streets during the highest crime period—8:00 p.m. to 4:00 a.m. More patrol officers are on the streets during weekend evenings and fewer during the day.

The patrol division is hierarchically organized and headed by an inspector who reports directly to the chief. The remainder of the patrol division is territorially organized on a precinct or station-house basis. Each precinct is headed by a captain who generally works only day watch. Consequently, each shift has a lieutenant and several sergeants assigned to it. The actual supervision of the patrol officers is the sergeant's responsibility.

Each shift begins with a roll call. Attendance is called and officers assigned squads and, if two person squads are used, partners. Since sergeants already know who is not going to be at work (officers are expected to call in before their shift and inform their sergeant they are ill) and because most officers work specific squads with regular partners, this part of roll call occurs over the din of conversations and jokes. Next, a report of serious crimes occurring in the precinct during the previous day is made. Special assignments or problems are noted and the officers are dismissed. Rarely are formal inspections held. Since roll call can take up to a half hour and since the officers on the watch going off duty tend to come in off the street before the end of their watch, there can be considerable periods of time each day when there are few, if any, patrol officers available. That is one of the reasons for the back-up or overlapping shifts used by many departments.

Once dismissed, a number of additional tasks remain before officers actually begin their work. If the department permits patrol officers to carry shotguns they must be collected and signed out before going on duty. Citation booklets are checked and in some departments rules require that the squad's equipment—lights, siren, and radio—be examined. The rules of nearly all departments also require patrol officers to search the backseat of their squad car before going out lest a citizen arrested by officers on an earlier shift has hidden a weapon or other materials in the car. Few officers bother to do this. Lastly, if the officers in the car during the last shift have left the remnants of their lunch or coffee in the squad or if the officers coming on duty are particularly tidy souls, a brief period of housecleaning is undertaken.[75]

At last nearly all is ready. In many departments the officers tell their dispatchers they are now clear to accept calls. The time they "clear" along with the weather and the mileage on the car are dutifully recorded in the squad's log. They will later record the mileage at the end of shift. If it is a busy night or if the squad is in a high-crime area, there may be a backlog of calls that the officers must handle. Perhaps there is a report to be written or some juveniles to be dispersed. If, however, the watch is slow or the officers work a relatively peaceful district, the officers begin their proactive cruising, searching for signs of disorder or criminality.

In most respects, then, bureaucratic structure is well suited to the demands placed upon contemporary police organizations. The operational center of the police bureaucracy, the dispatch room, permits citizens to make their needs known to police. And the bureaucratic structure of the patrol subdivision makes it possible for the department to respond to these needs. Although far from perfect, the bureaucratic structure facilitates the routine work of the patrol subdivision.

Bureaucratic structure also expedites one type of nonroutine police patrol work: rapid assembly in the face of public demonstration and riot. Demonstrations and riots were among the reasons that a police force grew in London, Washington, D.C., New York, and especially, Boston. From their inception, organized police were involved in the control of these activities and they proved relatively effective, if frequently brutal.[76] In 1873, a London writer described some of the ways in which bureaucratic structure aids police control of public demonstration and riot:

> As each police constable being along might easily be overpowered, and as the men of each section, or even division, might be inferior in numbers to some aggregation of roughs or criminals collected in a given spot, it is arranged that ... reserves of force can be gathered ... and concentrated upon the disquieted area, and as the commissioners command the whole district, and the force is organized and united, while roughs act in small areas, and have diverse and selfish interests, the peace of London may be held secure against violence.[77]

Technological advances have increased the speed with which patrol officers can be assembled.[78] The first of these advances—telegraph networks permitting slow communication between district stations and headquarters in the 1850s—allowed supervisory personnel in one district to secure additional officers from other districts. The call box of the 1870s made it possible for individual officers to request assistance. These were telegraphs and only allowed officers to signal and describe very simple needs, since officers were not taught Morse code. The telephone call box of about 1890 permitted two-way communication between patrol officers and their superiors. The advent of telephones (enabling citizens to communicate their needs to police) and the installation of two-way radios in patrol cars further increased the speed with which patrol officers could be gathered. Citizens can alert police to problem areas, dispatchers can mobilize the patrol officers, and, if need be, off-duty officers can be called and ordered to report to work.

Parenthetically, we are all well aware of the fact that rapid assembly of police may also exacerbate situations. The violent police–citizen confrontations during the 1960s and early 1970s clearly suggest this possibility.[79] The present point, however, is that bureaucratic structure and communicative technology make such convergence possible. What actually happens once officers are assembled and under the control of administrative superiors is another issue.

In sum: bureaucratic structure eases the routine and nonroutine operations of the patrol subdivision. Routine policing involves the bureaucratic linking of needy citizens with available police as mediated by the dispatch room. This same bureaucratic structure permits rapid assembly of personnel in the face of public demonstrations and riots.

Negative Consequences of Bureaucratic Structure

Bureaucratic structure is intended to permit efficient attainment of organizational goals. However, it is not sufficient to create an organization with bureaucratic characteristics and then assume that goals are being efficiently attained. Supervisors, members of the general public, and other elements of the criminal justice system desire evidence that the department is operating efficiently.

Statistical performance records are used by police supervisors, members of the general public, and others interested in assessing the efficiency of police. These simple counts of police activities constitute:

> the internal product of police work ... the statistical measure which the sergeant uses to judge the productivity of his men, the lieutenant to assure himself that the sergeant is properly directing his men, the captain to assure his superiors that he is capably administering his district, and the department administrators to assure the public that their taxes are not being squandered.[80]

From a distance, the assembly of these statistical performance records would appear to be simple. All one need do is count whatever someone else is or might become interested in and then show the results to the interested party. But, we have already learned how one such count— crime reported to the FBI for inclusion in the *Uniform Crime Reports*— is subject to alteration for organizational, administrative, and political reasons. Such miscounting is not limited to the *Uniform Crime Reports* data.

Deliberate alteration of statistical performance records occurs in a number of settings, including the case clearing work of detectives and the "activity"-generating behavior of precincts and patrol officers. The reasons are the same as those behind the adjustment of *Uniform Crime Reports* information. All statistical performance records have organizational, administrative, and political significance: "good numbers" reflect positively on individuals, subdivisions, the department, and the city. Accordingly, detective bureaus, precincts, and patrol officers modify their statistical performance records.

The Detectives. Television and movie accounts of what detectives do suggest that they spend a great deal of time investigating, putting criminals together with crimes. These popular accounts also suggest that their detection efforts are quite effective.

Detectives generally receive their cases in the form of reports of criminal incidents written by patrol officers. The statistical performance record used to evaluate the effectiveness of inquiry is the clearance rate. This record is the percent of offenses handled by detectives which are solved or cleared by an arrest of persons whom detectives believe to be responsible for the crimes. If burglary detectives cleared eight of ten burglaries by arrest, their clearance would be eighty percent, a figure in line with media portrayals of the successful detective.

However, the results of recent research and examination of the national clearance rate information published in the *Uniform Crime Reports* combine to suggest that fictionalized accounts grossly exaggerate the method and frequency of successful detecting. In 1975, for instance, the Rand Corporation released the results of its study of "the criminal investigative process."[81] The Rand study relied upon mailed questionnaires returned by 153 detective bureaus and follow-up visits to 25 police departments. The results do not support the mass media image of the detective. It was found that detectives spend most of their time involved in unproductive interviews with victims. It was also discovered that most cleared cases are the result of the identification of the offender at the time the offense is reported. For cases without offender identifications, routine clerical tasks such as checking mug-shot or modus operandi files produce the majority of additional clearances. The researchers concluded that approximately

half of the officers assigned to detective bureaus could be placed elsewhere
without impairing existing clearance rates.

William B. Sanders' 1977 study, *Detective Work,* advances essentially
similar conclusions.[82] Sanders observed detectives in a small county police department located in California. The "Mountainbeach" detectives
also cleared most of their cases by pursuing offender identifications available at the time the offense was reported. Additional cases were cleared
by working "leads" and "clues" available in the original report of the
incident or developed during interviews with victims. When reports or
interviews failed to produce leads, routine clerical tasks such as checking
field interrogation reports produced the majority of other clearances.

Sanders' account, however, differs from the Rand study in its implied
conclusions. The Rand researchers advocated reassignment of detective
personnel. Sanders' data suggest that such an action would be premature.
Leads and clues are not self-existing or even apparent social facts. They
are recognized and developed by detectives using skills reflective of experience. Routine clerical tasks are not as random or even as routine as they
appear. Organizational information and knowledgeable colleagues shape
search procedures. The Rand study also fails to devote systematic attention to proactive detecting, the stake-outs which occasionally produce
clearances. The Sanders' study is less drastic in implied conclusion, principally because it is richer in observed detail.

This is an important difference, but it should not blind us to a point of
essential agreement: victims provide the information fundamental to successful detecting. Crimes against persons (homicide, rape, aggravated assault, and robbery) generally involve knowledgeable victims who can
provide detectives with useful information. Clearances rates are therefore
relatively high for these offenses. In 1977[83] the national clearance rate for
homicide was 75 percent, 51 percent for rape, and 62 percent for aggravated
assault. Robbery is something of an exception, principally because the
violator frequently uses a disguise to reduce the probability of detection.[84]
Victims have less information and the national clearance rate for robbery
reflects this: 27 percent.

Crimes against property (burglary, larceny, and auto theft) generally
involve victims unable to provide detectives with useful information.
Clearance rates are therefore relatively low for these offenses. In 1977, the
national clearance rate for burglary was 16 percent, 20 percent for larceny,
and 15 percent for auto theft. As suggested by these figures, victim information is fundamental to successful detecting.

Victim information limits the amount that detectives can legitimately
accomplish with respect to their clearance rates. Despite these very real
and well-known limits, detective bureaus are under organizational, administrative, and political pressure to increase clearance rates. Detectives
therefore use illegitimate but reliable techniques to improve clearance
rates: "unfounding"[85] and "defounding."[86]

Unfounding is a declaration that a criminal incident previously thought to have occurred did not happen. It is an extremely reliable method of increasing clearance rates. Suppose that a detective bureau receives 3000 burglary reports from the patrol subdivision each year. If we assume that this particular detective division precisely replicates the national clearance rate for burglary—16 percent—it will make a total of 480 burglary arrests. If, however, the detective bureau unfounded 200 of these offenses, then the 480 arrests for 2800 offenses would yield a clearance rate of 19 percent.

Police departments are understandably reluctant to talk to researchers about unfounding. In one situation, however, a researcher was able to study the incidence of and reasons for unfounding. Jerome Skolnick studied the "Westville" department's detective bureau and found that detective bureau officers unfounded 32 percent of the burglary incidents and 8 percent of the robbery offenses. According to Skolnick, the reason the Westville detectives unfounded cases was to give the appearance of effective and efficient detecting since "any small statistical changes—on the order of say, 2 or 3 percent per year . . . is . . . suggested . . . in staff meetings, conferences, to outsiders—as evidence of a department's competence."[87]

Defounding is a declaration that a criminal act originally thought to be a felony is now a misdemeanor. Defounding has the same effect as unfounding. If a detective bureau receives 3000 felonious burglary reports and defounds 200 hundred of them to misdemeanors ("breaking and entering"), it has increased its burglary clearance rate to 19 percent.

In the early 1970s, Richard M. Nixon's "law and order" rhetoric led to the establishment of a national laboratory for crime in Washington, D.C.[88] The District was to be a model, an example of what could be done to combat crime, given sufficient money and police personnel. Crime statistics were used to measure the success of the program. And crime did go down, especially burglary and larceny, but not because of more money or police personnel. It went down because police defounded. David Seidman and Michael Couzens studied defounding in the District and concluded:

> that at least part of the decline in crime statistics for the District of Columbia is attributable to increased downgrading of larcenies and, to a lesser extent, of burglaries. This appears to be a pure case of the reactivity of a social indicator: the fact that the statistic is used as a measure of performance affects the statistic itself. The political importance of crime apparently caused pressures, subtle or otherwise, to be felt by those who record crime—pressures which have led to the downgrading of crimes.[89]

Defounding is thus a reliable way of "getting the crime rate down."

However, unfounding and defounding do have their limits, principally the skepticism of the public and the FBI. At one time, New York City's crime rate decreased while its clearance rate increased, both precipitously.

Rates for other cities were opposite. Even the FBI became skeptical and it refused to accept or publish New York City data in the *Uniform Crime Reports* until unfounding and defounding were brought under control. A reform administration reduced unfounding and defounding and the results were dramatic: a 200 percent increase in robbery and assault, a 300 percent increase in larceny, and a 500 percent increase in burglary. All of these increases occurred in a single month.[90]

The Precinct. Detective bureaus are not the only units under organizational, administrative, and political pressures to produce good statistical performance records. Police precincts as units are subject to evaluation by departmental administrators. Precinct performance records also are accumulated and presented to the public as an indicator of the overall performance of the department.

Like their colleagues in detective bureaus, precinct administrators have had to confront the results of recent research. Since the creation of police departments, the idea of preventive patrol has been a cardinal tenet. But as early as 1930, researchers noted that the preventive effects of routine patrol "lack scientific documentation."[92]

The Kansas City Preventive Patrol Experiment was intended to provide that evidence.[93] Three areas of Kansas City were chosen for the experiment: one received regular patrol, a second received double patrols, and a third received no routine patrol, with police entering only when citizens requested their presence or to make an arrest. The areas were then compared using a number of measures. The researchers reported there were essentially no differences between the three areas in measures which included rates of crime and police response times. Alternatives to routine preventive patrol were not suggested by the researchers.

Perhaps because of the lack of recommendations, precinct administrators and their superiors have ignored or condemned the Kansas City Experiment.[94] They also remain concerned with the production of good statistical performance records, ones that reflect positively on the precinct and on the department as a whole.

Certain activities which precinct administrators count are not easily controlled or altered. Arrests for serious offenses such as rape and aggravated assault result from the circumstances surrounding these acts, a victim who possibly can identify a violator, and good fortune as when a patrol car is inadvertently at or near the scene of a dispatched offense.[95] Arrests for these offenses rarely reflect superior administration or extra effort on the part of subordinates. On the basis of their own experiences, most precinct administrators and patrol officers know that the findings of the Kansas City Experiment are essentially correct.

The wise administrator, therefore, concentrates on those activities which can be controlled—meter, parking, and moving violations—

responds to the periodic requests for increases in rates of arrests for minor offenses such as public drunkenness, and hopes that everything does not go wrong at once in rates of arrest for serious offences.

In order to insure that the countable activities under the control of the administrator produce acceptable statistical performance records, sergeants typically take special precautions. A sergeant short of parking or meter citations will assign a silent car—one that dispatch does not know is out on the street—to do nothing but write citations. I once rode with a patrol officer in a silent car who wrote 32 parking citations in eight hours.[96] The officer took only a short lunch break and was exhausted when finished. The officer's sergeant and colleagues, however, were most pleased.

A sergeant in need of moving violations will also put a silent car out and may give the officer the privilege of leaving early provided a certain number of citations have been issued. In this circumstance, the officer typically goes to a location known to be productive of traffic law violations.[97] In most cities there are intersections with short yellow lights. Large numbers of motorists regularly go through on the red, thereby providing officers with a nearly inexhaustible source of moving violations.

Precincts, then, are subjected to evaluative pressures essentially similar to those experienced by the detective division. Much like detectives who unfound and defound, precinct administrators take special precautions to insure that their performance records are acceptable.

The Patrol Officer. The equivalent of the army's foot soldier, the patrol officer is at the very bottom of the police hierarchy. Consequently, he or she is under pressure to generate actions useful to others in their efforts to document effective policing. Patrol officers also are evaluated by superiors. The statistical performance records for officers generally include counts of felony and misdemeanor arrests and citations for moving and parking violations. In one city, monthly tallies of felony arrests and citations for moving violations by individual officers are posted in precinct roll call rooms.[98] The reactions of patrol officers to these bureaucratic and evaluative pressures are several.

Patrol officers and their superiors know that felony arrests are largely a matter of assignments and good fortune. They rarely occur as a result of individual effort. An officer working a district without much serious crime, one who is writing moving violations for a sergeant, or one who is simply experiencing a run of bad luck stands a good chance of coming up empty in felony arrests.

The solution is for patrol officers to share felony arrests.[99] A felony-in-progress call typically produces a number of responding units. If the officers involved are fortunate to arrive while a violator is still present, they have a felony arrest. In this circumstance, it is not at all unusual to observe officers deciding who will get credit for the arrest. In most situations several officers are credited for a single arrest.

Traffic law violations, however, are a different story. They are frequent and easily detected. The patrol officer's problem is not discovering traffic law violations since they are abundant. It is a defensive matter: care must be taken to avoid issuing too many tickets lest superiors come to expect more of the officer each month.

Sociologist David Petersen's study of police reactions to traffic law violators in a medium-sized city suggests the solution employed by patrol officers.[100] The department emphasized traffic enforcement and officers were under pressure to generate traffic citations. Patrol officers responded by establishing an informal quota of roughly 40 traffic citations per month —two per working shift. Patrol officers encouraged their colleagues not to deviate from this norm, although individual officers were free to determine how they acquired these citations. Some officers worked traffic on a regular basis. Others put off working traffic until the end of each month and then finished in a flurry of citations. Still others worked traffic aggressively early in the month and then tapered off, sometimes precipitously:

> On one occasion an officer and the writer sat in an immobile patrol car in a deserted parking lot in the city for more than three hours. "I'm a little tired tonight," the officer explained. "Besides, I've got thirty (citations) already this month, and it's only July 11th."[101]

In sum: the consequences of bureaucratic structure also are negative for police organizations and the public they serve. Means originally intended to facilitate goal attainment—statistical performance records—become ends in themselves in the face of political, organizational, administrative, and evaluative pressures. Personnel who might otherwise be involved in other activities spend their time generating good numbers. Specifically, the need for good numbers forces detective bureaus to unfound and defound cases, sergeants to assign silent cars, and patrol officers to share felony arrests and establish traffic citation quotas. Policing is thus rich in "little lies" intended to give outsiders the appearance of effective policing.

SUMMARY

The essential task of this chapter has been the presentation of a structural analysis of police organizations. Towards that end we examined the contradictory normative environment of police organizations, styles of policing and community context, and the bureaucratic structure characteristic of contemporary police and policing.

The overall argument advanced is that contemporary policing is shaped in important ways by structural forces. Normative contradictions, for example, shape labor negotiations involving police while community resources affect styles of policing. Bureaucratic structure imposes its own requirements on policing; some are positive, as in the case of routine patrol, and some are negative, as with the means–ends inversion of statistical performance records.

Notes

1. For a discussion of formal organizations, see Peter M. Blau and W. Richard Scott, *Formal Organizations* (San Francisco: Chandler, 1962).

2. Blau and Scott, *Formal Organizations,* especially pp. 40–57.

3. Blau and Scott, *Formal Organizations,* p. 57.

4. For a discussion of the other types of formal organizations identified by Blau and Scott, see their *Formal Organizations,* pp. 40–57.

5. Based upon Cyril D. Robinson, "The Deradicalization of the Policeman: A Historical Analysis," *Crime and Delinquency, 24* (1978): 129–151; and Francis Russell, *A City in Terror: The 1919 Boston Police Strike* (New York: Penguin Books, 1977).

6. Louis Radelet, *The Police and the Community,* 2d ed. (Encino, Calif.: Glencoe Press, 1977), p. 441; and Robert M. Fogelson, *Big-City Police* (Cambridge, Mass.: Harvard University Press, 1977), pp. 195ff.

7. For a discussion of police strikes prior to 1974, see Fogelson, *Big-City Police,* pp. 213ff. There undoubtedly have been other police strikes, and there will always be more. For instance, one newspaper reports that police in Cincinnati, Ohio, will strike unless wage offers are increased. See *The Columbus Dispatch,* February 17,1979, p. A-2.

8. Russell, *A City in Terror,* pp. 242–244; and Peter K. Manning, *Police Work* (Cambridge, Mass.: The M.I.T. Press, 1977), pp. 287–288. All of the material which follows on Baltimore is from these sources.

9. Based upon articles appearing in the *The Cleveland Plain Dealer* on the following dates - page numbers are noted in parentheses: December 14, 1977 (p. A-1 and A-10); December 16, 1977 (p. A-11); December 17, 1977 (p. A-1, A-6). All of the material which follows on the Cleveland strike is based upon these sources.

10. Based upon articles appearing in *The Christian Science Moniter* on the following dates - page numbers are noted in parentheses: August 15, 1978 (p. 2); August 17, 1978 (p. 6); August 18, 1978 (p. 6). All of the material which follows on the Memphis strike is based upon these sources.

11. Based upon articles appearing in *The Columbus Dispatch* on the following dates— page numbers are noted in parentheses: February 9, 1979 (p. A-10); February 10, 1979 (p. A-3); February 16, 1979 (p. A-3) and March 6, 1979 (p. A-3). Also based upon "The CBS Evening News," February 16, 1979. All of the material which follows on the New Orleans strike is based upon these sources.

12. Herman Goldstein, *Policing in a Free Society* (Cambridge, Mass.: Ballinger, 1977), p. 14.

13. For a discussion of this same process in the context of mental illness see Eliot Freidson, "Disability as Social Deviance," in Earl Rubinbton and Martin S. Weinberg (eds.), *Deviance: The Interactionist Perspective* (New York: Macmillan, 1968), pp. 117–120.

14. *The Wall Street Journal,* January 11, 1972, p. 1.

15. *Crime in the United States, 1977* (Washington, D.C.: Department of Justice, 1978), pp. 54–73.

16. See Manning, *Police Work,* pp. 179–185.

17. *Crime in the United States,* p. 3.

18. Radelet, *The Police,* p. 334.

19. For a representative sampling of police opinion, see Yale Kamisar, "When the Cops Were Not 'Handcuffed'," in Arthur Niederhoffer and Abraham S. Blumberg (eds.), *The Ambivalent Force* (Hinsdale, Ill.: The Dryden Press, 1976), pp. 319–324.

20. Jonathan Rubinstein, *City Police* (New York: Ballantine, 1973), pp. 390–391.

21. Niederhoffer and Blumberg , *The Ambivalent Force,* p. 244.

22. Niederhoffer and Blumberg, *The Ambivalent Force,* p. 244.

23. Edward Banfield, *The Unheavenly City Revisited: A Revision of the Unheavenly City* (Boston: Little, Brown, 1974).

24. Radelet, *The Police,* p. 336.

25. Radelet, *The Police,* p. 336.

26. We shall have occasion to question this argument later in the book.

27. Jerome Skolnick, *Justice Without Trial,* 2d ed. (New York: Wiley, 1975), p. 244.

28. James Q. Wilson, *Varieties of Police Behavior* (Cambridge, Mass.: Havard University Press, 1968).

29. See Mike Royko, *Boss: Richard J. Daley of Chicago* (New York: Signet, 1971); and Herbert Beigel and Allan Beigel, *Beneath The Badge* (New York: Harper & Row, 1977).

30. See Joseph R. Daughen and Peter Binzen, *The Cop Who Would Be King: Mayor Frank Rizzo* (Boston: Little, Brown, 1977).

31. Based upon Wilson, *Varieties;* James Q. Wilson, "The Police and The Delinquent in Two Cities," in Stanton Wheeler (ed.), *Controlling Delinquents* (New York: Wiley, 1968), pp. 9–30; and personal observation.

32. See Steven Keeney, "Research Becomes a New Battleground for Police," *Police Magazine* (Prototype Issue, Summer 1977): 54.

33. See James F. Ahern, *Police in Trouble* (New York: Hawthorn Books, 1972).

34. Skolnick's "Westville" is commonly identified as Oakland, California. See Skolnick's *Justice Without Trial* for a description of the department. See Peter K. Manning, "The Researcher: An Alien in the Police World," in Niederhoffer and Blumberg, *The Ambivalent Force,* p. 105, for a statement that "Westville" is Oakland. Skolnick, (*Justice Without Trial,* p. 251) asserts that guesses as to the identity of the city have thus far been incorrect. I am of the opinion that Manning is correct. Apart from all of this, Sherman identified Oakland and decribes it in largely legalistic terms. See Lawrence W. Sherman, *Scandal and Reform: Controlling Police Corruption* (Berkeley, Calif.: University of California Press, 1978), pp. xxx–xxxiv and passim.

35. Wilson, *Varieties,* p. 300.

36. Based upon Wilson, *Varieties;* Wilson, "The Police"; and personal observations.

37. Personal observation.

38. Wilson, *Varieties,* p. 200.

39. Personal observation.

40. The material which follows is based upon personal observations.

41. This material is based upon personal observations.

42. Royko, *Boss,* p. 111.

43. James Q. Wilson, "To Catch a Cop (A Review of *Beneath the Badge: A Story of Police Corruption* by Herbert Beigel and Allan Beigel)." *The New York Times Book Review Section* (Sunday, September 18, 1977), pp. 10 and 34.

44. For example, John A. Gardiner and David J. Olsen (eds.), *Theft of the City: Readings on Corruption in Urban America* (Bloomington, Ind.: Indiana University Press, 1974).

45. Max Weber, "The Theory of Social and Economic Organizations," in H. H. Gerth and C. Wright Mills (trans.) *Max Weber: Essays in Sociology* (New York: Oxford University Press, 1946), pp. 329–441.

46. For the organizational chart of the "Mountainbeach" sheriff's office, see William B. Sanders, *Detective Work: A Study of Criminal Investigations* (New York: Free Press, 1977), p. 32.

47. Sherman, *Scandal and Reform*, p. 128.

48. Arthur Niederhoffer, *Behind the Shield* (Garden City, N.Y.: Doubleday/Anchor Books, 1969), p. 44.

49. Sherman, *Scandal and Reform*, p. 128.

50. Egon Bittner, *The Function of the Police in Modern Society* (Washington, D.C.: U.S. Government Printing Office, 1970), p.56.

51. Rubinstein, *City Police*, pp. 41–42.

52. See John Webster, *The Realities of Police Work* (Dubuque, Iowa: William C. Brown, 1973).

53. See Richard J. Lundman, "Domestic Police – Citizen Encounters," *Journal of Police Science and Aministration, 2* (March 1974): 22–27.

54. See Donald J. Black, "The Social Organization at Arrest," *Standford Law Review, 35* (August 1970): 1087–1111.

55. Based upon personal observation. One sign of this is that patrol officers generally carry a briefcase in their squad cars. It contains copies of the report forms used by the department.

56. Skolnick, *Justice Without Trial*, pp.42–70.

57. James L. Walsh, "Professionalism and the Police: The Cop as a Medical Student," in Harlan Hahn (ed.), *Police in Urban Society*, (Beverly Hills, Calif.: Sage, 1971), pp. 225–246.

58. John P. Clark, "Isolation of the Police: A Comparison of the British and American Situations," *Journal of Criminal Law, Criminology and Police Science* (Fall 1965): pp. 307–319.

59. John Van Maanen, "Rookie Cops and Rookie Managers," *The Wharton Magazine, 1* (Fall 1976): 54.

60. Rodney Stark, *Police Riots* (Belmont, Calif.: Wadsworth: 1972): p. 228.

61. See Wilson, *Varieties*, p. 78.

62. T. A. Critchley, *A History of Police in England and Wales, 900–1966* (London: Constable, 1967), p. 52.

63. Kenneth G. Alfers, *The Washington Police: A History, 1800–1866* (unpublished Ph.D. Dissertation, George Washington University, 1975), p. 201.

64. Niederhoffer, *Behind the Shield*, pp. 35–43.

65. Thomas C. Gray, "Selecting for a Police Subculture," in Jerome Skolnick and Thomas C. Gray (eds.), *Police in America* (Boston: Little, Brown, 1975), p.47.

66. See Gray, "Selecting for a Police."

67. See Robert Rigoli and Donnell E. Jones, "The Recruitment and Promotion of a Minority Group into Established Institution," *Journal of Police Science and Administration, 3* (December 1975): 410–416.

68. See Anthony V. Bouza, "Women in Policing," *FBI Law Enforcement Bulletin, 44* (September 1975): 2–7.

69. See Richard H. Rowan and James S. Griffin, "St. Paul Police Department Minority Recruitment Program," *Police Chief, XLIV* (January 1977): 18–20; Goldstein, *Policing*, pp. 267–271; and Michael S. Serrill, "Urban Crisis is Making Police Vulnerable—And Angry," *Police Magazine* (Prototype Issue, Summer 1977): 2–16, passim.

70. Bittner, *The Function*, p. 57.

71. I am grateful to Peter K. Manning for sharing this observation with me.

72. Sue Titus Reid, *Crime and Criminology*, 2d ed. (New York: Holt, Rinehart and Winston, 1979), p. 374; and Serrill, "Urban Crisis," p. 4.

73. Serrill, "Urban Crisis," p. 4. Recent contract settlements have resulted in even higher starting salaries. In Columbus, Ohio, new officers now start at $16,900.

74. Rubinstein, *City Police*, pp. 73–74.

75. To some extent, these prestreet activities are delaying tactics. Few workers, professors included, begin their work as soon as their "shift" begins. Others have emphasized the danger-delaying and -denying implications of these actions. For a discussion of this latter point, see Niederhoffer, *Behind the Shield,* p. 61; and Manning, *Police Work,* pp. 300–332.

76. Center for Research on Criminal Justice, *The Iron Fist and The Velvet Glove* (Berkeley, Calif.: Center for Research on Criminal Justice, 1975), pp. 16–17.

77. Allan Silver, "The Demands for Order in Civil Society: A Review of Some Themes in the History of Urban Crime, Police, and Riot," in David J. Bordua (ed.), *The Police: Six Sociological Essays* (New York: Wiley, 1967), p. 8.

78. This section is based upon Rubinstein, *City Police*, pp. 15–25.

79. See *Report of the National Advisory Commission on Civil Disorders* (New York: Bantam Books, 1968).

80. Rubinstein, *City Police,* p. 44.

81. Peter W. Greenwood, Jan M. Ckahen, Joan Petersilia, and Linda Prusoff, *The Criminal Investigation Process, Vol. III: Observations and Analysis. Rand Corporation* (Washington, D.C.: U.S. Department of Justice, 1975), pp. 65–83.

82. Sanders, *Detective Work,* passim.

83. *Crime in the United States,* 1977, p. 161.

84. See Sanders, *Detective Work,* p. 179.

85. Skolnick, *Justice Without Trial,* p. 169.

86. I seriously doubt that I am the first to use the "defounding" phrase. But a relatively thourough search of the literature failed to yield a similar usage.

87. Skolnick, *Justice Without Trial,* p. 173.

88. David Seidman and Michael Couzens, "Getting the Crime Rate Down: Political Pressure and Crime Reporting," *Law and Society Review, 8* (Spring 1974): 457–493.

89. Seidman and Couzens, "Getting the Crime," p. 476.

91. See "Abuses in Crime Reporting," in Marvin E. Wolfgang, Leonard Savitz, and Norman Johnston (eds.), *The Sociology of Crime and Delinquency,* 2d ed. (New York; Wiley, 1970), pp. 114–116.

92. Steve Keeney. "Research Becomes a New Battleground for Police," *Police Magazine* (Prototype Issue, Summer 1977): 54.

93. George L. Kelling, Tony Pate, Duane Dieckman, and Charles E. Brown, *The Kansas City Preventive Patrol Experiment—A Summary Report* (Washington, D.C.: The Police Foundation, 1974).

94. Keeney, "Research Becomes," pp. 55ff.

95. See Manning, *Police Work,* p. 300.

96. Also see Rubinstein, *City Police,* p. 57.

97. See Rubinstein, *City Police,* p. 154. I have seen this same technique used in three different cities.

98. Personal observations.

99. Personal observations.

100. David M. Petersen, "Informal Norms and Police Practices: The Traffic Ticket Quota System," *Sociology and Social Research, 55* (April, 1971): 354–362.

101. Petersen, "Informal Norms," p. 359.

CHAPTER 4

Police
Socialization

INTRODUCTION

Socialization is the process whereby individuals learn the values and behavior patterns of a group.[1] Police socialization is the process whereby police recruits learn the values and behavior patterns characteristic of experienced police officers.

Until very recently, there existed a near consensus among social scientists that all police officers display a distinctive set of values and behaviors. For patrol officers, these values and behaviors were placed together under the general heading of an occupational or "working personality."[2] Although there was some variation according to the study one consulted, the attributes commonly said to be part of the patrol officer's working personality include: authoritarianism, suspicion, racism, hostility, insecurity, conservatism, and cynicism.[3] In the words of George Kirkham: "There are, of course, other things ... but these are the essence of what contemporary scientific research suggests are the hallmarks of the police personality."[4]

In an effort to discover the origins of these values and behaviors, initial research attention was directed toward the personality characteristics of new police officers. Researchers initially thought that policing attracted persons who were predisposed towards authoritarianism and the other attributes characteristic of the police personality. The results of this research consistently indicate that policing does *not* attract a distinctive type of personality.[5]

Researchers then turned their attention to the nature of police socialization, principally police selection and training practices. These studies appear to suggest the origins of the working personality of patrol officers:

1) selection procedures favoring whites and males at the expense of black and female applicants; 2) a quasi-military or "stress" training academy experience emphasizing "discipline, following orders ... and looking sharp;"[6] and 3) field training officers who encouraged a "hard-nosed" approach to policing.

Over the past few years, however, there have been a number of *slow* and *uneven* changes in police socialization practices. As compared to the largely white high school educated males of the recent past, more police recruits are black, female, and college educated. Quasi-military training is slowly giving way to less rigid alternatives. Some academies feature technical training with primary emphasis given to the maintenance of order under the rule of law. A minority of academies offer nonstress training featuring a condensed liberal arts curriculum. Some departments select "coaches" for new officers in terms of their police skills and adherence to a "softer" approach to policing. A possible effect of these slow and uneven changes is diversity in the working personalities of patrol officers.

Slow change is characteristic of police socialization practices. But data descriptive of the nature of these changes are scattered and fragmentary. Information on the possible effects of these changes are even more elusive. It is therefore necessary to be very cautious in assessing the consequences.

Purpose of the Chapter

The purpose of this chapter is to describe and analyze the effects of police socialization practices. Because slow change is characteristic of police socialization, our description and analysis will be divided into two general sections.

The first section focuses on the nature and effects of *traditional* police socialization practices. It emphasizes that until very recently nearly all police recruits were white males with a high school education. It describes the quasi-military training and abrupt transition to the world of the "street cop" characteristic of many contemporary training efforts and nearly all past efforts. It will be suggested that the major effect of traditional police socialization is to produce a distinctive working personality with attributes ranging from authoritarianism to cynicism. Most of the officers currently policing urban America and many of those currently being trained to take their place are the products of traditional police socialization practices.

The second part describes and cautiously analyzes the possible effects of the slow changes in socialization practices. It emphasizes that more police recruits are black, female, and college educated. It describes the uneven movement away from quasi-military training. It also describes the sometimes softer philosophies of the field training officers who coach new police officers. It suggests that a possible result of these gradual changes is diversity in the working personalities of patrol officers.

TRADITIONAL POLICE SOCIALIZATION

If police patrol officers display a distinctive working personality, an important question is: what are the experiences and other forces which give rise to a concern with authority, cynicism, and the other characteristics commonly identified as being part of a patrol officer? The goal of this section is to suggest that these attributes are a result of traditional police socialization practices.

Departmental Screening Procedures

All police organizations have a set of minimum requirements for applicants. Typically these include a minimum height and weight (five feet eight and 150 pounds), a minimum and maximum age (21 and 35), good health and eyesight as determined by a police physician, and a high school diploma or its equivalent.[7] Traditional height and weight requirements make it difficult for women to become police recruits.

Second, nearly all police organizations require persons who meet these criteria to take and pass a civil service examination. Traditional civil service exams basically are general intelligence tests and like many similar tests, they are biased in favor of the racial majority.[8] Civil service examinations make it difficult for black and other minority persons to become police recruits.

Third, persons who meet these criteria take a physical agility test. Although the specifics vary by department, a traditional test involves a timed run, evidence of an ability to carry a specified weight a certain distance, and a test intended to measure a person's ability to pull a trigger a fixed number of times in a certain period of time (for persons who are right-handed, 45 dominant hand trigger pulls and 15 left-handed trigger pulls in one minute—one "shot" a second).[9] Physical agility tests make it difficult for women to become police recruits.

Fourth, nearly all departments investigate the "character" of those who meet all of the above criteria. An applicant's occupational history, financial status, school and military records, and criminal and delinquency records are examined. Throughout this investigation, the traditional guiding principal is: "All doubts about a candidate should be resolved in favor of the department."[10] Persons with a serious and in some cases minor criminal records are therefore excluded. Black citizens, who generally are shown less leniency than white citizens by police, are often further excluded by reason of a criminal record.[11]

Finally, many departments use a battery of psychological tests and an oral interview. The latter frequently is the final hurdle and it generally consists of an interview of the applicant by police and civil service representatives. Questions are asked of applicants—"What would you do if ... " —and judgments as to suitability are made by those present. Such judgments are of necessity discretionary and factors such as race and gender almost certainly play a role.[12]

Taken together, traditional departmental screening procedures eliminate most applicants. In New York, for instance, only 15 percent of those who apply are ultimately accepted. The figures are 6 percent in Tucson, Arizona, and only 4 percent in Los Angeles.[13]

Demographic and Psychological Characteristics

The net effect of these screening procedures is the creation of a remarkable homogeneous group of individuals. Until very recently, nearly all police recruits have been white and male. In 1973 in New York City, for instance, black and Puerto Rican citizens accounted for 31 percent of the city's population, but only 8 percent of the 30,000 New York City police. In Boston, only 2 percent of the police were black; in Baltimore, 13 percent; New Orleans, 6 percent; Birmingham, 2 percent; Cleveland, 8 percent; Dallas, 2 percent; and Los Angeles, 5 percent.[14] Women have been even less visible. Of those who were police officers, most were essentially secretaries or worked with juveniles. In 1971, out of a total of nearly 500,000 police nationwide, "fewer than a dozen women police officers were patrolling city streets."[15]

In addition to race and gender, police recruits also are similar in several other respects: they have a high school education, they come from a blue-collar background, they are young, and they are attracted to policing because it offers job security.[16]

Psychologically, police recruits apparently are *not* inclined to authoritarianism, punitiveness, or cynicism before becoming police officers. Arthur Niederhoffer, for instance, compared police recruits with others and concluded that there was "no self-selection among authoritarian personalities prior to appointment."[17]

John McNamara reached a similar conclusion. He sought to determine whether there was evidence that police recruits were more punishment-oriented than other people.[18] McNamara gave police recruits a punitiveness scale developed in a previous study of community leaders. The questionnaire asked recruits to indicate which societal response—treatment or punishment—was most appropriate for various types of delinquent acts. As compared to community leaders, police recruits were significantly *less* punitively oriented: 37 percent of the community leaders were highly punitive as compared to only 19 percent of the police recuits. Moreover, 70 percent of the police recruits scored low in punitiveness as compared to 53 percent of the community leaders. A number of potential explanations exist, including the inevitable problem of paper-and-pencil data collection techniques—people choose responses in terms of their social desirability. But one explanation is that police recruits do not have an unusually punitive attitude upon entrance to a police academy.

Cynicism can be defined as "diffuse feelings of hate and envy, impotent hostility, and the sour-grapes pattern"[19] directed either towards people generally, the department, or both. Arthur Niederhoffer devised and administered a 20-item cynicism questionnaire to police recruits. He found that police recruits who had just entered the academy were not a cynical lot: three-quarters of naive recruits expressed confidence in the department they had just entered and in the training they were about to receive.[20]

Traditionally, the persons who become police recruits are a remarkably homogeneous group. They are almost exclusively white males with a high school education and a blue-collar background. They are also similar in their belief that policing is the best-paying job they can find and in their lack of the working personality of the patrol officer when they enter the academy. Instead, the elements of the working personality are taught during the quasi-military training characteristic of the police academy.

The Quasi-Military or "Stress" Academy[21]

The persons who enter police academies have good reasons to feel proud. They have been assessed mentally, physically, emotionally, and psychologically, and have been found acceptable. They also traditionally have been favored by discriminatory selection and testing procedures. Most of the others who began the application process with them did not meet the requirements or were not so favored.

Police academies rarely treat recruits as special. Instead, they almost immediately inform them that they will be watched constantly and that they can be dismissed for even minor infractions of the rules. They encourage recruits to eliminate signs of individuality and to identify with the department generally and the recruit class specifically. During the long classroom hours which take up most of the students' time, the academies treat them like recalcitrant high school dropouts. They tell them where and how to sit, what they can and cannot have on top of and in their desks, and, if it proves necessary, as it likely will, how to yawn properly. Lastly, elaborate rules govern the interaction between recruits and their superiors. In a large midwestern city, recruit–superior interaction is undertaken according to these procedures:

> When you ask permission to speak to, or are ordered to report to the Captain or Lieutenant through the chain of command, you will inform the secretary of your purpose, and she will announce your presence. When told to enter an office—the recruit shall approach the front of the desk by direct route and stop

at attention and state, "Recruit——has permission to speak to the Captain or Lieutenant, Sir," or "Recruit——reporting as ordered, Sir." You will remain at attention until given the command "At Ease." Upon leaving, you will again come to attention until given the command, do an "About Face," and then leave the office.[22]

Presumably the recruit also leaves by a direct route.

For the recruits who have been in the military, these experiences and rules are familiar. For those who have not had military experience, the initial academy experience is more novel and difficult. For both types of recruits, however, elation at being accepted and a dogged determination to survive combine to produce an eagerness to get on with the process of learning how to become a police officer.

This education involves a number of steps. First, the recruit has to become acquainted with the formal *rules* of the academy. To do otherwise is to invite a seemingly endless string of rule-violative activities. Second, the recruit has to master the *formal content* of the academy and generally give evidence of understanding the complexities of lawful arrest, search and seizure, and crime scene preservation. The recruit also has to learn how to use police weapons and to drive cars at high speeds. Third, the recruit learns to be especially attentive to the *informal content* of the academy. Paradoxically, it is largely through these informal mechanisms that police recruits first learn the nature of "real" policing. Fourth, recruits learn to deal with the feelings of *disenchantment* their quasi-military training occasions. Lastly, recruit disenchantment is confirmed during their *early street experiences.* The effect of quasi-military training appears to be creation of a distinctive *working personality.*

The Rules.   There is a rule or set of rules for almost everything the recruit does while at the academy. Nearly everything that others take for granted the police recruit has to reexamine in light of academy rules. Consider the nature of recruit behavior while in class. Unlike most of you in college and university classes (who sit where you please, posture as you see fit, and even read a newspaper, fall asleep, or simply leave during a particularly boring lecture), the classroom behavior of recruits is prescibed by rules. What follows are the classroom rules of a traditional police academy:[23]

Recruits must always be neat in personal appearance. Men will shave daily. Beards are prohibited. Hair styles will conform with current Divisional regulations.

A recruit does not chew gum . . . nor do you walk or stand with your hands in your pockets.

All recruits will stand Reveille ten minutes before mark on time and Retreat ten minutes before mark off time, on each school day. These formations will be in full recruit uniform unless otherwise specified.

Classes start on the even hour for a 50-minute duration, followed by a 10-minute break.

Recruits will be quietly seated at their desks before each class time.

Tardiness or Absence Without Leave will call for a letter of explanation.... Recruits will not be excused from classes for any reason unless permission is first granted through the chain of command....

Smoking will not be permitted in the classroom....

Recruits shall check the bulletin board in classroom daily....

Desks will be assigned to recruits in alphabetical order. Each recruit will occupy the same desk throughout the training period and be responsible for proper alignment and condition.

Whenever you wish to ask a question of the instructor during class, you will raise your hand and wait for recognition. You will stand, state your question and resume your seat immediately after stating the question. Questions must be limited to the subject under discussion at the time. Interruptions for questioning are encouraged and invited. Questions coming to mind that are irrelevant should be written down in your temporary notebook, then asked later at the proper time.

When called upon by an instructor, you will rise to answer. Recruits will be required to come to attention when a commanding officer of the rank of captain or higher enters the classroom. The first person observing such commanding officer will sound off with the command "Attention." Personnel will remain at attention until the command "Carry on" or "As you were" is given. Do not call attention if the class is in session.

There are many other rules—no chinning on shower rods and the soles and stitching of shoes are to be shown "no neglect." One effect is that the sheer number of rules makes "it highly unlikely that any recruit can complete the training course unscathed."[24] Indeed, a recruit who manages to remain unscathed for a period of time stands a good chance of being done in by other recruits or deliberately attentive academy personnel. Even the most conscientious recruit can inadvertently neglect soles and stitching.

The solution for the police recruit is to join with other recruits in an effort to minimize the effects of academy rules. Recruits assist one another

prior to inspections, share responsibility for taking the mandatory classroom notes, and occasionally prepare crib sheets for use during examinations. They also learn that not all infractions are noticed and that penalties
are randomly assigned. And as the academy experience progresses, rules
are relaxed in an effort to achieve some degree of continuity between the
recruit experience and the more informal routines of the precinct.

The consequences of the rules characteristic of quasi-military training
academies are several. In relying upon others as a solution to the problem
of extensive rules, police recruits develop a strong sense of in-group
solidarity. A distinctive "we–they" imagery begins to emerge, one that is
further developed in the academy and on the street. Police officers, especially those of the same rank, are the only persons who can really be
trusted because only they really understand.

Second, the rules of the academy and the ways in which they are
enforced suggest to recruits that departmental rules are something to be
gotten around rather than followed. In John Van Maanen's words: "Under
the impact of 'stress' training, the recruit . . . learns that the formal rules
and regulations are applied inconsistently; behavior that is punished in
one case is ignored in another."[25]

Third, the extensive rules characteristic of the quasi-military academy
make administrators into punishers rather than teachers. Academy personnel and "brass" generally are seen as people who do things to you, not
for you.

The rules of police academies are thus comprehensive and seemingly
rigid. They foster a strong group identity, a tendency to circumvent rather
then follow rules, and a view of administrators as punishers.

Formal Content. The classroom topics covered during quasi-military
training are disproportionately weighted towards two general issues: the
law and physical training.[26] The former emphasizes the kinds of laws
police officers enforce and the proper ways to enforce these laws. The
latter emphasizes the physical skills thought to be fundamental to policing. Recruits are taught the use of weapons, the handling of cars at high
speeds, and self-defense tactics.

The formal content of the quasi-military academy gives recruits a distorted image of policing. The amount of time devoted to law enforcement
suggests that patrol officers make large numbers of arrests. They do make
arrests, but not that often. As Albert J. Reiss, Jr., has noted: "No tour of
duty is typical except in the sense that the modal tour of duty does not
involve an arrest of any person. . . . "[27]

Stress training also fails to indicate that of the arrests which are made,
many are discretionary—that is, the citizen could just as easily have been
released. Laws generally contain words or phrases such as "A peace officer

may ... arrest a person ... whenever ... (there exists) ... *reasonable cause* to *believe* that the person ... has committed a public offense.... "[28] "May," "reasonable cause," and "believe" are all words and phrases which imply discretionary rather than automatic arrest. Additionally, over-crowded jails and courts make discretionary arrests a fact of life for patrol officers; there is simply not enough room in the criminal justice system for all who violate the law. Time is therefore needed to recognize discre-tion, to learn of its problems, and to suggest how it might be exercised. In the quasi-military academy, that precious time is spent memorizing laws.

The amount of time devoted to physical training, weapons use, high-speed driving, and self-defense also gives recruits a distorted image of police patrol work. It suggests that policing is a physically demanding and dangerous enterprise. It is, but not very often. Recruits clearly need to know how to do these things safely, but they also need to know when to use their weapons and how to weigh the generally remote benefits of a chase against the very real hazards of doing so on crowded city streets. Most importantly, a patrol officer needs to know how to talk so as to minimize the need for self-defense.[29] Talk can calm, ennoble, and suggest alternatives. The proper use of talk requires time. Time spent in physical training is time away from learning how to talk.

In most respects, then, the formal content of the traditional quasi-mili-tary academy is necessary but not sufficient. Patrol officers need to know the law and how to defend themselves. But they also need to understand that the law is discretionary and that talk is the major skill of the patrol officer. Quasi-military training tends to exclude these things; therefore, to the extent that this is the case, the formal content of this type of academy is insufficient.

Informal Content. The typical police recruit in a traditional academy is plagued by a variety of questions. They ask themselves and each other: "What is it really like out there on the streets? How do I arrest someone who doesn't want to be arrested? Exactly when do I use my nightstick and how do I do it? What do the other patrol officers expect of me?" The list of possible questions is almost endless, since the imagined possibilities are nearly infinite.

The quasi-military academy is poorly equipped to formally respond to these questions. The extensive rules the recruit is expected to follow fail to provide meaningful answers. Specific answers to these questions do not come from the long classroom hours devoted to technical topics. The outside speakers occasionally brought in from colleges and universities know even less, or so it seems. Academy instructors appear to have been away from the streets for so long that the only thing they know is the materials in the notebooks they lecture from. The formal content of the quasi-military academy generally does not answer the many questions which trouble recruits.

The informal information that they receive provides recruits with answers to their questions. The major vehicle for the delivery of these informal messages is the "war story." Their content frequently emphasizes defensiveness and depersonalization.

War stories.[30]   Instructors in police academies and in military boot camps encounter a similar problem. Although police recruits and military personnel know that their instructors have been there once, they remain skeptical that their instructors can really prepare them for their respective experiences. The solution for police and military instructors is essentially similar: war stories.

The war story is an episode which involves the person telling the story and establishes that the instructor was there (on the street for police instructors or in combat for military instructors) and acted in ways consonant with recruit images of proper action. The war story also may relate elements of the history of the department, important people, places, or events. Let us consider two brief examples of the war story and then turn to their general themes, defensiveness and depersonalization.

Richard Harris went through a recruit school for purposes of research. During a class break, he overheard a recruit who had been a police officer in another city and was now being retrained by the academy Harris was studying. His war story revolves around an emergency call and it illustrates the theme of defensiveness—a general distrust of persons not connected with policing.

Experienced Recruit:	You know, I got a call for my resuscitator. I never was taught how to use it, but I turned the corner on two wheels, skidded up to the house, jumped out and popped the trunk, and brought out the resuscitator. He was already dead, but the guy came up to me, "I'm glad they called you; you really know what you're doing!" And I never knew what to do!
Novice Recruit #1:	Sure it's a big con job. You go in, you see that he's pissed and crapped in his pants. You know he's dead, but you ... put the resuscitator on "one." It makes a lot of impressive noise....
Novice Recruit #2:	Shit, you go in and tell them he's dead....
Experienced Recruit:	You aren't a doctor. You have to take care of them until they're pronounced dead. How can you tell if he's dead or not? ... *You can't pronounce him dead, or you'll wind up behind bars for the rest of your life.*[31]

Historian and sociologist Jonathan Rubinstein went through the Philadelphia police academy, also for purposes of research. A self-defense instructor told recruits a war story which illustrates the theme of depersonalization—treating self and others as objects rather than people:

> ... A jack (a piece of lead in leather jacket, about 6 inches long) is a beautiful weapon, but it is very dangerous fellas. ... I remember once we were looking for a guy who had beaten up a policeman and escaped from a wagon. I found him hiding under a car. To this day I don't know if he was coming out to surrender or to attack me, but he was coming out before I told him to move. He was a real big guy and I didn't wait. I had my jack ready, and as he came up I hit him as hard as I could. I thought I killed him. He was O.K., but since then I haven't carried a jack unless I was going on some dangerous job. I don't want to beat someone to death, and with a jack you can never be sure. You should get yourself a convoy (a jack with a spring handle which creates a whipping action) and use it in your fist. *If you punch for a guy's heart, the whipping action of the spring will snap it forward and break his collarbone. Then you've got him.* [32]

Defensiveness.   An informal theme emphasizing a general distrust of persons and organizations outside the police department is characteristic of the quasi-military police academy. It was Richard Harris' experience that the manifestations of defensiveness during academy training were several.[33]

Departmental rules and regulations were constantly stressed. Recruits were told that the only way in which they could protect themselves from the inevitabl accusations of misconduct by outsiders was to give the appearance of doing everything by the book.

Recruits were also told that special police units have been created to protect the department and its officers from outsiders. The Community Relations unit was portrayed as a defensive response to accusations that the department treated certain segments of the community (for instance, minority and powerless citizens) improperly. Community Relations functioned to deflect these criticisms. And, recruits were informed that the Internal Inspection Squad had been created to protect the department from attempts to create a Civilian Review Board.

Further, recruits were constantly reminded that they had to be alert lest the "invisible eyes" which constantly monitor police actions discover an impropriety. Instructors indicated that real or imagined misbehaviors would almost automatically result in telephone calls to superiors, letters which become part of an officer's dossier, and occasionally civil suits demanding exorbitant amounts of money.

Lastly, defensiveness was manifested in the attitudes of instructors towards out-groups. Politicians were characterized as persons who did not know what they were doing. Black and other minority citizens were portrayed as criminal threats who denied the work ethic by living on welfare. Members of the press were described as deceitful and likely to distort any story involving police. Women were portrayed as causing special problems because of the possibility of accusations of sexual assault. In general, "anyone who was not a law enforcer was not to be trusted."[34]

One major informal theme of the quasi-military police academy is defensiveness. This theme is indirectly communicated to recruits in a variety of situations including the war story. The message or caution is always similar: the only people to be trusted are other police officers.

The informal emphasis given defensiveness has several effects. Recruits learn that one method of avoiding accusations of impropriety by outsiders is to give the *appearance* of proper policing. The alteration of crime statistics which we spoke of earlier is one example because it gives the general public the illusion of effective policing. A second illustration is keeping dead citizens "alive" until they are pronounced dead by a physician.

Recruits also learn that secrecy is a method of deflecting criticism. They quickly recognize that the only people who can be counted on in tight or problematic situations are other police officers. An early researcher, William Westley, described the "blue curtain" which surrounds many police organizations:

> Policemen are under explicit orders not to talk about police work with anyone outside the department; there is much in the nature of a secret society about the police; and past experience has indicated that to talk is to invite trouble from the press, the public, the administration, and their colleagues.[35]

Defensiveness also produces a number of legal deviations. For instance, many experienced police officers believe that there are people who would like to "off a cop." Police academy instructors frequently communicate this belief to recruits and encourage them to err on the side of caution. At the academy studied by Harris, recruits were told: "I'd rather use unnecessary force than have someone tell my widow I was afraid of his civil rights."[36]

Depersonalization.[37]   The quasi-military academy encourages recruits to view themselves and others as members of categories. Individual merits and idiosyncracies are ignored in favor of all-encompassing typologies. Complex issues are rendered simple and are simply resolved. Certain citizens are criminal because they choose to be evil. Punishment is the only appropriate response to persons who make such a choice. The sources and consequences of this depersonalization are several.

The public depersonalizes police officers. Recruits quickly learn that in the eyes of outsiders they have acquired a "master status."[38] While they were formerly many things to many people—spouse, parent, employee, friend, neighbor, homeowner, and customer—they quickly become one thing to many people—a police officer. The public treats police officers as members of a category. Much like grammar school children who have a difficult time envisioning *their* teacher doing things other than teach, police recruits experience a similar reduction in self. Where there was once diversity there is now homogeneity.

The new police of London were among the first to experience the effects of the master status of police officer. Writing in 1856, an English essayist observed:

> Amid the bustle of Piccadilly or the roar of Oxford Street, P.C.X. 59 stalks along, an institution rather than a man. We seem to have no more hold of his personality than we could possibly get of his coat buttoned up to the throttling point. Go, however, to the sectionhouse . . . and you no longer see policmen, but men. . . . They are positively laughing with each other! [39]

Grammar school children share the same sense of surprise when they become privy to the laughter and conversation of the teacher's lounge.

The consequences of the public's depersonalization of police are profound. Police recruits feel a loss of identity, a feeling of having been stripped of their individuality. They also experience a number of "unnormal restrictions" on various aspects of normal life. They turn inward and recreate with recruits and experienced officers, people who have experienced a similar loss of identity. Much like teachers who take pains to make certain their students do not gain access to the teacher's lounge, police recruits hide their recreation from outsiders. The somewhat exaggerated description of "choir practice" by Joseph Wambaugh is a result.[40]

A second source of depersonalization is the academy experience. Instructors categorize all class members as representative of a single category—recruits—thereby denying individuality. The extensive rules, authoritarian relations between administrative personnel and recruits, and the emphasis on standard operating procedures contribute to a loss of self. There is precious little room for individuality in the quasi-military police academy.

The major consequence of depersonalized academy training is to encourage recruits to depersonalize citizens. People are divided into two general groups—law-abiding and criminals. The precise labels vary—whites and hillbillies, blacks and niggers, students and radicals, good people and assholes—but the theme is constant: there are two kinds of people in the world, the good and the evil. Since they are themselves depersonalized by citizens and their academy, recruits in turn depersonalize the public, creating a dichotomized and frightening world to police.[14]

Disenchantment. Police recruits enter the quasi-military academy as a group of highly motivated young people. They generally have survived a rigorous screening procedure and frequently waited a long time for a recruit class to form. They are eager to have their questions answered and their fears calmed. They are intensely interested in learning how to become good police officers.

For these young people, the quasi-military training experience is almost always something of a disappointment. Long and dull classroom hours are part of the problem. There also are other problems: the ever-present possibility of messing up, the constant subservience, and the seeming irrelevance of academy training. Important questions are not answered and fears worsen. The academy has not taught them what they want to know.

These feelings of disenchantment have a measurable effect on police recruits. Arthur Niederhoffer devised a 20-item questionnaire to measure cynicism among police officers. Among the officers who filled out the questionnaire were recruits who had just entered the academy and recruits with two to three months of training completed.

As measured by Niederhoffer, just two or three months at the academy produced a "precipitous rise"[42] in the levels of cynicism evidenced by police recruits. For example, nearly half of naive or first-day recruits believed that the average police superior was "very interested in the welfare of his subordinates"; two months later, only 13 percent of the experienced recruits held that same belief.[43] Similarly, nearly 80 percent of first-day recruits believed that the department was an "efficient, smoothly operating organization"; two months later, less than a third of the experienced recruits held that same opinion.[44] Lastly, nearly three-quarters of new recruits believed that police academy training "does a very fine job of preparing the recruit for life in the precinct"; two months later, less than a quarter of the experienced recruits believed that was the case.[45] What Niederhoffer found was that quasi-military police academy training caused police recruits to become cynical about themselves, others, and the department they were jointing.

John Van Maanen undertook a study similar to Niederhoffer's, with parallel results. Van Maanen sought to determine how much a recruit's feelings about a department changed during police training. He developed a questionnaire to measure the motivational level and organizational commitment of recruits. The questionnaire was administered to succeeding waves of recruit classes at varying intervals so that a more or less constant monitoring of recruit beliefs was possible. Since Van Maanen also did participant observation, his research involved the use of "multiple methods." Consequently, we can be somewhat more confident about his results.

Van Maanen found that as the recruits' careers progressed, there were significant changes in attitudes and beliefs. Recruit motivation declined significantly as did organizational commitment. Van Maanen interprets the results of his study as follows:

The early stages of the person's police career are marked by some rather vivid attitude changes. First, motivational attitudes drop considerably never to rise again. Only personal rewards remained associated with working hard. This seems to indicate a growing realization on the part of recruits that a hard work ethic was not linked to most of the system rewards. Second, organizational commitment also fell sharply; yet remained relatively high vis-à-vis several other occupations. Third, the recruits were somewhat dissatisfied . . . with their experiences at the police academy. The degrading nature of the recruit's role during the academy's stress training serves to detach the newcomer from his old attitudes, resulting in a scaling down of high but unrealistic attitudes about the department.[46]

Van Maanen goes on to note that the recruits' solution to these changes is to "stay low and avoid trouble."[47]

The person who leaves the quasi-military police academy is clearly different from the person who enters. At the outset of the academy experience, the recruit identity is eagerly embraced; however, a few months later, the typical recruit is disenchanted with the recruit role and the department.

Early Street Experiences

New police officers arrive at their assignments disenchanted with what they have experienced and apprehensive about what they will experience. They arrive convinced that they do not know very much about policing, largely because of an irrelevant academy experience. They are eager to get on the street and learn, for the very first time, how to police.

In nearly all departments, the task of teaching rookies the practical side of policing is the responsibility of experienced officers. These officers, called Field Training Officers (FTOs)[48] in some departments, are almost always officers with considerable street experience. This is to some extent an advantage because they are in a position to pass along the rudiments of the folk-art of policing to rookies. It is also a disadvantage since having a lot of street experience means that an officer has elected not to attempt promotion to sergeant or has failed in that attempt. Traditionally, FTOs are among the most bitter, cynical, authoritarian, defensive, depersonalized, and depersonalizing officers in the department.

The tasks of the FTO are several: 1) to finalize the rookie's break with the academy experience; 2) to provide an example of how real police officers go about the job of policing; 3) to expand upon informal academy themes, including defensiveness and depersonalization; and 4) to evaluate the rookie's willingness to risk injury during "heavy" calls.

The first task is quite easily accomplished, since rookies are already disenchanted with their training experiences. Experienced officers capitalize on these feelings and quickly assure the rookie that the academy experience is a waste of time. There is near consensus among social scientists who have studied police socialization that FTOs tell recruits to "forget" their academy training.[49]

Rookies, however, want to forget only certain parts of the training. They feel they must remember how to use their weapons although they never may have occasion to do so. They will not forget the war stories they were told and their themes of defensiveness and depersonalization. War stories have that effect on people. They feel they must forget whatever elements of compassion may have been present during their academy training. Whatever good policing is, it does not appear to involve compassion. Policing apparently is too dangerous to risk being or seeming soft.

Having been assured that feelings of disenchantment are entirely appropriate, the FTO's second task (to provide an example of how real police officers work) is facilitated. Training has not helped the rookie, so perhaps the FTO can.

Rookies learn to police by watching and then, very slowly, by doing. At least initially, the rookie is expected to be "a good listener, quiet, unassuming, and deferential without being obsequious toward ... superior officers."[50] During husband–wife disputes, for instance, the rookie is silent and watches how the experienced officer handles the problem. In a watch-style department, the rookie learns that experienced officers police the domestic by separating the combatants, listening more patiently to the complaints of the wife, telling both to stop or by asking and telling the man to leave, and by warning both that if officers are called back more serious actions will have to be taken. The rookie also learns that if two officers are present, one should play the tough role by threatening formal action while the other should emphasize a softer approach, suggesting that unless the problem can be quieted, then formal action will "regrettably" have to be taken. Since most husbands and wives do not want formal action, rookies learn that threats are an effective police tool.

The rookie is slowly given the opportunity to handle problems under the supervision of the experienced officer. The rookie makes pedestrian and traffic stops, polices citizens who are publicly drunk or juveniles disturbing others, and warns the owners of barking dogs. In these and other situations the rookie learns, literally by doing, the craft or folk-art of routine policing.[57]

In teaching and showing the rookie the actual practices of policing, the FTO expands and illustrates the informal themes characteristic of the quasi-military academy. FTOs tell recruits that only police can be trusted and that the world is indeed populated by two kinds of people. For instance, during his very first tour of duty as a police officer, George Kirkham made a clumsy arrest of a chronic public drunkenness offender. The drunken citizen reciprocated by leaving a deposit of feces in the backseat of their squad car. The citizen was booked and jailed and while cleaning the backseat of the squad car, Kirkham's FTO observed:

> They ought to put them on an island somewhere. Treat 'em real good. Give 'em any damn thing they want. Then use 'em for parts.... You know like when some decent person—maybe a little kid—gets sick and needs, say, a lung or a kidney, take it off one of these assholes.[52]

"Decent people" and "assholes" populated this officer's world and they also came to dominate Kirkham's.

Of all the things the FTO does, the most important is to evaluate the rookie's response to "hot" or "heavy" calls.[53] These calls involve on-going or actual threats to the life of a citizen or police officer and are dispatched with a curious simplicity:

"Man with a gun."
"Shots fired."
"Silent (alarm), Seven-Eleven Store."
"D.K. (drunken) domestic, man with a gun."
"Officer needs assistance."

In the mind of experienced officers, these calls and others like them are what "real" policing is all about. The rest is simply to be endured. Because lives may be at stake, including those of police officers, the heavy call is a terribly important event in the early street experience of the new police officer. It is the crucial test. If the rookie is ever to be trusted it must be passed. A rookie need not be reckless; indeed, recklessness is looked upon with disfavor. But, the recruit must prove willing to risk injury when necessary.

The Effects of Traditional Police Socialization

All socialization is a continuous process. It is not something that begins with selection or a recruit's first encounter with academy rules and ends with the rookie's early street experiences. Police officers, students, and professors (even old ones) can learn new tricks. But traditional socialization practices almost certainly have a profound effect on the majority of the persons exposed.

The available evidence suggests that the primary effect is creation of a distinctive working personality. The nearly universal social science argument regarding police socialization is that patrol officers display a characteristic working personality, with elements ranging from authoritarianism to cynicism because of their training and early street experiences.

Our review of traditional police socialization practices provides support for this argument. Although the points of correspondence are far from precise, Table 4-1 suggests the origins of the patrol officers' working personality. Therefore, until there is evidence to the contrary it is suggested that traditional police socialization practices are responsible for the distinctive working personality of the patrol officer.

CHANGES IN POLICE SOCIALIZATION PRACTICES

During the last few years, there has emerged evidence of gradual and uneven change in traditional police socialization practices. However, the data descriptive of these changes and their possible effects are scattered and fragmentary. We shall proceed by pulling together the available evidence of change and then assess the possible effects.

Departmental Screening Procedures

There has been considerable change in screening procedures, primarily as the result of Congressional and court actions. In 1972, Congress

TABLE 4–1. Traditional Police Socialization and the Working Personality

Traditional Police Socialization	Working Personality
Demographic Homogeneity	
White	
Male	Conservatism
High-school Education	Racism
Blue-collar	Insecurity
Academy Rules	
Inflexible	Authoritarianism
Punishment Oriented	Hostility
Arbitrary Enforcement	Cynicism
Formal Content	
Law Enforcement	Conservatism/Authoritarianism
Physical Training	Suspicion
Informal Content	
War Stories	Authoritarianism
Defensiveness	Suspicion/Hostility/Insecurity
Depersonalization	Authoritarianism/Cynicism/Racism
Disenchantment	
Cynicism	Cynicism
Lower Motivation	Cynicism
Lower Organizational Commitment	Cynicism
Early Street Experiences	
Forget Training	Cynicism
"Real" Policing	Authoritarianism
Expand Informal Content	Defensiveness/Depersonalization
"Hot" Calls	Authoritarianism

amended Title VII of the Civil Rights Act of 1964 to apply to public agencies including police departments. As amended, the Act bars police organizations from "discriminating on the basis of race, creed, color, sex or national origins."[54]

Court decisions generally have been directed at increasing the representation of minority personnel in police departments. In most large cities, police departments currently are under court order to bring the percentage of minority personnel up to the percentage of minority citizens in the city.[55] The primary court-ordered mechanism for accomplishing this is to require that all new recruit classes be disproportionately (as compared to the composition of the city) composed of minority persons. In Columbus, Ohio, for instance, black citizens make up 19 percent of the city's population,[56] but are less than 4 percent of the city's police.[57] The department is under federal court order to have each new recruit class be a minimum of 45 percent black until such time as the department itself is 19 percent black.

Extending Title VII to police departments has forced modification of nearly all height and weight requirements since they function to discriminate against women.[58] Physical agility tests also have been modified. As compared to the discriminatory and inconclusive tests of the past, most large departments now offer tests which more accurately measure general physical fitness. In Louisville, Kentucky, all candidates must: 1) demonstrate cardiovascular fitness using a stationary bicycle; 2) demonstrate lower back and upper body strength through a series of specific exercises; and 3) be of acceptable weight, as measured by the percentage of a candidate's body which is fat.[59]

The effect of court decisions requiring departments to increase the number of minority personnel has caused fundamental changes in civil service testing. The civil service tests of the past were general intelligence tests which discriminated against minority citizens. In Berkeley, California, for instance, only a one-third of white applicants failed the civil service examination as compared to nearly 90 percent of all black applicants.[60]

In most large cities, civil service examination procedures have been modified in several respects. Many departments now use tests intended to measure a persons ability to perform the police role. Some departments also offer written examination tutorials for prospective applicants.[61] Lastly, separate eligibility lists for black and white applicants who pass the civil service examination are now kept. In order to comply with court orders, minority applicants are selected first, until the required level is achieved. Then white applicants are selected in terms of their performance on the examination. In the past, selection was solely the result of performance on discriminatory civil service examinations. Currently, selection reflects a combination of performance and minority group status.

What we find is evidence of change in nearly all screening criteria and procedures. The only criterion that remains unchanged is age. In nearly all jurisdictions, applicants must still be over 21 and under 35 years of age.

Demographic and Psychological Characteristics

Demographically, the changes in screening criteria and procedures have had predictable effects. There are more black and female recruits. In Chicago in 1975 for instance, a court order required the department to hire 200 black and female police officers to achieve some compliance with Title VII of the Civil Rights Act.[62] By 1975, 400 women were on patrol in New York City.[63] At the "Metropolitan South County Police Training Institute," a 1976 recruit class was 24 percent black and 29 percent female.[64] In Columbus, Ohio, the last three recruit classes have been approximately 35 percent black and 10 percent female.[65] In St. Paul, Minnesota, the department had been virtually all white (98.6 percent) prior to 1975, despite a minority population of 6 percent. The 1975 recruit class was 26 percent minority and the department now is nearly 5 percent minority.[66] In these cities, then, there is clear evidence of increases in minority and female police patrol officers.

There is also change along on one other demographic characteristic— educational level. In the past, very few recruits had taken any college courses and even fewer possessed an undergraduate degree. Most had a high school diploma or its equivalent. In 1967, however, the President's Commission on Law Enforcement and the Administration of Justice stated: "The ultimate aim of all police departments should be that all personnel with enforcement powers have baccalaureate degrees."[67]

One response was creation of criminal justice programs tailored for police at community colleges and universities. Table 4-2 documents the enormous increase in these programs. As can be seen in the Table, associate, baccalaureate, Masters, and Ph.D. programs increased dramatically between 1966 and 1976.

TABLE 4–2. Criminal Justice Programs in the United States, 1966–1976*

	Type of Program				
Year	Associate	Baccalaureate	Master's	Doctorate	Total Schools
1966–1967	152	39	14	4	184
1968–1969	199	44	13	5	234
1970–1971	257	55	21	7	292
1972–1973	505	211	41	9	515
1975–1976	729	376	121	19	646

*Source: Louis B. Fike, John P. Harlow, Jr., and Charles P. McDowell, "Criminal Justice Curricula: A Reflective Glance," *Journal of Police Science and Administration, 5:4* (December 1977), p. 459. Reprinted by permission of authors and publisher.

The effects are those that would be expected. More recruits have college backgrounds and more recruits have baccalaureate degrees. Of the 170 recruits in the 1976 "Metropolitan South County Police Training Institute" class, 49 percent had some college and 27 percent had their baccalaureate degrees.[68] In 1975, the St. Louis County Police Department recruit class had an average of three years of college.[69]

On this dimension, however, we have more than scattered evidence. In 1975, the Law Enforcement Assistance Administration (LEAA) released the results of a survey of educational levels of police recruits in California, Michigan, New Jersey, and Texas.[70] As can be seen in Table 4-3, 37 percent of police recruits in Michigan, New Jersey, and Texas had at least some college and 10 percent had completed four or more years of college. When the California figures are included, the figures become 45 percent with some college and 12 percent with four or more years of college.

The California figures are important because they suggest the likely impact of the increased numbers of criminal justice programs. California has been the leader in requiring college training for police recruits. In the words of the author of the LEAA report, Larry T. Hoover:

California was purposely selected for inclusion in the study in order that a comparison could be made between educational levels there and elsewhere, and thus obtain data which can be employed for projective purposes. *Information regarding police education levels in California is useful for anticipating the impact of law enforcement academic programs in other parts of the nation.*[71]

On the basis of the California data, it does not seem unreasonable to suggest that about half of all future police recruits will have two or more years of college.

However, it must be noted that court actions requiring departments to reverse the discriminatory hiring practices of the past are likely to temporarily blunt the impact of academic law enforcement programs. Public education also has been discriminatory, and minority young people less frequently attend college.[72] Minority recruits are therefore not as likely to possess a college background.

To sum the demographic data: as compared to the homogeneity of the academy classes of the recent past, contemporary police recruit classes in large urban areas are likely to contain a rich demographic mixture. Contemporary urban recruit classes are black as well as white, female as well as male, and college educated as well as high school educated. Demographic diversity has replaced homogeneity.

Psychologically, the contemporary police recruit is essentially similar to the recruit of the past. Based upon the available evidence, it seems accurate to say that they are no more or less authoritarian, cynical, or

TABLE 4–3. Level of Education of Police Recruits, 1972–1973*

Level of Education	California		Michigan		New Jersey		Texas		Total excluding California		Total	
	N	%	N	%	N	%	N	%	N	%	N	%
Four or more years of college	145	22	117	9	73	11	118	9	308	10	453	12
Two but less than four years of college	283	42	59	5	142	22	158	12	359	11	642	17
One but less than two years of college	124	19	214	18	138	22	163	13	515	16	639	17
High school or less than one year of college	116	17	890	68	286	45	840	66	2,016	63	2,132	55
Totals	668	100	1,280	100	639	100	1,279	100	3,198	100	3,866	101

*Source: Larry T. Hoover, *Police Educational Characteristics and Curricula.* Law Enforcement Assistance Administration, U.S. Department of Justice (Washington, D.C.: U.S. Government Printing Office, July 1975), p. 19.

suspicious at the outset of their training than police recruits of the past. The reasons for this are several.

The factors which attract minority citizens and women to policing do not appear to be different from those which attract white males. Job security and salary are the primary attractions. A recent survey of black and female police patrol officers provides support for this observation.[73] They were asked to rank in order of importance the factors they felt were effective in attracting black citizens and women to policing. Over half of the black males (55 percent) and exactly half of the white females listed pay as the most important factor; 25 percent of the black males and 15 percent of the white females listed job security as the second most important. Although the sample sizes were small (40 black males and 18 white females) and limited (black females were not included), these data do suggest that the factors which attract blacks and women to policing are not different from the factors which attract white males. That their psychological profiles appear to be similar is perhaps a function of the fact that their motivations are the same.

College training also appears not to have changed the psychological profiles of police recruits. At the very least, it seems that college education does not produce recruits who are authoritarian at the outset of their police training.[74]

To sum the psychological data: based upon the scattered and fragmentary information currently available, it appears that contemporary police recruits are not psychologically different from the recruits of the past. Policing continues not to attract a distinctive type of personality.

The "Nonstress" or "College" Academy[75]

The essential assumption underlying nonstress or college training is a belief that anything different is better than traditional academy training. Traditional training features extensive rules and arbitrary punishments. Nonstress training involves fewer rules and counseling regarding their infraction. Traditional preparation concentrates primary attention on law enforcement and physical training. Nonstress instruction covers these topics, but it also includes meaningful sections on psychology, black studies, urban sociology, poverty, community relations, and civil rights. Traditional education relies upon a lecture format and most lecturers are police officers. Nonstress schooling uses buzz groups, simulations, role playing, and sensitivity training. Frequently, sections are taught by college and university professors and others who have no police experience. Traditional training either ignores or devotes very little attention to the exercise of arrest discretion. The nonstress program alerts recruits to the problems of discretion and uses buzz groups and role playing to allow recruits to learn the possible consequences of various decisions. Traditional training frequently involves "war stories" emphasizing defensive-ness and depersonalization. Nonstress courses also may involve the telling of war stories, but they are more frequently used to ennoble rather than denigrate. Traditional instruction ignores or minimizes the impor-tance of problems such as police corruption and police brutality. Nonstress education admits that these problems exist and provides opportunities to discuss them. Traditional teaching encourages an exaggerated sense of masculinity, one that emphasizes that the police officer can take it. And recruits trained in this way frequently do take it. They take it out on themselves in the form of excessive drinking, heart disease, suicide, and on their families in the form of divorce.[76] Nonstress preparation seeks to alert recruits to the problems of being a police officer and encourages them to be open about them.

How many contemporary police academies offer nonstress or college-type training? The tentative response is that most continue to offer what is essentially a traditional program. Some academies are less stressful than others and a minority display most of the features just described. But no police training academy offers a college experience. By this we mean that the recruit, unlike the college student, does not, choose the courses to be taken, their general sequence, or the times at which they will be taken; and has none of the rights of the student who is critical of the professor's ability (the rights to drop a course, to miss lectures, or even to fall asleep). This is not to say that recruits should have these rights, since it would not be in the public's best interest if recruits decided not to attend classes on, for instance, lawful searches and seizures. It means that while nonstress training is different from traditional training, it occurs in a police rather than college environment.

Early Street Experiences

Police departments which offer some of the elements of nonstress edu-cation also generally seek to have the FTO reinforce and expand basic academy themes. The field training experience is seen as an extension of the academy experience. FTOs are carefully selected and occasionally are given special training.[77] A young police officer describes his FTO:

> My coach . . . helped me to put to use what I had learned at the academy and as different situations would arise he was there to answer questions and assist. Those who felt that "the academy is a waste of time" were not chosen as coaches. In the substation if I heard this comment I could look at the officer, the officer's actions, and dealings with citizens, and immediately see the statement had little validity.[78]

However, FTOs continue to be sensitive to signs of a new police officer's willingness to risk injury during hot calls. Policing is occasionally dangerous and when it is, officers need to be able to rely upon their partners and colleagues for assistance. During the field experience, the new police officer is the training officer's partner. The training officer therefore looks for signs of dependability for reasons of personal safety and as information to be passed to others. The hot call remains the crucial test for the new police officer and it still must be passed.

The Possible Effects of Recent Changes

In 1977, William K. Muir provided limited evidence of the possible effects of the gradual changes characteristic of police socialization practices.[79] Muir's data are limited by a small sample of officers (n = 28) and they must therefore be interpreted with caution. They do suggest, however, that a possible effect of recent changes is *diversity* in the working personalities of patrol officers.

Muir studied patrol officers in an unidentified West Coast police department, "Laconia." Using questionnaires, interviews, and observations to collect his data, Muir identified four different types of working personalities. The first two, which Muir called "enforcers" and "avoiders," displayed characteristics traditionally described as part of the working personality of the patrol officer. Enforcers emphasized the authoritarian, suspicious, and hostile nature of their work, enjoying the conflict generated by their heavy-handed style of policing. Avoiders were cynical believing that neither they or anyone else could really accomplish anything. They retreated from their work, policing only when forced by citizens, colleagues, or administrators. Muir reported that 12 (43 percent) of the 28 patrol officers he studied were enforcers or avoiders.

The other sixteen officers epitomized two additional types of working personalities. Muir called them "reciprocators" (n = 6) and "professionals" (n = 10). Reciprocators showed few of the characteristics traditionally associated with the patrol officer. They were rescuers, seeing the potential for good in every person and situation. They spent a great deal of time searching for good and were somewhat discouraged when they could not find it. They preferred slow beats and were "soft," often extremely so. Many had made a personal decision not to use force, even when it was necessary to do so. They also did not carry their share of policing because their style took so much time. Others were forced to do what they should have been doing. They were "do-gooders" in a world where doing good is an admirable but not universally applicable style of policing. They were different but incomplete police officers.

Professionals were total police officers. They were different in that they did not rely upon force or avoidance to resolve situations; talk, emphasizing alternatives, was their primary tool. They were not cynical, defensive, or depersonalized; they did not classify people as either good or bad. All people were cut from the same cloth; some just found themselves in-

volved in particularly troublesome situations. These situations occasionally inclined these people in a violent direction. But even most of these
people could be talked to and reasoned with, but not extensively. There
were others who were troubled and needed help. Reasons and alternatives
had to be quickly pointed out and citizens left to do their own restoration.
Occasionally, however, troubled citizens could not be talked to because
their inclinations to violence overwhelmed them. When that happened,
force had to be used. Avoidance or doing good simply invited needless
injury.

The reasons for the diversity in the working personalities of the patrol
officers studied by Muir may have had something to do with the nonstress
education they received. Muir describes it as follows:

> In police circles the department was regarded as a model in the extensive
> professional training it provided its officers. . . . The schooling period for a
> recruit lasted a full thirty-eight weeks. It consisted of twenty weeks of class-
> room work, where the . . . (recruit) . . . mastered the criminal code, learned
> how to observe human events and write reports about them, discussed (for
> six intensive weeks) the sociology of the city, took part in simulations of
> critical street incidents, and underwent training in using firearms. In the
> succeeding eighteen weeks, each rookie received individual instruction from
> a specially trained recruit–training officer who chaperoned and evaluated . . .
> in the field.[80]

Muir's study is important because it provides evidence of the possible
effects of changes in police socialization practices. But Muir's data are
limited by a small sample of officers and they must therefore be interpreted with caution. All that can be said is that this study suggests that
an effect of recent changes in police socialization practices is diversity in
the working personalities of patrol officers.

This deliberately cautious interpretation receives some additional support when the results of a recent study by John J. Broderick are examined.[81] Using questionnaires, interviews, and participant observation,
Broderick studied a small number of police officers in three different
police settings: a 200-person department in a manufacturing city, a 20-
officer state police station, and a 40-person department located in a resort–
residential community. Broderick reported that diversity rather than
homogeneity is characteristic of police personalities. Although enforcers
and avoiders were present among the officers studied, Broderick also encountered and described reciprocators and professionals.

Broderick is less certain than Muir as to the origins of the diversity in
police personalities. He sees nonstress instruction as a way of furthering
diversity, but he does not identify it as a cause of such variation. Instead,
Broderick observes that while traditional police socialization practices
shape working personalities, certain officers somehow manage to rise

above enforcer or avoider approaches to policing. How these officers manage to do this is not made clear.[82]

Broderick's study is thus comforting in one sense, troubling in another. It provides additional evidence of diversity in the working personalities of police officers, but it makes no clear causal connection between changing socialization practices and diversity in working personalities. Indeed, Broderick's data suggest that such a connection is premature and may well be spurious. It is necessary therefore to be cautious in assessing the possible effects of changes in police socialization practices.

SUMMARY

An important characteristic of contemporary police socialization practices is slow and uneven change. Demographic homogeneity among police recruits is slowly giving way to diversity. Quasi-military academy and field training experiences are slowly being modified in the direction of less stressful alternatives. A possible effect of these slow and nonuniform changes is diversity in the working personalities of patrol officers.

However, it is necessary to emphasize three additional points. First, these changes are all very recent and the evidence of their effects is scattered and fragmentary. We would do well, therefore, to suspend judgment until such time as additional and more comprehensive data are available. To do otherwise is to reach premature closure on issues we know very little about.

Second, because these changes are recent, most of the persons patrolling the streets of our cities are the products of traditional police socialization practices. Most patrol officers are white males with a high school education; most also went through a quasi-military training academy and had FTOs who told them to forget their academy experiences. Most therefore display the traditional working personality of the patrol officer.

Third, police socialization is a continuous process, not a fixed entity. Some of the officers studied by Broderick became reciprocators or professionals after having been exposed to traditional training practices. Some of the officers studied by Muir became enforcers or avoiders despite exposure to a less stressful training experience. Undoubtedly, some of these changes reflect the nature of routine police work, which is the focus of the next chapter.

Notes

1. For a discussion of socialization, see any introductory sociology text, including Ronald Fernandez, *The Promise of Sociology* (New York: Praeger, 1975), pp. 68–80.

2. Jerome Skolnick was among the first to advance the working personality notion. See his *Justice Without Trial* (New York: Wiley, 1966), pp. 24–69.

3. George Kirkham, *Signal Zero* (New York: Ballantine, 1977), p. 3.

4. Kirkham, *Signal Zero,* p. 4.

5. Arthur Niederhoffer, *Behind the Shield* (Garden City, N.Y.: Doubleday Anchor Books, 1969), p. 159.

6. John J. Broderick, *Police in a Time of Change* (Morristown, N.J.: General Learning Press, 1977), p. 179.

7. For a typical description of these requirements, see Thomas C. Gray, "Selecting for a Police Subculture," in Jerome Skolnick and Thomas C. Grays (eds.), *Police in America* (Boston: Little, Brown, 1975), p. 47.

8. For a discussion of these, see Robert Regoli and Donnell E. Jones, "The Recruitment and Promotion of a Minority Group into an Established Institution: The Police," *Journal of Police Science and Administration, 3* (December 1975): 410–416.

9. Prior to 1977, these were some of the requirements in Columbus, Ohio.

10. Niederhoffer, *Behind the Shield,* p. 36.

11. See Irving Piliavin and Scott Briar, "Police Encounters with Juveniles," *American Journal of Sociology, 70* (September 1964): 206–214.

12. See Gray, "Selecting for a Police Subculture."

13. Niederhoffer, *Behind the Shield,* p. 38.

14. Center for Research on Criminal Justice, *The Iron Fist and The Velvet Glove* (Berkeley, Calif.: Center for Research on Criminal Justice, 1975), p. 60.

15. Michael Kiernan and Judith Cusick, "Women on Patrol: The Nation's Capital Gives Them High Marks," *Police Magazine, 1* (Prototype Issue, Summer 1977): 45. Published by Correctional Information Service, Inc., 801 Second Avenue, New York, N.Y. 10017.

16. Rodney Stark, *Police Riots* (Belmont, Calif.: Wadsworth, 1972), pp. 171–172.

17. Niederhoffer, *Behind the Shield,* p. 159.

18. John H. McNamara, "Uncertainties in Police Work: The Relevance of Police Recruits' Backgrounds and Training," in David Bordua (ed.), *The Police: Six Sociological Essays* (New York: Wiley, 1967), pp. 163–252.

19. Niederhoffer, *Behind the Shield,* pp. 98–99.

20. Niederhoffer, *Behind the Shield,* pp. 199–248.

21. The material which follows is based on Richard Harris, *The Police Academy: An Inside View* (New York: Wiley, 1973); John Van Maanen, "Observations on the Making of Policemen," *Human Organization, 32* (Winter 1973): 407–418; John Van Maanen, "Police Socialization: A Longitudinal Examination of Job Attitudes in an Urban Police Department," *Administrative Science Quarterly, 20* (June 1975): 207–228; John Van Maanen, "Rookie Cops and Rookie Managers," *The Wharton Magazine, 1* (Fall 1976): 49–55; John Van Maanen, *Pledging the Police: A Study of Selected Aspects of Recruit Socialization in a Large, Urban Police Department* (unpublished Ph.D. dissertation, University of California, Irvine, 1972); and Stanley Cross, *Social Relationships and the Rookie Policeman: A Study of Becoming a Policeman in Illinois* (unpublished Ph.D. dissertation, University of Illinois, 1973).

22. From *Student Guide, _____* Division of Police, Training Academy, 1975, p. 1. The department wishes to remain anonymous.

23. *Student Guide,* pp. 2–7. This academy has since moved in a less stressful direction.

24. Van Maanen, "Observations on the Making," p. 411.

25. Van Maanen, "Rookie Cops," p. 51.

26. Based upon personal observations of three police academies. Also see Harris, *The Police Academy,* p. 18.

27. Albert J. Reiss, Jr., *The Police and the Public* (New Haven, Conn.: Yale University Press, 1971), p. 19 (emphasis in original not included here).

28. William K. Muir, *Police: Streetcorner Politicians* (Chicago: University of Chicago Press, 1977), p. 231.

29. Based upon Muir, *Police,* pp. 163–164, 169, and 227–235.

30. Based upon Van Maanen, "Observations."

31. Harris, *The Police Academy,* p. 63 (emphasis added).

32. Jonathan Rubinstein, *City Police* (New York: Ballantine, 1973), p. 282 (emphasis added).

33. Harris, *The Police Academy,* pp. 53 ff.

34. Harris, *The Police Academy,* p. 53.

35. Cited in Niederhoffer, *Behind the Shield,* p. 65.

36. Harris, *The Police Academy,* p. 65.

37. Harris, *The Police Academy,* pp. 39 ff.

38. Based upon Howard S. Becker, *Outsiders: Studies in the Sociology of Deviance* (New York: Free Press, 1963), p. 33.

39. Cited in Allan Silver, "The Demand for Order in Civil Society: A Review of Some Themes in the History of Urban Crime, Police, and Riot," in David J. Bordua (ed.), *The Police: Six Sociological Essays* (New York: Wiley, 1967), pp. 13–14.

40. Joseph Wambaugh, *The Choirboys* (New York: Delacorte, 1976).

41. Muir, *Police,* p. 22.

42. Niederhoffer, *Behind the Shield,* p. 238.

43. Niederhoffer, *Behind the Shield,* p. 216.

44. Niederhoffer, *Behind the Shield,* p. 220.

45. Niederhoffer, *Behind the Shield,* p. 221.

46. Van Maanen, "Police Socialization," pp. 207–208.

47. Van Maanen, "Police Socialization," p. 222.

48. Van Maanen, "Observations"; and personal observations.

49. Van Maanen, "Observations," p. 42; Kirkham, *Signal Zero,* p. 35; and personal observations.

50. Niederhoffer, *Behind the Shield,* p. 55.

51. Van Maanen, "Rookie Cops," p. 52.

52. Kirkham, *Signal Zero,* p. 76.

53. Rubinstein, *City Police,* pp. 317–318; and Van Maanen, "Observations," p. 414.

54. Anthony V. Bouza, "Women in Policing," *FBI Law Enforcement Bulletin, 44* (September 1975): 2.

55. Richard H. Rowan and James S. Griffin, "St. Paul Police Department Minority Recruitment Program," *The Police Chief, XLIV* (January 1977): 18.

56. *1970 Census of the Population, Ohio* (Washington, D.C.: Department of Commerce, April 1973), Table 23, p. 37–95.

57. In 1975, the Police Athletic League published *Columbus, Ohio, Division of Police: Police History* (Columbus, Ohio: Police Athletic League, 1975). It contains photographs of all police personnel. Visual inspection of the 1143 photographs revealed that as of 1975, 42 (or 3.6 percent) of Columbus Police personnel were black.

58. Bouza, "Women," p. 3.

59. Bryant A. Stamford, Jack Kley, David Thomas, and John Nevin, "Physical Fitness Criteria—An Avant Garde Approach," *The Police Chief, XLIV* (January 1977): 59, 70–71, and 80.

60. Regoli and Jerome, "The Recruitment," p. 412.

61. Rowan and Griffin, "St. Paul," p. 20.

62. Bouza, "Women," p. 4.

63. Bouza, "Women," p. 5.

64. David M. Rafky, Thomas Lawley, and Robert Ingram, "Are Police Recruits Cynical?" *Journal of Police Science and Administration, 4* (September 1976): 352–360.

65. Personal observation.

66. Rowan and Griffin, "St. Paul," p. 20.

67. President's Commission on Law Enforcement and Administration of Justice, *The Challenge of Crime in a Free Society* (Washington, D.C.: U.S. Government Printing Office, 1967), p. 107.

68. Rafky, Lawley, and Ingram, "Are Police Recruits Cynical?" p. 354.

69. Lewis J. Sherman, "An Evaluation of Policewomen on Patrol in a Suburban Police Department," *Journal of Police Science and Administration, 3* (December 1975): 435.

70. Larry T. Hoover, *Police Educational Characteristics and Curricula* (Washington, D.C.: U.S. Government Printing Office, 1975).

71. Hoover, *Police Characteristics,* p. 19.

72. David K. Cohen, "Schooling, I.Q., and Income," in Lee Rainwater (ed.), *Inequality and Justice: A Survey of Inequalities of Class, Status, Sex, and Power* (Chicago: Aldine, 1974), pp. 124–134.

73. Ohio Peace Officer Training Academy, *Minority Recruitment Manual for Ohio Police Officers* (London, Ohio: Ohio Peace Officer Training Academy, 1976), pp. 62–64.

74. For a general discussion of this, see Norman L. Weiner, "The Educated Policeman," *Journal of Police Science and Administration, 4* (December 1976): 451; Louis B. Fike, John P. Harlan, and Charles P. McDowell, "Criminal Justice Curricula: A Reflective Glance," *Journal of Police Science and Administration, 5* (December 1977): 459; and J. Hoffman, "Can College Make Better Cops." *College Management, 14–16* (1972): 15.

75. This section is based upon my observations and Muir, *Police,* p. 9 ff.; Brian A. Grossman, *Police Command: Decisions and Discretion* (Toronto: Macmillan, 1975), pp. 66–73; and Broderick, *Police in a Time of Change,* pp. 179–187.

76. See Niederhoffer, *Behind the Shield,* pp. 101 ff.

77. Muir, *Police,* p. 244.

78. Field notes, May 10, 1978.

79. Muir, *Police.*

80. Muir, *Police,* p. 9.

81. Broderick, *Police in a Time of Change.*

82. Broderick, *Police in a Time of Change,* p. 8

CHAPTER **5**

Routine
Policing

INTRODUCTION

In many respects, patrol officers do society's "dirty work" for us.[1] They do the things that we do not want to do, because of fear, repugnance, or shame. Consider the problem of policing public drunkenness offenders. This is not pleasant work. Some drunken citizens are belligerent and if chronic inebriates, their clothes and smells are very unpleasant. Urine soaked and perhaps covered with the effects of a recent stomach disturbance, the trip downtown to jail or to the detoxification center is best made with all windows open. Even this precaution may not be sufficient, as we learned from George Kirkham's experiences.[2]

The dead represent another dirty job routinely encountered by police officers. One July 4 several years ago, two police officers began what they assumed and hoped would be an uneventful day watch. Immediately after a large lunch, the officers received a call to check a "D.O.A." A man who had not seen his brother for two weeks had gone to pick him up for a Fourth of July picnic. No one answered the door and there was a strange odor coming out of the apartment. The officers got a key from the building manager, lit big cigars to help cover the smell of a ripe D.O.A., and entered the apartment. The smells and sight of a body dead for two weeks were overwhelming. The coroner, who was on his own picnic, did not appear for almost two hours and the officers were forced to sit in the apartment until the coroner arrived. They consoled the dead man's brother and later watched a televised baseball game with him. The open windows and perhaps the cigars helped cover some of the smell.

We also assign our police the task of apprehending persons desperate enough to attempt to acquire money or reputation illegally. In 1977, a young police officer who had graduated at the top of his academy class responded to an armed robbery-in-progress call. The officer sped to the scene—the parking lot of a grocery store. Upon arriving, he got out of the squad car and walked toward a man and woman who were arguing. The officer's gun was drawn. The man saw the officer approaching, spun around and fired once, hitting the officer in the stomach. The officer and his partner fired at the man, wounding him slightly. The officer who was hit is now in a wheelchair, crippled for life. The bullet severed his spine, paralyzing him from the waist down. Our minds run from thoughts of doing such dirty work ourselves.

Lastly, we call our police to handle annoyances which we cannot be bothered with: loud parties, televisions, radios, and stereos; children throwing snowballs, playing baseball in the street, or turning on fire hydrants during hot summer days; and barking dogs. "Calling the cops" is the solution for these and many of the other minor disturbances characteristic of the urban experience. In these and other ways, police patrol officers do our dirty work for us.

However, police officers are under an additional burden: they are expected to accomplish such tasks *efficiently.*[3] Because police organizations are bureaucracies, police officers experience organizational pressures to handle our problems quickly. The numerous logs and reports kept by patrol officers, dispatchers, and administrators are all used as measures of police efficiency.

Police organizations and officers also experience external pressures to handle cases efficiently. Citizens who use the telephone to call the police place an enormous burden on most large police organizations. Moreover, some departments seek additional work by encouraging citizens to call police about anything they believe to be suspicious. The result is a staggering volume of cases and complaints.[4]

The largest burden, and hence the greatest demand for efficiency, is borne by the patrol officers. They respond to most calls to the police by citizens. They also generate the "activity" desired by sergeants, administrators, and the public. In most high crime precincts, and in many police precincts on Friday and Saturday nights, there are so many calls that officers begin their shift by responding to the backlog which accumulated during shift change. New calls are continually dispatched and there is hardly time to eat or leave post for "personal necessity."

It is virtually impossible for patrol officers to practice a style of policing emphasizing responsiveness to particular people and their unique problems. If individual responses were attempted, officers would be "off the air" talking, writing reports, and going through booking procedures almost from the moment they began their shift. Individualized policing is a luxury most patrol officers cannot afford.

Urban patrol officers therefore confront a serious problem: they are assigned too many calls to permit individualized policing of particular people and their troubles. That would interfere with efficiency. At the same time, they are constantly assigned calls requiring contact with particular people who regard their difficulties as unique. Patrol officers construct and apply "typifications" and "recipes for action" as solutions to this problem.

Purpose of the Chapter

The purpose of this chapter is to analyze routine policing. The two concepts which will guide our analysis are typifications and recipes for action. The nature and meaning of these concepts occupy our attention in the first section of the chapter. The second section provides a description of routine policing and the ways in which typifications and recipes for action guide the work of the patrol officer. Specific attention is given to the problems, encounters, and decisions characteristic of routine policing.

TYPIFICATIONS AND RECIPES FOR ACTION

One of the earliest uses of the typification notion was by David Sudnow in his study of public defenders.[5] Sudnow observed that one of the diagnostic tools employed by public defenders to efficiently process a crushing volume of cases was a "normal crimes" typification or image of criminality and criminals. Sudnow describes how normal crime characterizations are built up by public defenders across time:

> In the course of routinely encountering persons charged with "petty theft," "burglary," "assault with a deadly weapon," "rape," "possession of marijuana" ... the [public defender] gains knowledge of the *typical* manner in which offenses of given classes are committed, the social characteristics of the persons who regularly commit them, the features of the setting in which they occur, the types of victims often involved, and the like.[6]

Typifications are constructs or formulations of events based upon experience. They represent what is typical or common about routinely encountered events. For public defenders, experience generates events known as normal crimes—typical burglaries, assaults, and rapes. A typification is a conceptual shorthand, one which permits identification of specific events as representative of a more general class of events.

The advantage of normal crimes classification for public defenders is that it permits efficient, nonindividualized processing of cases. Once a case has been identified as representative of one type of event, public defenders know what is usually or typically done with that kind of offender. Categorizations have guides or recipes for action as one of their features. These procedures inform the plea-bargaining process (the exchange of a guilty plea for a less serious charge and sentence). Given a representative case, the public defender knows what the prosecutor and judge will accept as an appropriate reduction in exchange for a guilty plea.

Recipes for action are constructs or guides for behavior based upon experience. They represent what is ordinarily done to certain offenders. For public defenders, experience generates actions such as appropriate charge and sentence reductions for normal cases or crimes—child molestation to loitering in a schoolyard, public drunkenness to disturbing the peace, and burglary to petty theft. A recipe for action also is a kind of conceptual shorthand, one which permits the efficient processing of specific cases as representative of more general classes of events.

Thomas Scheff has expanded upon Sudnow's efforts.[7] Scheff notes that public defenders are not alone in their use of typifications and recipes for action. Employees of hospitals, universities, police departments, and most large organizations where members work primarily with people experience external and internal pressures to do their work efficiently. And they respond to these pressures in the same way public defenders respond: they construct and apply typifications and recipes for action.

However, there exists considerable variation across organizations in the nature of the classifications and subsequent procedures in routine use. Organizations vary in the sources, negotiability, and number of categories and routines. For instance, nurses and physicians employed by hospitals construct and apply a relatively large number of assortments (diagnoses) and methods (treatments). As we will learn, police officers construct and apply a small number of typifications and recipes for action. A minimum of three factors are thought responsible for this variation: the amount of scientific knowledge backing an organization, the ability of an organization to process clients in the absence of their consent, and the status of the clients processed by the organization. The effects of these factors will now be described in the form of three propositions.[8]

The first suggestion is that organizational members have access to a minimum of two sources of information on how to process clients: scientific knowledge and work experience. If an organization and its members are backed by a body of scientific knowledge, then work experience is less frequently used to construct typifications and recipes for action. If, however, an organization does not rely on scientific knowledge, then work experience is used for classification and remediation.

Policing is not based on scientific knowledge, principally because the social sciences have failed to provide police with useful information. Social scientists cannot tell police what causes crime[9] or how to prevent or control it.[10] Practically the only thing social scientists do tell police is that standard police procedures appear to be ineffective.[11] Police are therefore forced to resort to their work experiences to construct the guidelines fundamental to efficient policing.

Second, the greater the ability of an organization to assign and respond to clients in the absence of their consent, the less negotiable the categories and reactions. When clients are unable to negotiate their fate, organization members tend to use their work experiences to construct inflexible classifications and responses. Because the law-violating clients of police organizations are routinely processed in the absence of their consent, it can be predicted police officers construct and apply nonnegotiable stereotypes and procedures.

Third, the more inferior and different the status and power of clients compared to organizational members, the smaller the number of typifications and recipes for action. The power of clients in relation to organizational members affects the number of classifications and responses employed by the members. Marginal or relatively powerless clients are not able to demand accuracy in assignment to a category or in treatment received. One would predict a small number of very broad categories and responses when an organization works primarily with powerless clients. Because the law-violating clients of police organizations are generally or situationally inferior in status to police, the specific prediction is that patrol officers construct and apply a small number of very general classifications and methods.

The research efforts of Sudnow and Scheff provide the basis for a series of propositions descriptive of routine policing. These propositions are as follows:

1. Police organizations and officers are under external and internal pressure to handle cases efficiently.
   A. Individualized treatment interferes with the efficient processing of cases.
   B. Typifications and recipes for action permit efficient processing of cases.
   C. Therefore, typifications and recipes for action are important components of routine policing.
2. Policing is not backed by a substantial body of scientific knowledge.
   A. Therefore, police officers use their work experiences to construct typifications and recipes for action.
3. Police organizations and officers process their law-violating clients in the absence of their consent.
   A. Therefore, police officers construct and apply *nonnegotiable* typifications and recipes for action.

4. The typical law-violating client in contact with a police organization is generally or situationally inferior in status as compared to
a police officer.
    A. Therefore, police officers construct and apply a *small number*
    of nonnegotiable typifications and recipes for action.

The next section establishes that the contours of routine policing follow
these propositions.

ROUTINE POLICING

We now turn to the task of describing and analyzing the problems,
encounters, and decisions characteristic of routine policing. We shall proceed by providing data descriptive of each aspect of routine policing and
then turn to an analysis of these data in terms of the above propositions.

The Problems

Although it might appear that patrol officers initiate the majority of
encounters with citizens, the truth of the matter is that police organizations are highly dependent upon citizen input. Police officers are legally
constrained from independent observation of private places such as homes
or apartments, unless they have reason to believe that a felony has been
or is about to be committed. They also are restricted from routine observation of semipublic places such as bars or restaurants by the uneasiness
their presence causes proprietors and customers.[12] As a consequence, police-initiated or proactive encounters are restricted to public places such
as sidewalks and streets and they rarely involve serious criminality. It has
been estimated that the average patrol officer will witness a burglary-in-
progress once in every three months of patrol and a robbery-in-progress
once every fourteen years.[13]

Police organizations are therefore highly dependent upon citizens for
reports of situations requiring police presence. Although the figures vary
slightly depending upon the particular study one examines, it is clear that
approximately three-quarters of all police-citizen encounters are initiated
by citizens who use the telephone to call the police.[14] If police-initiated
traffic stops are excluded from the total of police-citizen contacts, the
proportion of citizen-initiated encounters approaches 90 percent.[15]

The kinds of problems citizens call upon police to handle are seemingly
diverse. It is not an exaggeration to suggest that for every possible problem you can imagine, a patrol officer has been called upon to deal with it.
Although not intended to be representative—we will attend to that in a
moment—police officers have on more than one occasion removed an owl

from a family room; responded to calls involving children attacked by squirrels, cats, and dogs; captured escaped pet snakes; lifted senior citizens back into their beds; and helped countless people locked out of homes and automobiles.[16] They also do many of the things we expect them to do, such as issuing traffic citations, breaking up fights, and occasionally making arrests. But it is important not to lose sight of the fact that they provide a variety of services they are not necessarily trained to perform. Few police academies provide instruction on owl removal or snake capture.

In order to fully comprehend the problems handled by patrol officers, however, it is not sufficient to provide a list of activities. Such a list would be nearly infinite. Instead, it is necessary to attempt to place patrol activities into a finite number of mutually exclusive categories. Several social scientists have suggested classificatory schemes, and we will review their ideas. Then we will turn to the typifications and recipes for action constructed by patrol officers as they deal with the problems characteristic of routine policing.

Classification by Social Scientists   Elaine Cumming, Ian Cumming, and Laura Edell were among the first to study the problems commonly handled by patrol officers.[17] They stationed themselves in the telephone and dispatch room of a metropolitan police department and listened to incoming calls. A total of 801 calls, 652 of which resulted in the dispatch of a patrol car, were overheard. Their technique did cause them to miss the police-initiated encounters observable only in the field. However, because the majority of patrol activities are initiated by citizen calls to police, their classificatory scheme encompasses the bulk of routine policing.

They divided incoming calls into two general categories on the basis of the *content* of the call. The first, "calls about things," accounted for about one-third of all calls and nearly 40 percent of the calls requiring dispatch of a squad car. These calls "include traffic violations, reports of losses or thefts, calls about unlocked doors, fallen power wires and so on."[18] The second category, "calls for support," accounted for nearly one-half of all calls and 60 percent of those requiring a patrol car. They divided this second general category into two subcategories: persistent personal problems (health services and children's problems) and periodic personal problems (disputes and quarrels). The second subcategory also contained criminal offenses. There were approximately 80 such calls, accounting for 12 percent of the 652 calls resulting in the need for a squad car.[19] As a consequence of their research, Cumming, Cumming, and Edell concluded that the urban police officer acts primarily as a "philosopher, guide and friend." Although patrol officers sometimes deal with crime, their primary activities are order maintenance and service provision.

Sociologist Albert J. Reiss, Jr., used the same technique and reached a similar conclusion.[20] Reiss monitored the calls received by the Chicago

Police Department. The majority of the calls received concerned disputes, breaches of the peace, or requests for assistance. Less than a quarter of the calls concerned crimes against persons or property. In this study also, the vast majority of the patrol officer's time was spent maintaining order and providing assistance.

Criminologist John Webster used a slightly different technique to identify the problems handled by patrol officers.[21] He studied the logs most patrol officers use to record the calls they receive or initiate and the amount of time they devote to each activity. Webster examined logs kept by patrol officers in a large west coast city across a 54-week period. He found that less than 17 percent of the problems and less than 18 percent of activities of patrol officers were devoted to crimes against persons or property. Also important is Webster's finding that nearly three-quarters of patrol activities were citizen-initiated.

Observation of police patrol work in a large midwestern city provides evidence of essentially similar activity.[22] Law enforcement calls accounted for only one-third of the problems handled by patrol officers. The remaining problems, in order of frequency, involved order maintenance, traffic and parking violations, service, and information gathering. Moreover, three-quarters of the problems handled by "Midwest City" patrol officers were citizen-initiated. When police-initiated traffic and parking problems are excluded from the total, nearly nine out of ten of the remaining problems are citizen-initiated.

In sum: independent of the techniques or classification schemes employed by social scientists, two points are clear. First, most police patrol activities do not involve criminal incidents. Second, routine policing is largely reactive. Citizens initiate most of the problems patrol officers deal with.

Typifications and Recipes for Action.   The perspectives of the patrol officers who actually handle these calls are different from the classificatory schemes imposed on their work by social scientists. Police officers typify the nearly infinite variety of problems they handle. They also employ varying recipes for action depending on the general class of events a particular problem represents.

Police officers see themselves as handling only two types of incidents: those requiring "real police work" and a much larger but residual class of events occasionally lumped together under the general heading of "bullshit."[23] John Van Maanen recounts a patrol officer's description of real police work:

> It's our main reason for being in business. Like when somebody starts busting up a place, or some asshole's got a gun, or some idiot tries to knock off a cop. Basically, it is a situation where you figure you may have to use the tools

of your trade. Of course, some guys get a little shaky when these incidents come along; in fact most of us do if we're honest. But, you know deep down that is why you're a cop and not pushing pencils somewhere.[24]

The specific types of problems which are thought to require real police work by patrol officers are those which involve a substantial threat of injury to persons or damage to property. These problems include, but are not limited to, people with weapons, serious felonies such as rapes or assaults, less serious felonies such as burglaries or robberies reported to be "in progress," and all calls involving an officer requesting assistance.

The response associated with these calls is emergency speed, lights, and siren. Generally, these calls are prefaced by an alarm tone of some type and then a description of the call, an address, and the number of the squad assigned the call. Other cars near the call are expected and encouraged to reply. The experiences of two patrol officers and their colleagues illustrate the real police work category and the reaction associated with it.

It was a warm summer evening and the officers were patrolling a middle-income district. Their precinct, however, was adjacent to a low-income precinct and they shared the same radio band as the officers who worked that area. The officers listened and sipped their coffee as a squad in the adjacent area accepted a call to "check a disturbance" at a restaurant. The officer who was driving commented that it was a "rough place" and began to drive, still very slowly, towards the adjacent precinct. Although a good three miles from the scene of the call, it seemed that the decision had almost been made unconsciously. The officer continued to drive slowly and his partner continued to check cars and buildings, as is the habit of most patrol officers.

A large number of police officers were thinking and doing the same thing. The area recently had been tense, and for several summers it had been the site of occasionally violent confrontations between police and citizens. Consequently, two other cars had gone to the call with the assigned squad, and literally tens of other squads were slowly and almost casually moving in the same direction.

The officers continued to patrol, but they were now well outside their assigned district. They also listened intently as the dispatcher called and was told: "We've got about two hundred people here and I guess we could use some help." The dispatcher responded quickly but the officers did not wait. The hand which had already been hovering over the buttons flicked on the emergency lights and siren. The siren, along with the sounds of car accelerating rapidly in low gear, partially covered the sound of the alarm tone and "officer needs assistance" statement which followed it. Coffee spilled to the floor as the car rocketed to assist the other officer.

The restaurant was bathed in revolving red lights; as squads arrived, officers piled out and entered the crowd. Sergeants were already present, and within minutes several lieutenants arrived. They ordered their patrol colleagues out of the crowd and a skirmish line was formed. Helmets and riot batons were taken out of trunks by those who had remembered to put them in. Ultimately, the crowd was dispersed not by force but by a night-watch inspector who talked over a loud-speaker for a half hour as the assembled patrol officers watched nervously.

However, most routine policing only infrequently involves "real police work." Consequently, most calls are placed into a second and much larger residual class of events. As one patrol officer observes: "You could give most of what we do around here to any idiot who could put up with the insanity that passes for civilized conduct."[25] The reaction associated with the residual call is to hope that it goes away by itself. In the context of husband–wife disputes, for instance, police generally respond without emergency speed, signal lights, or siren. They also proceed to the scene of the domestic in a deliberate manner in the hope that it will be settled prior to their arrival.[26] Minor auto accidents also represent residual work. When assigned an accident not involving injury, patrol officers generally respond slowly, hoping that the people involved will grow tired of waiting, exchange information in the absence of police assistance, and leave.[27] The same is true of juvenile trouble, landlord–tenant arguments, noisy parties, and the many other calls patrol officers are assigned. Unless modified to suggest a serious threat to life or property (for instance, "juvenile trouble, shots reported"), police officers believe that they have little or nothing to do with real policing.

What we find is relatively clear evidence that patrol officers construct and apply typifications in the course of their work. Recipes for action are associated with these typifications. The bulk of the problems are responded to slowly to allow for their resolution without police aid.

The classifications and responses constructed by patrol officers also appear to follow from the propositions advanced earlier. They permit efficient handling of problems. Energy, attention, personnel, and equipment are all reserved for situations where they are most clearly needed. They are constructed using work experiences since social science classificatory schemes are arbitrary and add nothing to what patrol officers learn through experience. They also are relatively inflexible and they are clearly small in number.

The Encounters

Most police work does not involve real policing and most calls are therefore answered slowly. Many citizens, however, are patient and they await arrival of a squad car. If citizens do wait, or if the problem is police-initiated, what follows is an *encounter* or period of interaction between police and citizens.

The nature of these encounters is the focus of this section. We shall proceed by describing citizen interaction during encounters and by considering the factors which influence citizen behavior. Then we will turn to an analysis of the typifications and recipes for action employed by patrol officers during their encounters with citizens.

Citizen Interaction.   Recently, students in my classes were asked to describe the typical police-citizen encounter. They were asked to indicate how often they thought citizens were impolite in their interaction with police, how often they got angry, and how often encounters declined to the level of potential or actual violence. Relying upon mass media portrayals and perhaps their own experiences with traffic stops, most believed that citizen interaction with police was characterized by impoliteness. They also believed that displays of anger and violence were quite common.

If you share these beliefs, you will understand the need to extensively document the following point: *the communicative acts of citizens involved in encounters with police are primarily polite, nonviolent, and delivered in the absence of displays of anger.* Review of the results of six different studies provides support for this assertion.

The first study is "Police Encounters with Juveniles," by Irving Piliavin and Scott Briar.[28] Piliavin and Briar sought to determine whether a juvenile's demeanor, along with factors such as the seriousness of the alleged offense, related to police arrest decisions. They found that demeanor was important in that cooperative juveniles tended to be released while uncooperative juveniles were arrested. They also found that over two-thirds of the juvenile suspects they observed were "cooperative" or polite in their interaction with police.

The second study, "Police Control of Juveniles," by Donald Black and Albert J. Reiss, Jr., also sought to determine whether a juvenile's attitude, along with other factors, played a role in police arrests.[29] The relationship between demeanor and arrest was again confirmed. Also confirmed was the fact that the overwhelming majority of juvenile suspects are polite in their encounters with police: slightly over 80 percent of the juvenile suspects observed were "civil" or "very deferential" in their dealings with police.

The third study, "Police Control of Juveniles: A Replication," repeated the earlier study by Black and Reiss.[30] Although the replication was conducted in a different city some six years later, the findings were nearly identical: 83 percent of the juveniles observed were polite or deferential in their relations with police.

In the fourth study, "Production of Crime Rates," Donald Black examined the relationship between the demeanor of an adult crime victim and police writing of a report of the incident.[31] Black found that polite victims had reports written more frequently than impolite victims. He also found that fully 96 percent of the victims observed were polite in their conversations with police.

In these first four studies, we find evidence that most police-citizen dealings are polite. However, the skeptical among you may argue that because these studies involved juvenile suspects or adult victims they do not accurately represent *adult violator* interaction with police. The next two studies consider this type of encounter and the findings are essentially similar to those we have just examined.

The fifth study, "Routine Police Arrest Practices," sought to identify the factors associated with a police officer's decision to arrest a person who was intoxicated.[32] Since we will be examining the actions of citizens who were drunk, a few words about the effects of alcohol on behavior are in order. The following is a typical, but not uncontested, interpretation:

> The apparent "stimulation" from alcohol is the result of the lower brain centers being released from higher brain controls. This reduces inhibitions, and behavior which is untoward when the individual is sober becomes acceptable. For example ... an always proper ... [person] ... may become obscene ... when intoxicated.[33]

If you were forced to predict a type of encounter in which citizens would be impolite, angry, and perhaps even violent, then the public drunkenness encounters would appear to be a good choice.

The data in Table 5–1 suggest that if you had actually made such a prediction you would have been wrong. Fully 80 percent of the public drunkenness offenders observed in this study displayed little or no anger during their encounter with police. Similarly, 97 percent of the encounters contained little or no violence on the part of the citizens involved. Further, over two-thirds of the publicly intoxicated citizens involved in these encounters evidenced little or no impoliteness in their interaction with police. Finally, most complied with the orders given them by police officers.

The final study, "Police Work with Traffic Law Violators," attempted to identify the factors which are important in a police officer's decision to issue a traffic citation to motorists stopped for traffic law violations.[34] Since we all have our favorite traffic stop story and since most of these are recounted in heated, if not argumentative tones, all we need note is that traffic stops and citations are said to be major sources of friction between police officers and citizens. However, the majority of motorists stopped for traffic law violations were *not* impolite in their interaction with police. Specifically, 87 percent of the motorists offered little or no verbal resistance to the police officers they interacted with.

TABLE 5-1. Percent of Public Drunkenness Encounters According to Indicators and Level of Respect Shown Police by Citizens*

Indicator and Level[a] of Disrespect	Percent
A. Temper	
Low	80
High	20
	100
	(195)
B. Violence	
Low	96
High	4
	100
	(195)
C. Impoliteness	
Low	68
High	32
	100
	(195)
D. Noncompliance	
Low	82
High	18
	100
	(195)

[a] Low = $0 \leqslant X_1 \leqslant \overline{X}$

High = $X_1 > \overline{X}$

*Source: Richard J. Lundman, "Routine Police Arrest Practices: A Commonweal Perspective," *Social Problems*, 22:1 (October 1974), p. 135. Adapted and reprinted by permission.

These six studies clearly suggest that the communicative acts of citizens involved in encounters with police are primarily polite, nonviolent, and even-tempered. Only a minority of encounters involve departures from civility. Despite the fact that such actions are relatively infrequent, it is instructive to consider the circumstances which precipitate impoliteness and verbal or physical abuse of police by citizens.

Factors Influencing Citizen Interaction.   The circumstances surrounding the start of an encounter appear important. Police-initiated encounters generally involve a perception on the part of the patrol officer that real policing is called for or, at the very least, that a quantitative product of police work will emerge. Police officers therefore enter proactive encounters with a greater sense of determination. The citizens present quickly learn of this as they are questioned, searched, and perhaps issued a traffic citation or arrested. Since very few citizens enjoy being searched and even fewer enjoy being ticketed or arrested, police-initiated interactions are productive of departures from civility.

Police-initiated encounters also represent situations in which the consensus surrounding the legitimacy of the officers' intervention is considerably less. In reactive situations, police have been called to the scene of an encounter by a citizen. Although the complaining citizen may not actually be present, the officer can and frequently does announce that someone has complained. In proactive encounters, an officer is acting alone and must independently establish the legitimacy of the intervention. In doing so, the officer stands a greater chance of causing some of the trouble characteristic of proactive encounters.

A second factor which affects police-citizen interaction is the way an officer *approaches* a citizen. Although approach is clearly related to the proactive-reactive variable, recent research suggests that it deserves independent attention.

Mary Glenn Wiley and Terry L. Hudik focused their research attention on proactive or police-initiated encounters.[35] They began by noting what we have just considered: "one of the touchiest aspects of police community intervention is that of field interrogation."[36] They speculated whether the "touchiness" characteristic of proactive encounters could be reduced by altering the way police officers approach the citizens involved in them.

They hypothesized that citizens react negatively to their involvement in police-initiated encounters for three reasons. Police sometimes fail to tell citizens why they are being interrogated. This gives citizens the impression that officers are harassing rather than seeking information. If police do provide reasons for the interrogation, citizens still may feel that the problems they are questioned about are unimportant. Still others who are told the reason they have been stopped know themselves to be innocent and find an interrogation embarrassing. Wiley and Hudik then hypothesized that if the structure of proactive encounters could be altered such that citizens perceived them as more rewarding, then negative citizen reactions would be reduced.

To assess the accuracy of their hypotheses, they first interviewed a sample of persons representative of the kinds of citizens involved in proactive encounters. They asked them how important they thought certain police activities were. From these citizens they learned that police investigations of crimes against persons were viewed as an important activity. Crimes against property were seen as less important and victimless crimes (gambling, narcotics) were ranked as least important.

They then went on to the crucial phase of their research: a field test of their hypotheses. They created or allowed to emerge the following four types of proactive encounters:

1. Citizens were told that they had been stopped because a crime against a *person* had been committed and they or their car resembled the description which had been given.
2. Citizens were told that they had been stopped because a crime against *property* had been committed and they or their car resembled the description which had been given;
3. Citizens were told that they had been stopped because a *victimless* crime had been committed and they or their car resembled the description which had been given;
4. Citizens were not given any information as to the reason they had been stopped.

They then measured the amount of time the citizens in each of these four circumstances willingly and politely interacted with police.

As can be seen in Table 5–2, the findings follow from the hypotheses advanced by the researchers. Based upon their earlier interviews, when crimes were perceived as important by citizens and when they were told the reason for the inquiry, they willingly and politely interacted with police for considerable periods of time. By contrast, when citizens considered the reason for their stop less important or when they were not told why they had been stopped, they interacted with police for significantly shorter periods of time. Wiley and Hudik observe:

> The police-citizen encounter is a two-way exchange. If the citizen acts in a negative or abusive manner, police . . . are likely to respond in kind. However, the officer often sets the tone for the interaction. A positive relationship can be established by such simple and low-cost behaviors as providing explanations.[37]

We have thus far established that two factors affect citizen interaction: proactivity and the nature of the officer's approach to the citizens involved in police-initiated encounters. However, a number of other factors also are important, among them the classifications and responses patrol officers employ in their encounters with citizens.

TABLE 5–2. Average Length (in Minutes) of Willing Cooperation Evidenced by Citizens in Field Interrogations by Type of Approach Used by the Officer

Type of Approach	Minutes of Cooperation	N
Reason given, crimes against persons	4.73	50
Reason given, crimes against property	1.78	50
Reason given, victimless crimes	.45	50
No reason given	.31	50

*Source: Mary Glenn Wiley and Terry L. Hudik, "Police–Citizen Encounters: A Field Test of Exchange Theory," *Social Problems*, 22:1 (October 1974), p. 124. Reprinted by permission.

Typifications and Recipes for Action.   Nearly all social scientists who have studied police officers agree that they categorize citizens in terms of a single overriding classification: "attitude." Citizens are said to possess a good or bad attitude. Those with a "good attitude" are polite in their interaction with police and show respect for the power the officer represents. Citizens who possess a "bad attitude" are impolite or disrespectful in their relations with police and appear indifferent to the power the officer represents.

Associated with these typified images of citizens are recipes for action.[38] Citizens with a good attitude are responded to politely and nonviolently. If they have violated the law in some minor way they also are treated leniently. Citizens who have a bad attitude because of what has happened to them (a mugging victim) or because they appear to have lost control over their actions (the "mental case") are ignored or isolated. Citizens who have no good reason to be angry and have control over their actions are treated impolitely and less leniently. They also are responded to more violently.

The data supportive of these assertions are strong and without contradiction. We now will examine the relations between citizen attitude and police interaction, reserving our analysis of the relations between attitude and leniency for later in the chapter. Relations between attitude and police violence will be explored in the next chapter.

In 1968, James Q. Wilson published the results of his study of police work in eight different police jurisdictions. The attitude typification was present in all of the departments Wilson studied, and it had an important effect on police behavior. Wilson reports:

> The implicit conception of justice the patrolman brings to his task is quite different from that assumed to operate in "the administration of criminal justice" or "law enforcement." Treating equals equally in a courtroom means to assume that all who enter there are equal before the law. . . . The patrolman, however, sees these people when they are dirty, angry, rowdy, obscene, dazed, savage, or bloodied. To him, they are not in these circumstances "equal," they are *different.* What they deserve depends on what they *are.* "Decent people" and "bums" are not equal; "studs" and "working stiffs" are not equal, victims and suspects are not equal. . . . To be just to these people means to give each what he deserves and to judge what he deserves by how he acts and talks. . . . A "wise guy" deserves less than a "good guy"; a man who does not accept police authority, and thus legal authority, deserves less than a man who does.[39]

In 1972, Rodney Stark released the results of his study, *Police Riots.* In it he described the importance of attitude among Los Angeles police officers:

Virtually all studies of the Los Angeles Police Department report that the "attitudes test" is a common part of L.A. police argot, and that for a policeman to say that a suspect "failed the attitudes test" justifies to other officers his use of violence, harassment, or bringing "chicken shit" citations and charges. The "attitudes test" in Los Angeles indicates that in police–citizen interactions the police impose certain standards of deference and respect and failure to meet this test merits reprisals.[40]

Most recently, William K. Muir's sophisticated analysis of the importance of attitude for patrol officers was published.[41] Muir establishes not only that attitude continues to be an important part of routine policing, but he also tells us the reason. Police officers work with all kinds of people, most of whom are amenable to police authority. He labels this group "governables." A minority of citizens (Muir's estimate is 20 percent)[42] resist police authority, thereby threatening not only the stability of an encounter, but potentially the safety of the officers and other citizens who might be present. These "rebels" represent a menace to police officers, and attitude is one of the earliest and most reliable signs of their rebelliousness. Attitude tests are a universal part of routine policing because patrol officers use them to distinguish governable and rebellious citizens. In Muir's words; "Ever since God investigated Adam, police . . . have performed "attitude tests" because they have always had to make judgments."[43]

Reactions by police are associated with the results of attitude tests. In general, citizens who signal their governability by passing attitude tests are treated politely by patrol officers. Citizens who act rebellious, thereby flunking attitude tests, are treated less civilly by officers.

One of the earliest and best studies of the relations between citizen attitude and police responses was directed by Albert J. Reiss, Jr.[44] Reiss placed 36 observers with patrol officers in high crime police precincts in Washington, D.C., Boston, and Chicago. The observers were attentive to a number of things, including the general nature of the interaction or conversation between police officers and citizens involved in encounters. Fundamental to Professor Reiss' analysis is an assumption that at least initially police officers respond to all citizens in a civil manner. Therefore, any deviation from civil interaction is assumed to be a function of the attitude of the citizens present during an encounter.[45]

The data in Table 5–3 are from the Reiss study, and they strongly suggest that a police officer's interaction is closely related to the attitude of the citizens they encounter. Fully nine out of ten of the officers confronted by very polite citizens were themselves polite or good-humored and jovial; the same is true of officers who confronted polite citizens. Courtesy on the part of a citizen most often resulted in reciprocal treatment on the part of an officer. A citizen's antagonism clearly altered police

TABLE 5–3. Percentage Distribution of General Demeanor of Citizen, by General Demeanor of Police Officer*

General Demeanor of Citizen	General Demeanor of Police Officer			
	Good-Humored or Jovial	Polite	Antagonistic	Totals
Very Polite[a]	26	64	10	100 (1,647)
Polite	20	76	4	100 (11,143)
Antagonistic	6	52	42	100 (1,149)

[a] The data in this row should be used as follows: 26 percent of the officers involved in encounters with very polite citizens responded in a good-humored or jovial manner, 64 percent responded politely, and 10 percent responded antagonistically.

*Adapted from Table 1.6, "Percentage Distribution by General Demeanor and Race of Citizen, by Conduct of Police Officers toward Citizen and Type of Mobilization of Police," from Albert J. Reiss, Jr., *The Police and the Public* (New Haven, Conn.: Yale University Press, 1971), p. 50. Adapted and reprinted by permission of author and publisher.

responses. Only a minority of police officers responded to antagonism with good humor or joviality. Slightly over half managed to maintain a civil tone while 42 percent responded to antagonism with antagonism.

The data in Table 5–4 are the same as those in the preceding table, presented in a slightly different manner. Looked at in this way, these data suggest that police demeanor is closely but not entirely related to citizen attitude. Thus, almost all of the good-humored or jovial officers were responding to polite or very polite citizens; only 2 percent were responding to antagonistic citizens. Similarly, almost all of the polite officers were responding to polite or very polite citizens; only 6 percent were responding politely to antagonistic citizens. For the minority of officers who responded antagonistically, less than half (44 percent) were responding to antagonistic citizens. The remainder responded to polite or very polite citizens in an antagonistic manner. Citizen attitude therefore is not the sole determinant of police interaction. Factors other than attitude relate to police demeanor.

It is likely that these factors include the seriousness of the alleged offense, the number of citizens in the crowd witnessing the encounter, and the characteristics of the officer who responds to the call. For example, certain officers respond antagonistically to nearly all citizens, even those who are polite. They seem to work on the premise that the only way to police effectively is to take charge of every situation. They use hostility, anger, and threats as their principal tools. Muir describes one such officer:

> Kip's style in everything he did was to overwhelm others with the might of his tongue, his spirit, his body, and his weaponry. Not that he was unaware of the virtues of explanation, discussion, and manipulation, it was just that

TABLE 5-4. Percentage Distribution of Police Officer Demeanor by General Demeanor of Citizen*

General Demeanor of Citizen	Distribution of Police Officer Demeanor		
	Good-Humored or Jovial Officers[a]	Polite Officers	Antagonistic Officers
Very Polite	16	10	15
Polite	82	84	41
Antagonistic	2	6	44
Totals	100 (2,726)	100 (10,120)	100 (1,094)

[a] The data in this column should be used as follows: 16 percent of the officers who were good-humored or jovial were responding to very polite citizens, 82 percent were responding to polite citizens, and 2 percent were responding to antagonistic citizens.
*Adapted from Table 1.6, "Percentage Distribution by General Demeanor and Race of Citizen, by Conduct of Police Officers toward Citizen and Type of Mobilization of Police," from Albert J. Reiss, Jr., The Police and the Public (New Haven, Conn.: Yale University Press, 1971), p. 50. Adapted and reprinted by permission of author and publisher.

... he invariably concluded that the better thing to do was to leap right in. The crowds were too problematic to be trusted to help, it was better to keep them at bay by keeping them "confused" and cowed by a display of might and a preemptive attack. . . . He enjoyed fights, they released tensions which built up in him whenever the streets got too quiet. He had to have a sense of total control. The more chaos he created, the greater his sense of self-control.[46]

What Reiss' data suggest is that police responses are closely related to citizen attitude. If we assume that patrol officers classify citizens in terms of attitude, and if we assume that they follow recipes for action associated with that typification, then the data in Tables 5-3 and 5-4 are supportive of both assumptions. It must be emphasized, however, that the Reiss data only *suggest* support for these assumptions. Fortunately, there is a more recent instance of research which also speaks to this issue.

Richard E. Sykes and John P. Clark also sought to determine what factors influence police behavior during encounters with citizens.[47] In their analysis, they advance an expanded image of attitude, one that includes actions and identities as signs of governability or rebelliousness. They also emphasize that patrol officers and citizens enact roles during encounters and that norms or rules structure relations between these roles. Sykes and Clark observe:

Police behavior must be explained in terms of the rules which order their relations with civilians and which are usually mutually acknowledged by both officers and civilians. Among these rules we posit the influence of an interpersonal norm governing police-civilian relations which we shall term an asymmetrical status norm. . . . Police are of higher status than many citizens. . . . We hypothesize then that this difference in status influences the flow of deference so that it is expected that it will be expressed differently downward or upward.[48]

What they are hypothesizing is that in encounters with citizens who display a bad attitude, police will be less deferent than the citizens with whom they interact. This is what they mean by the asymmetrical or unequal status norm governing police-citizen encounters.

There are several reasons that Sykes and Clark advance this hypothesis. Citizens who have violated the law are said to have displayed a bad attitude by reason of their actions. By becoming alleged law violators, they have displayed signs of rebelliousness. Citizens also suggest potential rebelliousness by becoming involved in domestic, landlord–tenant, customer–proprietor, and many other disputes which patrol officers are routinely called upon to deal with. Although these persons may not have violated the law, they have rebelled against the informal rules which constitute the fragile social order of the urban environment. Their potential for general rebellion is thus suggested. The Sykes and Clark prediction is that police officers will be less deferent than citizens who, by their actions, have displayed a bad attitude.

However, independent of a person's words and deeds, citizens bring other characteristics or elements of self to their encounters with police. Some of these characteristics, especially gender, race, age, and social class, are viewed by patrol officers as additional indicators of attitude and hence governability. Many police patrol officers view males, black citizens, young people, and lower-class citizens as displaying a greater potential for a bad attitude. Sykes and Clark hypothesize that patrol officers will be less deferent than citizens who give off signs of possible rebelliousness.

The data to assess the accuracy of these hypotheses were collected during a quantitative field study of police in a large midwestern city and two of its suburbs. A group of observers traveled with police and among the aspects of encounters recorded were the verbal statements of police and citizens. Each statement made by a police officer or citizen during an encounter was coded as either deferring or disrespectful. Crucial to the hypotheses advanced by Sykes and Clark is evidence that police are consistently less deferent in their interaction with particular types of citizens across many encounters.

The data in Table 5–5 are representative of those advanced by Sykes and Clark. In all situations examined by the researchers, patterns of deference flow are in the directions predicted by reference to our discussion of typifications (attitude) and recipes for action (an assymmetrical status norm). In those encounters where citizens showed signs of governability, the differences between the absolute levels of deference displayed by police and citizens averaged only 4 percent—on the average, police were 4 percent less polite than citizens. But in those encounters where citizens

TABLE 5-5. Differences in Absolute Levels of Deference between Police Patrol Officers and Citizens, by Signs of Attitude Given and Given Off (n = 1,466)*

Attitude	Difference (%)
"Governable"	
Dispute or service call	−3.0
Only a complainant present	−1.5
Only middle-class citizens present	−4.4
Only white citizens present	−6.5
Average difference	−3.85
"Rebellious"	
Crime against person or property call	−8.5
Violator present	−14.7[a]
Only lower-class citizens present	−7.3
Only black citizens present	−4.6
Average difference	−8.77

[a] These data should be interpreted as follows: assume that across all encounters involving violators, 80 percent of the total statements made by these citizens were deferent (polite). The 14.7 percent difference in levels of politeness means that across all of these encounters, 65.3 percent of the total statement made by the police patrol officers present were deferent—80.00 percent minus 65.3 equals an absolute deference level of 14.7 percent. The differences are all negative because police officers were less deferent in all encounters, on the average.

*Source: Richard E. Sykes and John P. Clark, "Deference Exchange in Police–Civilian Encounters," American Journal of Sociology, 81:3 (November 1975), p. 593. Reprinted by permission.

displayed signs of rebelliousness, the differences between the absolute levels of deference displayed by police and citizens was 9 percent. The greatest difference in absolute levels of deference occurred where citizens gave the clearest sign of their rebelliousness by being violators; here the difference was almost 15 percent. Sykes and Clark thus provide additional evidence of the existence of an attitude typification and an associated recipe for action—an asymmetrical status norm.

However, it would be unwise to encourage premature closure on this issue. As noted, certain police officers ignore the typifications and recipes for action of what appears to be the majority of their colleagues. They act antagonistically no matter what type of attitude citizens assume. There is also the troublesome issue of whether police officers or citizens independently or jointly control the flow of deference. Although our best guess would be that police officers enforce the asymmetrical status norm, we should recognize that it would be just that—a guess. Finally, our quantitative empirical support consists of only two studies. We must therefore be cautious in our conclusions.

Given the available data and the absence of evidence to the contrary, it appears that patrol officers typify citizens in terms of an "attitude" classificatory scheme and act by reference to an associated recipe for action—an asymmetrical status norm. Unless and until contradictory evidence is presented, we will accept this as an adequate description of most police–citizen encounters.

The Decision

Discretion exists when patrol officers are in a position to decide to terminate an encounter in more than one way. In the typical traffic-stop encounter, an officer can terminate the encounter by issuing a citation or by verbally warning the motorist. In an encounter with an alleged misdemeanor violator, an officer can either arrest or release the suspect. Discretion thus refers to an officer's ability to choose between two or more mutually exclusive dispositional alternatives.

It is common for social scientists to describe patrol work as largely discretionary.[49] Most of them emphasize that patrol officers frequently find themselves in encounters where more than one outcome is possible.[50] Many scholars also stress that patrol officers abuse their discretion by treating lower-class citizens differently than middle-class citizens, and blacks differently than whites.[51] These are largely accurate observations.

However, the essential accuracy of these observations has had an unfortunate effect. In describing police patrol work as largely discretionary, social scientists have inadvertently ignored or minimized the constraints which surround police exercise of discretion. The nature of these constraints will therefore occupy our immediate attention. We then will examine the typifications and recipes for action which guide the discretionary decisions of patrol officers and police abuse of discretion.

Constraints on Police Discretion. A minimum of three factors constrains police exercise of discretion. These factors are: 1) the circumscribed nature of the police mandate; 2) citizen actions prior to the start of an encounter; and 3) the problems patrol officers are called upon to deal with. Analysis of these restrictions will help remedy the inadvertent neglect shown this topic in the past.

The Police Mandate.[52]   It was earlier argued that police departments were created by and for elites. One sign of elite control of early police is found in the circumscribed nature of the police mandate. Police were charged with the task of controlling the criminality, public intoxication, and riot of the dangerous classes. They were not concerned with elite crime. Servants did not police their masters.

Elites continue to define the limits of policing. Police forces are primarily concerned with attempting to control only certain types of crimes. They are greatly concerned with crime in the streets. They are little concerned with elite crimes, sometimes called "crime in the suites."[53]

Consider the problem of theft.[54] You undoubtedly would be concerned by the loss of $50 during a mugging. You also likely would be reassured that police appear to share your concern. If you call, a car generally will be sent. If you wish, the responding officer will write a report of the incident. If you can provide a description of the violator, and if detectives have time to investigate such a minor loss, there exists the possibility of arrest.

If you lost $50 because of price-fixing, however, the story would be quite different. It is highly unlikely that you would even know that you had lost the money. If you somehow did find out and become concerned, it is doubtful that police would share your concern. If you called, a squad car would not be sent, even though price-fixing is illegal. Instead, the police operator would likely inform you that price-fixing is not a police matter. At the very most, you might be referred to another agency. But even this is debatable, since the typical police operator does not know who is responsible for controlling price-fixing.

Police discretion is thus limited by elites, principally by limiting the areas that the police can control. Common street crimes such as mugging are a central component of the contemporary police mandate. Common suite crimes such as price-fixing are not.

Citizen Actions Prior to an Encounter.   Citizens determine whether patrol officers will be in a position to dispose of an encounter in more than one way. Routine policing is largely reactive, with police highly dependent upon citizens for reports of criminal incidents. Unless citizens call, the police generally do not even know that a crime has occurred. Research results suggest that in about half the number of cases, citizens elect not to report their victimization to the police.[55]

Citizens further constrain police exercise of discretion by their willingness to remain at the scene of an encounter until police arrive. If a violator is not present and a citizen complainant or witness leaves, fails to appear once police arrive, or otherwise deliberately avoids contact with the police, there is little an officer can do. For example, two patrol officers received a call to "see the lady" along with an address. They drove to the address and knocked on the door. No one answered and the officers returned to their car. Once in the car, one officer flipped on the emergency lights saying, "If someone wants us, they'll find us." After about 30 seconds, they turned off their lights and told the dispatcher that the call was "GOA" (gone on arrival). Research results suggest that about one in five radio calls result in no police contact with a complaining citizen.[56] These GOAs further limit police exercise of discretion.

Citizens therefore restrict police exercise of discretion. They can elect not to alert police to criminal incidents, and approximately half of the criminal incidents known to citizens are not reported to the police. If they do call the police, citizens can elect not to interact with responding officers. In general, then, for every encounter in which it appears possible for a police officer to exercise discretion, there is at least one other that never took place because a citizen chose not to call the police or decided not to interact even though a call had been made.

Problems as Constraints.   Police exercise of discretion is further limited by
the nature of the problems police officers are called upon to deal with. If
we take discretion to refer to the choice between two or more mutually
exclusive dispositional alternatives, then patrol officers are involved in a
significant number of encounters where only one outcome is possible.
Service requests involving sick calls, lock-outs, and nonvehicular accidents constitute limited discretion encounters. Police officers may alter
the quality or quantity of the services rendered, but for all except the most
obnoxious of citizens, they have little choice but to render some degree
of service.

Felony encounters consisting of a suspect and sound evidence or credi-
ble witnesses also represent a limited discretion situation. Although patrol officers may elect to release felony suspects, they are constrained in
doing so. Patrol officers continue to be evaluated by the number of felony
arrests they make and this severely limits their ability to release felony
suspects. Most felony calls produce several responding squads and officers
expect to be able to share felony arrests. A released suspect obviously
cannot be shared. Sergeants and other administrators depend upon their
patrol officers to help give an appearance of effective policing by arresting
those felony suspects they are lucky enough to apprehend. Generally
speaking, therefore, only naive or very fortunate officers are in a position
to release felony suspects. It is probably more accurate to note that meaningful choice among dispositional alternatives is not present in felony
encounters containing suspects: arrest is the nearly universal outcome.

Police exercise of discretion is thus constrained by a minimum of three
factors: the circumscribed police mandate, citizen action prior to an encounter, and the problems police officers are called upon to resolve. It is
within limits imposed by these three factors that patrol work can be said
to be largely discretionary. Specifically, police discretion is routinely
present in two general types of encounters: 1) those containing only victims or complainants, wherein the officer can choose to handle the situation formally by writing a report of the incident or informally by not
writing a report; and 2) those involving alleged misdemeanants where the
issue is arrest or release. It is in these two types of encounters that
patrol officers are in a position to dispose of a problem in more than
one way. They are also able to abuse their arrest discretion in these situations.

Typifications and Recipes for Action.   At first glance, it appears extremely difficult to identify the factors influencing police choices among
dispositional alternatives. This is because many social scientists have
provided answers and their answers conflict. What follows is a partial listing of variables previously identified as influencing police decisions:

1. Characteristics of the citizens present including demeanor, gender, age, social class, race, style of dress, family status, and for juveniles, school status.[57]
2. Characteristics of the problem and encounter including legal seriousness, situational availability of evidence, presence or absence of complainants, victims, witnesses, or bystanders, and the location and visibility of the encounter.[58]
3. Characteristics of the department including the style of policing in evidence—watch, legalistic, or service, and whether the department maintains a formal or informal quota system for certain offenses such as traffic law violations.[59]
4. Characteristics of the officers involved including beliefs about certain citizens, attitudes toward court and court personnel, and feelings about working overtime or appearing in court the next day.[60]

Despite this conflict, there exists general agreement on one point: police officers classify citizens in terms of attitude and apply associated standard procedures. In the context of the two general types of decision-making situations we are concerned with, citizens with a good attitude either have reports of criminal incidents written or are released even though they allegedly violated the law in some minor way. Citizens who have a bad attitude have reports written less frequently or are more frequently arrested for minor offenses. The data supportive of these assertions are strong and without contradiction. Table 5–6 summarizes the results of seven studies of police decision making.

In the first study, "Police Encounters with Juveniles," by Irving Piliavin and Scott Briar, only 13 percent of the juveniles who passed the attitude test ("cooperative" juveniles) were arrested. By contrast, nine out of ten flunking the attitude test ("uncooperative" juveniles) were arrested.

The second study, "Police Control of Juveniles," by Donald Black and Albert J. Reiss, Jr., also provides evidence of the importance of attitude. However, the difference in rates of arrest for those juveniles who passed the attitude test ("civil" juveniles) as compared to those who failed ("antagonistic" juveniles) are much less dramatic than those reported by Piliavin and Briar: 12 percent of the civil juveniles were arrested as compared to only 18 percent of the antagonistic juveniles. The Black and Reiss study also contains evidence that overly polite ("very deferential") juveniles were arrested at a rate essentially equal to the rate for antagonistic juveniles. Although the reason for this is somewhat unclear, it does appear reasonable to suggest that extreme deference is inappropriate in certain encounters.

The third study, Donald Black's "Production of Crime Rates," suggests that extreme deference is inappropriate when expressed by alleged violators. If we assume that a written report is a desirable outcome for a complainant involved in an encounter with police, then nine out of ten

TABLE 5-6. Summary of Selected Studies of Police Exercise of Discretion

Source	Focus of Article	Demeanor and Outcome of Encounter				Other Factors Related to Outcome
			Percentage of Outcomes			
		Demeanor	Arrest	Release	Totals	
Irving Piliavin and Scott Briar, "Police Encounters with Juveniles," American Journal of Sociology, 70 (September 1964): 206–214	Factors affecting the arrest or release of juvenile suspects in a West Coast city.	Cooperative	13	87	100 (45)	1. Offense seriousness 2. Prior record 3. Race 4. Style of dress 5. Group membership
		Uncooperative	90	10	100 (21)	
		Totals	38 (25)	62 (41)	100 (66)	

| | | Demeanor | Percentage of Outcomes | | | |
			Arrest	Release	Totals	
Donald Black and Albert J. Reiss, Jr., "Police Control of Juveniles," American Sociological Review, 35 (February 1970): 63–77	Factors affecting the arrest or release of juvenile suspects in Boston, Chicago, and Washington, D.C.	Very deferential	17	83	100 (30)	1. Offense seriousness 2. Complainant preference 3. Situational evidence
		Civil	12	88	100 (148)	
		Antagonistic	18	82	100 (44)	
		Totals	14 (31)	86 (191)	100 (222)	

Donald Black, "Production of Crime Rates," *American Sociological Review*, 35 (August 1970): 733–748.

Factors affecting the writing of a report of a criminal incident in Boston, Chicago, and Washington, D.C. The encounters examined include those where violators were not present and the complainant requested that a report be written.

Demeanor	Percentage of Outcomes		
	Report	No Report	Totals
Very deferential	91	9	100 (35)
Civil	73	26	99 (206)
Antagonistic	30	70	100 (10)
Totals	74 (185)	26 (66)	100 (251)

1. Offense seriousness
2. Complainant preference
3. Relational distance between complainant and alleged violator
4. Social class (felony situations only)

Richard J. Lundman, "Routine Police Arrest Practices: A Commonweal Perspective," *Social Problems*, 22 (October 1974): 127–141.

Factors affecting the arrest or release of public drunkenness offenders in a large midwestern city.

Demeanor	Percentage of Outcomes		
	Arrest	Release	Totals
Low level of impoliteness	26	74	100 (132)
High level of impoliteness	44	56	100 (63)
Totals	31 (61)	69 (134)	100 (195)

1. Offense conspicuousness (proactivity, downtown location, or closed public location such as a library)
2. Offender powerlessness (race and social class)

Richard E. Sykes, James C. Fox, and John P. Clark, "A Sociolegal Theory of Police Discretion," in Arthur Niederhoffer and Abraham S. Blumberg (eds.), *The Ambivalent Force*, 2d ed. (Hinsdale,

Factors affecting the arrest or release of persons who have committed a minor misdemeanor in a large midwestern city and two suburbs of that city (includes some of the cases examined above in context of public drunkenness).

Demeanor	Percentage of Outcomes		
	Arrest	Release	Totals
No impoliteness	10	90	100
Less than average impoliteness	23	77	100
Greater than average impoliteness	11	89	100

1. Offense seriousness
2. Departmental policies

TABLE 5–6. (Continued)

Source	Focus of Article	Demeanor and Outcome of Encounter	Other Factors Related to Outcome
III.: Dryden Press, 1976), pp. 171–183.		Much greater than average impoliteness: 41	59	100 (282)	

Source	Focus of Article	Demeanor	Arrest	Release	Totals	Other Factors Related to Outcome
Richard J. Lundman, Richard E. Sykes, and John P. Clark, "Police Control of Juveniles: A Replication," *Journal Research in Crime and Delinquency*, 15 (January 1978): 74–91.	A replication of the Black and Reiss research (see above). The factors affecting the arrest or release of juvenile suspects in a large midwestern city. Excludes felonies.		*Percentage of Outcomes*			1. Departmental policies 2. Offense seriousness 3. Complainant preference 4. Situational evidence
		Very deferential	30	70	100 (10)	
		Civil	5	95	100 (141)	
		Antagonistic	23	77	100 (31)	
		Totals	9 (17)	91 (165)	100 (182)	

Source	Focus of Article	Demeanor	Citation	Release	Totals	Other Factors Related to Outcome
Richard J. Lundman, "Organizational Norms and Police Discretion: An Observational Study of Police Work with Traffic Law Violators," *Criminology*, 17 (August 1979), pp. 159–171.	Factors affecting the citing versus release of traffic law violators in a large midwestern city.		*Percentage of Outcomes*			1. Quota saliency (departmental policies) 2. Social class 3. Race
		Little or no verbal resistance	47 (120)	53 (136)	100 (256)	
		Above average verbal resistance	51 (19)	49 (18)	100 (37)	
		Totals	47 (139)	53 (154)	100 (293)	

very deferential complainants had reports written. Citizens who were simply civil had reports written in nearly three-quarters of their encounters with police. Complainants who flunked the attitude test by being antagonistic had reports written in only 30 percent of their encounters with police.

The fourth study, "Routine Police Arrest Practices: A Commonweal Perspective," examined the role of citizen demeanor in public drunkenness encounters. Most public drunkenness offenders are essentially polite in their interaction with police and only about a quarter of public drunkenness offenders with a good attitude were arrested. By comparison, almost half of those who flunked the attitude test were arrested.

In the fifth study, "A Socio-Legal Theory of Police Discretion," the role of citizen demeanor in a variety of minor misdemeanor encounters is examined. As is clear, the greater the level of impoliteness, the greater the probability of arrest. Only one of ten minor misdemeanants who were entirely polite in their interaction with police were arrested. However, somewhat less than half (41 percent) of those who evidenced a "much greater than average impoliteness" were arrested.

The sixth study is a replication of Donald Black and Albert J. Reiss, Jr.'s "Police Control of Juveniles." As with any replication, the intent was to discover the extent to which the earlier findings hold at a different time and place. Table 5–6 suggests that the findings are the same as those reported earlier by Black and Reiss. Only 5 percent of those juveniles who possessed a "good attitude" ("civil") were arrested by police as compared to nearly a quarter of the antagonistic juveniles. Also similar to Black and Reiss' was the finding that very deferential juveniles were arrested at a rate similar to that for antagonistic juveniles. This suggests that extreme deference on the part of alleged *violators* may be seen by police as inappropriate. It should be emphasized that a great deal more research needs to be done before we can be confident of this interpretation.

The final study summarized in Table 5–6, "Police Work with Traffic Law Violators," examined the factors affecting the citing versus release of traffic law violators. In this study, demeanor plays a role but its impact is minor: 47 percent of the motorists displaying little or no verbal resistance received a traffic citation, as compared to 51 percent of those who evidenced above-average verbal resistance. The difference is in the expected direction, but it is very small.

Across these seven studies we find additional proof that police officers employ a classification technique called the "attitude test." These studies also suggest that there is a response associated with this stereotypical imagery of citizens: those who display a "bad attitude" are treated differently than those who display a "good attitude."

We are also in a position to suggest the reasons that patrol officers are so sensitive to the attitudes displayed by citizens. The available evidence suggests that police officers believe that effective policing requires citizen acceptance of police authority.[61] Because authority is seen as central to the police role, citizens who question or resist that authority represent a serious challenge to police officers and the organizations they represent. Specifically, challenges by persons displaying a "bad attitude" are not taken lightly because they are seen as threatening an officer's ability to accomplish assigned tasks. Officers respond to these perceived challenges by treating citizens less leniently. In responding in this manner, they abuse their arrest discretion.

Police Abuse of Arrest Discretion. "Abuse" is not a neutral term and it is important to be as precise as possible about what it is intended to suggest. We can begin by noting that in a society which is at least rhetorically democratic, police departments are commonweal organizations intended to serve the best interests of the public at large. Among the norms surrounding police organizations are expectations that police patrol officers will follow the rule of law and be consistent or generally equitable in their treatment of citizens. Abuse of arrest discretion, therefore, refers to arrest decisions based upon factors outside the rule of law or upon factors which favor certain citizens at the expense of others.

The late O. W. Wilson, a leading advocate of police professionalism and a reform police administrator in Chicago, established that attitude as a factor affecting arrest is outside the rule of law. Wilson cautioned:

> The officer ... must remember that there is no law against making a policeman angry and that he cannot charge a man with making him angry.[62]

There also exists general agreement that factors such as social class, gender, and race should not play a role in police decision making. This is because these factors violate norms emphasizing consistency or general equitability. One group's advantage is another's disadvantage.

Looked at in this way, the data in Table 5–6 suggest that police abuse of discretion is frequent. Across the nearly 15 years represented by the studies summarized in the table, there is clear evidence that patrol officers routinely operate outside the role of law by basing arrest decisions on attitude. Although there is no law against having a bad attitude, arrest for "contempt of police" is a frequent occurrence.

The studies summarized in Table 5-6 also suggest that police officers normally make decisions which are biased toward certain citizens and against others. Factors such as prior record, race, style of dress, group membership, complainant preference, relational distance between the alleged violator and victim (strangers versus family members), social class, and offense conspicuousness all are reported as playing a role in decision making. Specifically, citizens without prior records, whites, the conventionally dressed and affiliated, victims of attacks by strangers, middle-class citizens, and those who are discreet in their actions are benefited; former criminals, blacks and other minorities, the unconventionally dressed and affiliated, citizens victimized by friends and family members, lower-class citizens, and those who are conspicuous in their actions are at a disadvantage.

The data in Table 5–6 indicate that routine police decision making occurs outside the rule of law (attitude). The data also show that decisions are made on the basis of factors which are beneficial to only some people. On the basis of the available data, it appears that police abuse of discretion is common.

SUMMARY

Police officers are expected to do our dirty work efficiently. Typifications and recipes for action permit efficient policing. The nature of the categories and procedures constructed by patrol officers reflect their grounding in work experiences. This is because social scientists have consistently failed to provide police with useful information.

Patrol officers construct and apply a small number of nonnegotiable typifications and recipes for action. This is because police are able to process clients in the absence of their consent. It is also because the typical law-violating client in contact with a police organization is generally or situationally inferior in status to a police officer.

In the context of routine policing, patrol officers classify and respond accordingly to the problems they handle, the encounters they are involved in, and the decisions they make. The many different kinds of problems citizens call upon police to handle are placed in two general categories: those involving real policing and a much larger residual category. Recipes for action follow from this typification; problems requiring real policing are responded to quickly and aggressively.

The attitude test is the general technique used by patrol officers to guide their interaction during encounters and to shape their decisions in situations where discretion exists. Citizens who display a good attitude are responded to politely and, if they have violated the law in some minor way, they are treated leniently. Citizens with a bad attitude are responded to impolitely and are shown less leniency.

The data also suggest that police misconduct in the form of abuse of discretion is common. Patrol officers routinely base their discretionary decision on factors outside the rule of law or upon factors which benefit only a portion of the population. However, police misconduct is not limited to abuse of discretion. Policing is rich in opportunities for additional types of misbehavior. The next chapter therefore examines the general problem of police misconduct.

Notes

1. For a discussion of the concept of dirty work, see Everett C. Hughes, "Good People and Dirty Work," in Howard S. Becker (ed.), *The Other Side: Perspectives on Deviance* (New York: Free Press, 1964), pp. 23–36.

2. George Kirkham, *Signal Zero* (New York: Ballantine, 1976), pp. 43–46.

3. The thrust towards efficiency is one feature of a bureaucracy. For a discussion of this, see Peter M. Blau and W. Richard Scott, *Formal Organizations* (San Francisco: Chandler, 1962). pp. 60–73.

4. See Albert J. Reiss, Jr., *The Police and The Public* (New Haven, Conn.: Yale University Press, 1971), p. 12; and Jonathan Rubinstein, *City Police* (New York: Ballantine, 1973), p. 74.

5. David Sudnow, "Normal Crimes: Sociological Features of the Penal Code in a Public Defender Office," in Richard Quinney (ed.), *Crime and Justice in Society* (Boston: Little, Brown, 1969), pp. 308–335.

6. Sudnow, "Normal Crimes," p. 314.

7. Thomas J. Scheff, "Typification in Rehabilitation Agencies," in Earl Rubington and Martin S. Weinberg (eds.), *Deviance: The Interactionist Perspective* (New York: Macmillan, 1973), pp. 128–131. All of the materials on Scheff are from this source. It should be noted that Scheff was working out of Meadian tradition while Sudnow was working from the phenomenological perspective. The former emphasizes interpretive processes while the latter stresses constructive processes. For a discussion of this difference, see William B. Sanders, *Detective Work* (New York: Free Press, 1977), pp. 6–12. The discussion which follows seeks synthesis of these two approaches to the problem of meaning, at least as it exists and is solved in police organizations. For a similar attempt at synthesis employing the ideas of typifications and recipes for action, see Peter K. Manning, *Police Work* (Cambridge, Mass.: The M.I.T. Press, 1977), pp. 236–238. Finally, I want to thank William B. Sanders and Joan Neff Gurney for their helpful criticisms of earlier versions of this discussion.

8. These propositions are partially based upon Scheff, "Typification."

9. We have a large number of theories of the causes of crime, but none has repeatedly escaped rejection. See, for example, Ruth Rosner Kornhauser, *Social Sources of Delinquency: An Appraisal of Analytic Models* (Chicago: University of Chicago Press, 1978).

10. The single best source of support for this statement is Robert Martinson, "What Works? Questions and Answers about Prison Reform," *The Public Interest, 35* (Spring 1974): 22–54. Martinson's answer is that "nothing works."

11. See Rand Corporation, *The Criminal Investigation Process, Volume III: Observations and Analysis* (Washington, D.C.: U.S. Department of Justice, 1975); and Police Foundation, *The Kansas City Preventive Patrol Experiment—A Summary Report* (Washington, D.C.: Police Foundation, 1974).

12. For a discussion of this, see William J. Chambliss and John T. Liell, "The Legal Process and the Community Setting," *Crime and Delinquency, 12* (1966): 310–317.

13. The President's Commission on Law Enforcement and Administration of Justice, *The Police* (Washington, D.C.: U.S. Government Printing Office, 1967), p. 14.

14. See Richard J. Lundman, "Police Patrol Work: A Comparative Perspective," in Richard J. Lundman (ed.), *Police Behavior: A Sociological Perspective* (New York: Oxford University Press, 1980).

15. Lundman, "Police Patrol Work."

16. These examples are from my observations.

17. Elaine Cumming, Ian Cumming, and Laura Edell, "Policeman as Philosopher, Guide and Friend," in Quinney (ed.), *Crime and Justice,* pp. 147–160.

18. Cumming et al., "Policeman as Philosopher," p. 151.

19. Cumming et al., "Policeman as Philosopher," p. 151.

20. Reiss, *The Police and the Public,* p. 71.

21. John A. Webster, *Police Task and Time Study* (unpublished Ph.D. dissertation, University of California, Berkeley, 1968).

22. Lundman, "Police Patrol Work."

23. Donald J. Black, *Police Encounters and Social Organization: An Observational Study* (unpublished Ph.D. dissertation, University of Michigan, 1968), p. 55.

24. John Van Maanen, "Observations on the Making of Policemen," *Human Organization, 32* (Winter 1973): 413.

25. Van Maanen, "Observations," p. 413.

26. Richard J. Lundman, "Domestic Police-Citizen Encounters," *Journal of Police Science and Administration, 2* (March 1974): 25.

27. Rubinstein, *City Police,* p. 98.

28. Irving Piliavin and Scott Briar, "Police Encounters with Juveniles." *American Journal of Sociology, 70* (1964): 206–214.

29. Donald Black and Albert J. Reiss, Jr., "Police Control of Juveniles," *American Sociological Review, 35* (1970): 63–77.

30. Richard J. Lundman, Richard E. Sykes, and John P. Clark, "Police Control of Juveniles: A Replication," *Journal of Research in Crime and Delinquency, 15* (January 1978): 74–91.

31. Donald J. Black, "Production of Crime Rates," *American Sociological Review, 35* (March 1970): 733–748.

32. Richard J. Lundman, "Routine Police Arrest Practices: A Commonweal Perspective," *Social Problems, 22* (October 1974): 127–141.

33. Charles H. McCaghy, *Deviant Behavior: Crime, Conflict, and Interest Groups* (New York: Macmillan, 1976), p. 264. The statement is not uncontested in that certain social scientists argue that *expression* of the effects of alcohol consumption is culturally determined. McCaghy discusses this in the pages following this quotation.

34. Richard J. Lundman, "Organizational Norms and Police Discretion: An Observational Study of Police Work with Traffic Law Violators," *Criminology* (forthcoming).

35. Mary Glenn Wiley and Terry L. Hudik, "Police–Citizen Encounters: A Field Test of Exchange Theory," *Social Problems, 22* (October 1974): 119–127.

36. Wiley and Hudik, "Police–Citizen Encounters," p. 119.

37. Wiley and Hudik, "Police-Citizen Encounters," p. 125.

38. The material in this paragraph is based upon John Van Maanen, "The Asshole," in Peter K. Manning and John Van Maanen (eds.), *Policing: A View From the Street* (Santa Monica, Calif.: Goodyear, 1978), especially p. 232.

39. James Q. Wilson, *Varieties of Police Behavior* (Cambridge, Mass.: Harvard University Press, 1968), pp. 36–37.

40. Rodney Stark, *Police Riots* (Belmont, Calif.: Wadsworth, 1972), p. 61.

41. William K. Muir, *Police: Street Corner Politicians* (Chicago: University of Chicago Press, 1977).

42. Muir, *Police,* p. 167.

43. Muir, *Police,* p. 160.

44. Reiss, *The Police,* p. 50ff.

45. Reiss, *The Police,* p. 48.

46. Muir, *Police,* pp. 107–108.

47. Richard E. Sykes and John P. Clark, "Deference Exchange in Police–Civilian Encounters," *American Journal of Sociology, 81* (November 1975): 584–600.

48. Sykes and Clark, "Deference Exchange," p. 586.

49. For example, Wilson, *Varieties,* pp. 7–10.

50. Herman Goldstein, *Policing in a Free Society* (Cambridge, Mass.: Ballinger, 1977), p. 93.

51. Goldstein, *Policing,* p. 102; and Lundman, "Routine Police Arrest Practices."

52. I want to thank William B. Sanders for calling this point to my attention.

53. McCaghy, *Deviant Behavior,* p. 203.

54. The examples which follow were inspired by McCaghy, *Deviant Behavior,* p. 205.

55. See Phillip Ennis, "Crime, Victims, and the Police," *Trans-Action* (1967): pp. 36–44.

56. Richard E. Sykes and John P. Clark, *Terminal Progress Report: Quantitative Analysis of Police Encounters* (Minneapolis: Minnesota Systems Research, 1972), Appendix V, Table 5.

57. See, for example, Nathan Goldman, "The Differential Selection of Juvenile Offenders for Court Appearance," in Arthur Niederhoffer and Abraham S. Blumberg (eds.), *The Ambivalent Force: Perspectives on the Police,* 2nd ed. (Hinsdale, Ill.: the Dryden Press, 1976), pp. 183–187.

58. See, for example, Black and Reiss, "Police Control of Juveniles"; Lundman, "Routine Police Arrest Practices"; and Lundman, Sykes, and Clark, "Police Control of Juveniles: A Replication."

59. See, for example, Wilson, *Varieties;* and Lundman, "Organizational Norms."

60. See, for example, Piliavin and Briar, "Police Control of Juveniles."

61. For example, Wilson, *Varieties,* pp. 36–37.

62. Cited in Stark, *Police Riots,* pp. 59–60.

CHAPTER **6**

Police
Misconduct

INTRODUCTION

Police misconduct is a difficult topic to discuss. Some people still work with what is essentially a dangerous classes image of the persons responsible for crime. They see police as a "thin blue line" standing between civility and anarchy. For people who maintain this image, mention of police corruption or unnecessary police force is taken as evidence of a willingness to encourage the forces of anarchy. To propose to systematically discuss police misconduct is to earn the label "antipolice."

Other people continue to see police as a fundamental threat to individual liberty. For people fearful of police, mention of police misbehavior reinforces and inflates stereotypical images of the forms and frequency of improper actions. To propose to systematically discuss police misconduct is to confirm what the fearful think they already know: all police are corrupt and brutal.

Both positions are without foundation. To systematically discuss police misconduct and to be openly critical of it is not antipolice.[1] In an organically solidary society police departments are important agencies of social control. They do the things we can not or will not do ourselves. Because they are so important, it is necessary to be critical of improper police actions. To be critical of the corruption of police in Seattle,[2] Chicago,[3] and Philadelphia,[4] or the brutality of police in Houston,[5] is to encourage civility. To ignore or minimize these actions is to encourage anarchy. Police are not the enemy of democratic society; corrupt and brutal police are.

To argue that all police are immoral and abusive also is without foundation. Many patrol officers bring integrity and compassion to their work and our lives.[6] William K. Muir describes the "Laconia" police department:

> Nor was there, generally speaking, any corruption. . . . In the 1950's the department had suffered serious scandal, in which several police . . . had gone to prison for shakedowns and bribery. Long since then, graft had been rooted out. Even a free cup of coffee transgressed departmental regulations , and the chief made several harsh examples of police . . . who violated the rules against accepting gratuities.[7]

Purpose of the Chapter

The purpose of this chapter is to consider the problem of police misconduct. The concept which guides our analysis is the idea of organizational deviance. The nature and meaning of that concept occupies our attention in the first section of the chapter. The second section directs attention towards police corruption and unnecessary police force as instances of organizational deviance.

ORGANIZATIONAL DEVIANCE

The essential hypothesis to be advanced is that in certain situations police misconduct is best understood as a form of organizational rather than individual deviance. It is suggested that organizational processes rather than individual pathologies are at the heart of police misbehavior.

The Position of Individuals in Organizations[8]

At first blush, it may appear difficult to study the deviance of an organization while basically ignoring the individuals who make up that organization. After all, one can assert that individual persons act in ways that ultimately produce police misconduct. How can we study the whole of police organizations while generally ignoring individual officers and their specific behaviors?

The answer is that we can do this in the same way that we can study the overall functioning of an automobile without studying specific individual parts, or how the human brain functions without studying each individual cell. The common feature these other objects have with police organizations is that they are all systems composed of parts. These parts are interrelated and they constrain and interact with one another. For instance, the decision of where to deploy marked patrol cars is not made by individual officers. It is made by various segments of police subdivisions including patrol, planning and research, and community relations.

This is because no single officer or division has the necessary information on personnel, requests for police presence, and community sentiments needed for such a determination. The decision to deploy patrol cars is the result of the joint actions of many interdependent parts.[9]

Within such a structure, individual police officers are relatively unimportant. Officers occupy social roles within police organizations. These roles are the smallest subunits of organization and associated with each role are formalized expections regarding actions and attitudes.[10] These expectations or positions are integrated with other social roles, typically in a hierarchical fashion with some roles answerable to other roles. The "chain of command" characteristic of police organizations is representative of this hierarchical role integration.

In a very real sense, individual officers are marginal to police organizations. They are replaceable, and those that replace them learn what to do during recruit training, interaction with field training officers, and the informal and formal rules which survive the departures of their predecessors. Officers who leave their department learn this retrospectively. The department functions quite nicely without them.

Consider, for a moment, a more familiar illustration of this point: the college or university most of you are attending and two roles within it, student and professor. Although you and your professor (and the author) may want to resist the idea, if we think candidly about the issue we will recognize that all of us are replaceable. Other people could easily enact the roles which we currently occupy. If all are replaced in a short period of time, your college or university would not change dramatically. Indeed, the turnover each year due to graduation or the replacement of one professor of criminal justice or sociology with another, causes suprisingly little alteration in the functioning of criminal justice or sociology courses from year to year. A course as a component of a college or university is as real as the individuals who make it up. The specific people, however, are rather marginal to the institution.

For persons who study large organizations, individuality is virtually irrelevant as a topic of study. Marvin Olsen observes:

> The process of social organization . . .incorporates social interactions and relationships, patterns of social order, and shared cultural ideas. Actions of individual persons, insofar as they behave as autonomous personalities, are not directly relevant. . . .To the extent that people behave idiosyncratically, in terms of personal motive, goals, and meanings, and without regard for existing social orders or cultures, they do not contribute to social organization.[11]

This suggests that it is possible to study police misconduct on the organizational rather than individual level. This is because specific persons are marginal in contemporary police oranizations. They are but parts functioning in roles in a larger organizational setting.

Organizations as Deviants[12]

Having suggested that individuals are subordinate to police organizations, the next task is to describe the circumstances in which police departments are deviant acting units. It is tentatively suggested that five conditions must be met for a deviant action to be the product of organizational rather than natural persons. These conditions identify the circumstances in which police departments are deviant acting units.

First, for an action to be organizationally deviant *it must be contrary to norms or rules maintained by others external to the police department.* An organizational act is deviant only if it contradicts public definitions of appropriate police behavior. For instance, there exists general aggreement that police power should be used to further societal rather than departmental or individualistic goals. Police officers are not expected to use their power to benefit themselves financially by accepting money and free or discount services for ignoring or tolerating behavior (narcotics sales) they are sworn to take legal action against. These actions are contrary to the norms surrounding police organizations.

There also exists a general but frequently imprecise normative consensus regarding police use of force. Minimally, the expectation is that a police function is to apprehend, while courts establish guilt and prisons punish. Police actions which involve punishment rather than apprehension, "curbstone justice," contradict the norms characteristic of democratic society.

Second, for police misconduct to be organizational rather than individualistic in origin, *the deviant action must be supported by internal operating norms which conflict with the police organization's formal goals and rules.* For instance, formal departmental rules may forbid officers from accepting gratuities while informal norms encourage acceptance of free or discount meals. Formal rules also may restrict the circumstances in which weapons may be used, yet internal norms may function to encourage officers to use their weapons in situations considered inappropriate by departmental standards. Formal goals and rules in each of these instances conform with the norms which comprise police organizations. But police officers fail to act in accordance with them because of internal operating norms.

These two conditions, violation of external normative expectations and internal operating norms at variance with formal goals and rules, constitute the minimum conditions under which an act can be defined as organizationally deviant. Other conditions, however, help to further substantiate the organizational origins of police misconduct.

For one, because the deviance under discussion is a distinctly organizational phenomenon, new members of police departments may not be prepared to participate. Consequently, *compliance with the internal operating norms supportive of police misconduct must be ensured through recruitment and socialization.* Socialization of new members involves an introduction to norms supportive of impropriety, an opportunity to learn and practice the rationalizations or justifications supportive of these actions, and an evaluation and reward structure based on compliance with them.

A fourth and related condition for organizational deviance is that *there must be peer support of the misbehavior of colleagues.* This approval may be active when all officers at a particular level engage in a particular form of misconduct (for instance, when they routinely accept free or discount meals). Peer support also may be largely passive as when a "code of secrecy" required officers at a particular level to remain silent about the improper actions of colleagues.

Finally, for improper behavior to be organizationally deviant, *it must be supported by the dominant administrative coalition of the police organization.* In most police organizations, the dominant coalition includes the chief, inspectors, captains, and lieutenants. These persons are seen by outsiders as representing and being responsible for the entire department. Without the support of the dominant administrative coalition, improper police actions cannot be considered organizationally deviant.

As with peers, support by administrative personnel may be active or passive. Support is active when members of the dominant administrative coalition encourage, cover for, or ignore misconduct or when they engage in actions essentially similar to those of their subordinates. Administrative support of police misconduct is passive when administrators fail, for whatever reason, to take reasonable precautions to ensure compliance with external norms and the formal goals and rules of the department. Passive support exists whenever a reasonable person taking reasonable prudent precautions would and could, in the course of routine events, be expected to encounter evidence that would lead a similarly situated person to undertake investigative and corrective action. If misconduct is effectively hidden from police administrators exercising reasonable precautions, then the behavior constitutes deviance within but not by the organization.

Therefore, *police misconduct is organizational deviance when actions violate external expectations for what the department should do. Simultaneously, the actions must be in conformity with internal operating norms, and supported by socialization, peers, and the administrative personnel of the department.*

It is perhaps useful to provide a brief illustration of police wrongdoing as organizational deviance. Provision of illegal but widely demanded services such as gambling and narcotics are lucrative enterprises in contempory society. They also can be risky, since police organizations are charged with the arrest of persons who offer these services. The solution is to pay police to ignore these actions. But it is not sufficient to purchase arrest immunity from a single officer or even a small group of officers. Any unpaid officer can then disrupt these activities. Equally, new police officers may stumble upon such operations or members of the dominant administrative coalition may order that arrests be made. Meaningful arrest immunity only occurs when an entire department is deviant. Lawrence W. Sherman provides a useful description of the organizational nature of this type of misconduct:

> Police departments in which corruption is so systematic that criminals can purchase immunity from arrest are deviant organizations, as distinct from organizations in which deviance occurs. . . . Where such extensive cooperation among officers occurs . . .[we can] . . . label the police department itself, and not just its officers, as corrupt: a deviant organization.[13]

POLICE MISCONDUCT AS ORGANIZATIONAL DEVIANCE

All police officers are exposed to opportunities for misconduct. In even the sleepiest of suburban patrol districts, there exists opportunities to accept money for not issuing a traffic citation and to render "street justice" to verbally aggressive citizens. Given the rates of work-based deviance by persons in occupations ranging from factory work to medicine,[14] it should not surprise us that police officers also engage in occupational misconduct.

However, the frequency and patterning of police misconduct varies between departments. In some departments there are only a few officers who accept bribes and render street justice. They do these things alone and hide their actions from most colleagues and and superiors. In these departments police misconduct is infrequent and unpatterned, and is a form of individual or subcultural deviance.

In other departments large numbers of officers engage in misconduct. Patrol officers routinely accept bribes and involve themselves in other types of corrupt activities. Officers also routinely assault verbally aggressive citizens. They do these things together and do not attempt to shield their actions from most colleagues and superiors. In these departments police misbehavior is frequent and patterned, a form of organizational deviance. This is the type of misconduct of concern in this chapter.

Police Corruption

Police corruption exists when officers accept money, goods, or services for actions they are sworn to do anyway.[15] It also exists when police officers accept money, goods, or services for ignoring actions they are sworn to invoke legal procedures against.

Types of Police Corruption. Of the various typologies of police corruption that have been advanced, one developed by Thomas Barker and Julian Roebuck is most useful.[16] As compared to other typologies, Barker and Roebuck's is less unwieldy: it contains only eight categories.[17] The Barker and Roebuck model also contains an indicator of seriousness and it was developed in an organizationally sensitive manner. It emphasizes that most forms of corruption are supported by internal operating norms, socialization, peers, and administrative personnel. For these reasons the Barker and Roebuck paradigm will be used to lay the groundwork for our analysis of police misconduct as organizational deviance.

Barker and Roebuck identify eight types of police corruption.[18] These types, arranged on a continuum from least to most serious, are as follows:

1. Acceptance of free or discount meals and services
2. Acceptance of kickbacks for referrals for services
3. Opportunistic theft from helpless citizens or unsecured premises
4. Shakedowns
5. Protection of illegal activities
6. Acceptance of money to fix cases
7. Planned theft

The eighth type of corruption, "assignment and promotion based upon internal payoffs," is not part of their seriousness continuum. It does, however, represent an extreme form of corruption, one that involves only police. We now will consider examples of each form of corruption.

Meals and Services.[19] Free or discount meals are avilable to police in most cities. Certain nationwide restaurant chains have a policy of giving police free meals. Other nationwide restaurant chains offer police meals at half price. Owners of many local restaurants also offer police free or discount meals. Police in most cities find it difficult to pay for meals in these restaurants. They literally are told either that they cannot pay at all or that they cannot pay full price for a meal.

Owners and operators at a variety of other commerical establishments also offer "police discounts." Next to restaurants, dry cleaning shops are probably the type of establishment which most routinely offers police discounts. Many other businesses desire police patronage and make special efforts to attract it. Officers readily exchange information on these establishments prior to roll call and over coffee.

It is likely that many of the people who provide police meals and services do so out of respect and gratitude. It is equally likely that many are simply buying the "deterrent presence"[20] of uniformed officers. They believe that a robbery is unlikely when a marked squad car is parked outside and an officer in uniform inside. They also believe that well-fed and dressed police are more likely to respond quickly to their calls for assistance and to make themselves available during higher risk times such as closing.

These strategies are generally effective. It is highly doubtful that a person would decide to rob a restaurant or store when a police officer is present. Police officers also acknowledge their obligations. They attempt to respond more quickly to calls and make themselves available at closing.

Kickbacks.   Acceptance of money in exchange for referrals also is available for patrol officers in most large cities. Towing companies, for instance, stand to benefit from police referrals and some are willing to pay police officers for doing so. Former New York City police officer Edward F. Droge, Jr., reports that officers received two types of kickbacks from towing companies.[21] The first was for ignoring illegal attempts to solicit repair work at the scene of an accident. The second and more lucrative kickback was received when patrol officers reported accidents directly to towing companies. According to Droge, this was worth between $20 and $30.

Other opportunities for kickbacks exist, including those from undertakers. Chicago newspaper journalist Mike Royko describes this type of kickback:

> On Skid Row, somebody had died—an old pensioner in a flophouse. The paddy wagon men hauled him into their van and drove as fast as they could to a funeral home about two miles away. They went past a couple of funeral homes along the way. The one they were going to paid the best prices for stray bodies.[22]

Opportunistic Theft.   James Spradley asked men in the Seattle city jail who had been arrested for public drunkenness: "Have you ever personally witnessed the Seattle police rolling, clipping, or stealing from a drunk or someone picked up for drunk?"[23] Of those interviewed, exactly one-third said they had witnessed this type of opportunistic theft. In one situation, an offender reported that a friend had cashed a check and the two had gone drinking. As they were leaving a bar, two police officers stopped and searched the pair, relieving the one of his money. When he objected, he was told to forget the incident or go to jail. He withdrew his objection and the suddenly more affluent police went on their way.

The possibility of opportunistic or unplanned theft from unsecured premises also is frequent for patrol officers. The actions of several officers provide an example of this type of activity.

It had been a relatively quiet middle watch and the officers had every reason to believe that it would continue to be quiet. It was a weekday and they were working a comfortable working-class area. At about 7:00 P.M. they received a call to "check some unclaimed property" at the rear of a beer warehouse. The night before the warehouse had been broken into and some beer had been taken. The call seemed to suggest that perhaps some beer had been left behind. At least, the officers hoped that was the case.

The officers in one other squad apparently thought the same thing and the two squads arrived almost simultaneously. A brief search of the tall weeds in the rear of the warehouse yielded a "treasure": 13 cases of malt liquor apparently left behind the night before. Without hesitation one officer said, "Let's split it." The beer was carried to the squad cars and exactly six and one-half cases of malt liquor were placed in the truck of each squad. The next step was to transfer the cases to their personal cars and they began to drive to the precinct station.

As the cars drove off, one of the officers noticed that an officer in the other squad had left his keys in the lock of the trunk of the car. Failing to recognize the consequences of his upcoming action, he picked up his microphone and said, "_____, your keys are still in the trunk." Once off the air, the officer then said, "Oh, shit," realizing what he had done. The dispatcher, quick to confirm his worst fears, came on the air and said, "I take it there will be a property report on that call?" The officer was quick to recover and respond by saying, "Yep, could I have the number for it?" The officer received the number and both squads proceeded to the precinct station. Now, however, the malt liquor would be placed in the property room, where it would be claimed by a representative of the warehouse.

Upon arriving at the station, several of their colleagues and a lieutenant greeted them. One said, "On the air he says 'your keys.'" Another observed, "It was a dumb piece of police work." The officers essentially agreed; after all, they *had* blown an opportunity for some free malt liquor.

The problem was that the officer who told the other squad that the keys were still in the trunk also told anybody else who was listening, including superiors, that *something* (most probably beer, given the location and the burglary of the night before) had been placed in the trunk. The dispatcher immediately recognized the problem and gave the officers a way out by assuming that a report would be forthcoming. And the officers who greeted the squad at the precinct were absolutely correct: it had been dumb to put something like that out over the air. Of such mistakes are opportunistic thefts blown.[24]

Shakedowns. Police officers shake down citizens by accepting money from them for withdrawing an arbitrary threat to enforce the law.

Chicago police routinely shake down tavern owners by threatening to enforce obscure liquor laws. Herbert Beigel and Alan Beigel provide a description of the "club's" operation and how it affected one tavern owner:

> She had been approached . . . by . . . [police] . . . and told that a club was being formed to service the . . . taverns. If she wanted to . . . avoid problems that could cause the loss of her liquor license, she would be wise to pay a reasonable sum of money once a week—$25. Each week an officer stopped by . . . to collect the payment. [25]

At this point in the Barker–Roebuck typology, it is necessary to note that it is possible for individual police officers to engage in each of these first four types of corruption in the absence of organizational support. Most patrol officers work alone or with a trusted partner. Most routine policing remains outside the scrutiny of immediate superiors, and especially, administrative elites. Many citizens who "suffer" from corrupt practices either encourage these actions (for example, restaurant and tow company owners) or are in a poor position to effectively object to them (such as public drunkenness offenders). And the "code of secrecy" which surrounds police and policing protects individually corrupt officers. The result is that it is possible for individual police officers who are so inclined to become individual entrepreneurs by soliciting kickbacks and engaging in opportunistic thefts and shakedowns on their own.

Entrepreneurial corruption is possible but it is not easy. Partners periodically change because of illness, different days off, and vacations. Sergeants occasionally observe patrol officers as they work and they may acquire evidence of corrupt activities. Citizens sometimes complain to administrators about the amount of money and services they are providing police. The individually corrupt officer must therefore be constantly alert lest new partners, inquisitive sergeants, or knowledgeable administrators acquire discrediting information. It is difficult to keep one's eyes and ears open, but it is possible.

Kickbacks, opportunistic theft, and shakedowns are both possible and easy when an officer is a member of a deviant department. Nearly all partners can be trusted; the least that can be expected is silence. Sergeants and administrators also can be trusted, either because they share their subordinates' improper income or they are busy creating and maintaining their own. The other types of corruption identified by Barker and Roebuck are also both possible and easy in a deviant department.

Protection of Illegal Activities.   Effective protection of illegal activities, such as gambling and narcotics, requires that officers in divisions other than patrol be involved. This is because the other divisions are largely responsible for policing these activities.[26] Vice and narcotics officers ostensibly function to control, if not eliminate, organized gambling and narcotics operations. Moreover, citizens frequently complain of illegal activities located in their neighborhoods.[27] Consequently, administrative superiors in police organizations inevitably know about these activities. Because of this division of labor and input from citizens, individual patrol officers can offer little more than the promise that *they* will not intervene. That is not a very effective system of protection.

But when officers in special function divisions such as vice and narcotics and administrative superiors agree to protect illegal activities along with patrol officers, then effective protection can be guaranteed. The price, however, is generally steep. In New York, for instance, the Knapp Commission found that plainclothes officers in five divisions "collected regular biweekly or monthly payments amounting to as much as $3,500 from each of the gambling establishments in the area under their jurisdiction, and divided the take in equal shares."[28] In the area of narcotics "enforcement," payments were said to be less systematic but more lucrative: a single payment totalled $80,000.[29]

William J. Chambliss has presented an essentially similar portrait of police in Seattle.[30] The owner of a restaurant (legal) and card room (illegal but protected) told Chambliss of the price of his "pay to stay" protection. Each month, a patrol officer collected $250 for distribution to appropriate officers. Administrators had their own "bag man," and he too appeared monthly. Chambliss also reports that Seattle police were paid to protect prostitution, drug distribution, pornography, and usury operations.

Case Fixing.   Traffic ticket fixing is likely the most common form of case fixing and often it does not even involve a monetary payment. According to John Gardiner, tickets are fixed in Massachusetts in one of several ways.[31] The cited motorist's "best bet" is to know someone who is a member of the police department which issued the ticket. Failing that, calls to "any" chief of police, police officer, or politician are said to be effective. Friends of these people are a last but sometimes effective resort.

Ticket fixing also is the least offensive type of case fixing. It pales by comparison with case fixing of organized crime. Nicholas Gage described case fixing in the state of New York:

Paul Vahio, who is listed by the Justice Department as a captain in the Mafia family of the late Thomas Luchese, pleaded guilty before Supreme Court Justice Domenic S. Rinaldi to commerical bribery of a police officer. Vahio, whose criminal record dates back to 1925 ... could have been given up to a year in jail. Instead, Judge Rinaldi fined him $250.00. ... Vahio is not the only Mafioso who has fared better than ordinary defendants in New York State courts. ... [The] rate of dismissals and acquittals for racketeers was five times that of other defendants.[32]

Although it is likely that case fixing by police and other members of the criminal justice system has declined since the era of Prohibition,[33] it remains a fixture in certain police jusrisdictions.

Planned Theft.   Direct involvement by police in criminal activities is not as uncommon as one might imagine. What follows is only a partial list of cities since 1960 in which police burglary rings and other forms of direct criminal activity by police have been reported: Denver, Colorado; Chicago, Illinois; Nassau County, New York; Des Moines, Iowa; Nashville, Tennessee; Birmingham, Alabama; Cleveland, Ohio; Bristol, Connecticut; Burlington, Vermont; Miami, Florida;[34] "Mid-City";[35] New York City; Philadelphia, Pennsylvania; Buffalo, New York; New Orleans, Louisiana;[36] and Newburgh, New York.[37]

The extent of organizational support for police burglary rings and other forms of direct criminal activity by police is unclear.[38] It seems accurate to suggest that passive support is present in most situations. However, if knowledge of these activities becomes public, even deviant departments generally respond in a forceful manner. As Barker and Roebuck note, "departments that tolerate other forms of corruption will usually prosecute and send to prison officers discovered engaging in forms of direct criminal activities."[39]

Assignment and Promotion Based upon Payoffs.   In this circumstance, police activities and rewards are bought and sold by police officers; there are no outside corruptors. Barker and Roebuck describe this type of corruption:

> Officers who administer the distribution of assignments and personnel ...
> collect fees for assigning officers to certain divisions, precincts, units, details,
> shifts, and beats and for insuring that certain personnel are retained in,
> transferred from or excluded from certain work assignments ... officers in
> certain assignments have little opportunity to engage in other types of cor-
> rupt activities. Internal pay-offs provide these officers with an illegitimate
> opportunity structure.[40]

Barker and Roebuck thus identify eight types of corruption. Their typology contains an indicator of seriousness and also allows for entrepreneurial corruption. They emphasize, however, that most of the types of misbehavior identified involve the active or passive support of patrol officers, special function police, and administrative superiors. They therefore encourage analysis of police corruption as organizational deviance.

Factors Related to the Incidence and Seriousness of Police Corruption

Few police organizations display all or even most of the types of corruption identified by Barker and Roebuck. Observation of patrol officers in a large midwestern city several years ago revealed that they routinely and unhesitatingly took advantage of the numerous opportunities for free or discount meals and services. They also "liberated" the meager resources and unopened hard liquor of chronic drunkenness offenders. Least frequently, they took advantage of burglary and break-in calls by helping themselves to a variety of items. The other types of corruption identified by Barker and Roebuck were not evident.

An early journalist, however, described this city as "wide-open." The city administration and the police department were said to have been "sold" to racketeers. It was only after a reform mayor was elected that the rackets were closed down. Since that time, corruption apparently has remained at the level described.

Other police departments evidence signs of more serious and persistent corruption. The New York City Police Department (NYCPD) is an example. At remarkably regular 20-year intervals, starting in 1894 and ending in 1971 with the Knapp Commission, NYCPD officers have been found to be extensively involved in corrupt activities.[41] This situation has been serious and persistent.

Still other departments present strong evidence that it is possible to eliminate chronic corruption. In the early 1950s, Oakland's police were as thoroughly corrupt as those in New York.[42] Their actions ranged from acceptance of free meals to planned theft. By 1960, however, corruption had been completely eliminated and the department has remained free of corruption.[43]

This contrast shows the variation in the amount of wrongdoing in police departments. The questions that emerge are several:

1. What factors determine whether or not a department is corrupt (for example, Oakland versus New York)?
2. If corrupt, what factors determine the seriousness of corruption (for instance, the midwest city versus New York)?
3. What factors relate to persistence in patterns of corruption (Oakland versus New York)?

Review of the available literature suggests that *partial* answers to each of these three questions arise when one examines the environment external to police organizations and the internal responses to that environment.

External Factors. Sociologist Lawrence W. Sherman has studied police corruption in Europe and the United States, and is author of two books on the topic.[44] Sherman suggests that three factors external to police organizations help determine the presence and seriousness of police corruption. He develops his suggestion by advancing three propositions:

1. There will be less police corruption in a community with little anomie.. . .
2. There will be less police corruption in communities with a more public-regarding ethos (among elected officials).
3. There will be less corruption in a community with less culture conflict.[45]

Let us briefly examine the content and implications of each of these propositions.

Community Anomie.   The role of anomie in the generation of social deviance has been considered by a number of social scientists, including Émile Durkheim and Robert K. Merton. Their ideas will be used to lay the groundwork for an analysis of Sherman's description of the role of anomie in the generation of police corrruption.

Durkheim coined and applied the notion of anomie in the context of his study of suicide rates.[46] Durkheim observed that a number of factors were related to increases in rates of suicide. They included economic catastrophes as well as sudden economic gains, declines in the control afforded persons by traditional religions, and increases in the proportion of persons working in industry or in professions such as teaching. Durkheim then sought to determine what was common or central to each of the factors causing increases in suicide rates. The answer Durkheim advanced was that each represented a condition or situation in which the social controls which surround the members of a society have been weakened. He termed this condition anomie or normlessness and argued that anomic suicide "results from man's activity's lacking regulation and his consequent sufferings."[47]

Robert K. Merton's essential contribution was to broaden the meaning of anomie and to extend it to forms of deviance other than suicide.[48] Merton defines anomie as a gap between important goals and legitimate means of reaching those goals. Merton then argues that rates of criminality and deviance are higher among groups of persons denied easy access to legitimate means of reaching cultural goals; the gap leads some individuals to use illegitimate or criminal means of achieving societal or situationally important goals.

What Lawrence W. Sherman is suggesting is that rates of police corruption may be higher in communities where large numbers of people are denied easy access to legitimate means of attaining goals. As Merton predicts, groups of persons in communities such as this frequently turn to innovative means. Gambling, prostitution, and narcotics services represent three of these means.

Outlook of Elected Officials.   Sherman notes that the level of anomie characteristic of a community affects the outlook or perspective of elected officials. Community anomie frequently produces a sense of normlessness among officials. Instead of attempting to serve in the best interests of the public-at-large, there exists a privatization or segmentation of commitment among local leaders. They are responsive to elite community members and to the persons who provide illegal but widely demanded services such as gambling and prostitution. Frequently elected officials are responsive to this latter group of persons because they are paid to ignore their actions. Richard J. Daley's Chicago was such a community:

> The city's dramatic physical redevelopment has been a boon to the political world as well as the private investors. There are so many deals involving ranking members of the Machine that it has been suggested that the city slogan be changed from *Urbs In Horto*, which means,"City in a Garden," to *Ubi Est Mea*, which means "Where's mine?"[49]

Sherman is suggesting that in Chicago, Philadelphia, Seattle, and other cities characterized by a privatization of perspective among governmental officials, police corruption may be present. This is because elected leaders are concerned with protecting and promoting special interests. As long as the activities of others, including those that are illegitimate, do not interfere with the interests of another group, they are tolerated or ignored. Police corruption may flourish in such a situation because the opportunities for it are present and because police are seen as simply another privatized or segmented interest group.

Culture Conflict.   Sherman is here sensitizing us to the differences in the *sentiments* attached to certain laws. The state has traditionally attempted to use the law to define and control the "morality" of its citizenry. Biblical injunctions against sodomy, for instance, guided English and Puritan laws which attempted to regulate the sexual activities and preferences of consenting adults.[50] Currently, most communities try to control the sale of intoxicating beverages,[51] and many still seek to restrain the sexual activities of consenting adults.[52] Laws governing gambling, prostitution, and drug use constitute additional examples of contemporary efforts to define and regulate morality.

The problem is that laws intended to govern morality are almost always met with mixed reaction. Many citizens, and especially those personally affected by these laws, resent and resist state attempts to control their actions. Other citizens believe that the state should not be in the business of attempting to regulate morality. Still others see these laws as creating opportunities to provide for the many citizens who desire these services. Since provision of most of these illegal services requires police tolerance, culture conflict creates additional opportunities for police corruption.

As a consequence of Sherman's three propositions, we are now in a position to identify the circumstances in which police misdeeds may be

present. In communities characterized by anomie, privatization or segmentation of interest, and culture conflict over the propriety of certain
laws, numerous opportunities for police corruption exist.

However, most of our large cities fit the above description. The urban
poor, black, and young routinely experience problems in gaining easy
access to legitimate means of reaching their goals. Many of our cities are
governed by less than public-minded officials. And many citizens dis-
agree over whether the state has the right to direct their morality. Obviously something more is needed to explain organized police corruption.

Internal Factors.   In cities characterized by anomie, segmentation of interest, and culture conflict, police departments generally display either a
legalistic or watch style of policing.[53] It is a department's type of policing
which is the prime determinant of its response to external opportunities
for corruption.

Legalistic Departments.   Officers in legalistic departments generally fail to
respond in an organized fashion to opportunities for corruption. Legalistic
departments typically do not contain internal operating norms supportive
of corruption. Police socialization emphasizes adherence to the law for
both police and citizens. And administrators are intolerant of improper
actions of either citizens or police. The corruption which does exist is of
the entrepreneurial or "rotten pocket" variety.[54]

It is important to recognize, however, that legalistic policing does not
mean that external opportunities for corruption have been eliminated or
even lessened.[55] In communities rich in opportunities for corruption,
legalistic policing frequently emerges in the wake of scandal and it represents an attempt at reform. But reform policing of a legalistic nature
cannot and does not change community patterns of anomie. Large numbers of citizens continue to be denied access to legitimate means of achieving goals. Reform policing of a legalistic nature also cannot and does not
bring consensus to community sentiments about laws intended to define
and regulate public morality. Large numbers of people still wish to engage
in these actions and others remain willing to serve those so inclined. The
successful and largely legalistic reforms of policing in Oakland, California, Newburgh, New York, and New York City can hardly be said to be
the result of lessened anomie or culture conflict.[56]

Extensive opportunities for corruption are thus available to police in
large cities. Officers in legalistic departments, however, do not respond to
these opportunities in an organized manner. Their failure to respond
reflects membership in a nondeviant department.

Watch Departments.   The internal characteristics of watch-style departments encourage organized responses to external chances for misbehav-

ior. Internal operating norms are supportive of involvement in corruption and they provide justifications for such action. Police socialization involves introduction to and evaluation in terms of the norms supportive of corruption. And watch department administrators are involved in their own dishonest activities, supportive of the corrupt activities of subordi-. nates, or both. We will now briefly examine the ways in which these internal factors facilitate the organized corruption characteristic of watch-style departments.

In these departments, the internal operating norms of the department provide patrol officers and others with rationalizations and justifications for corrupt actions. Officers learn that it is acceptable to utilize free or discount services or to accept kickbacks because of their deterrent presence, more frequent proactive observation, quick responses to calls for police presence, and more frequent referrals. From this perspective, store owners and others are simply paying for a level of service over and above that received by other citizens.[57]

Police officers who opportunistically steal from citizens or shake them down do so because of additional rationalizations. Officers who illegally confiscate the property of chronic drunkenness offenders *explain* that the items were almost certainly obtained illegally. Officers who release beer-drinking juveniles, but not their beer (it is saved for consumption after work in a backroom of the precinct station), note that they are giving the released juveniles a break.[58]

The most serious forms of corruption characteristic of watch departments require other rationalizations. In the context of protecting or fixing arrests for illegal gambling operations and liquor law violations, the distinction between these "clean" sources of corrupt income (as compared to the "dirty" money associated with narcotics and gun sales) appears to have been an important justification for this type of activity. Writing in 1965, Jerome Skolnick noted that police in the watch department he studied ("Eastville") took protection money from bookmakers and numbers operators. They did not take money from those who sold narcotics because they "felt that narcotics use posed a serious danger to the community and restrictions upon its use were not nearly severe enough."[59]

However, the traditional distinction between clean and dirty money in watch departments appears to be changing. In the words of the Knapp Commission Report of Police Corruption in New York:

> more relaxed attitudes toward drugs, particularly among young people, and the enormous profits to be derived from drug traffic have combined to make narcotics-related payoffs more acceptable to more and more police....[60]

In watch departments narcotics money is increasingly being rationalized as clean.

The most serious form of corruption—planned theft—as well as internal payoffs appear to be less a function of specific norms supportive of these activities. Instead, related but more general factors are of paramount importance.

The emergence of planned theft and internal payoffs appears to require the existence of most, if not all, of the other forms of corruption we have examined. Planned theft is an extreme action, engaged in by what some have called the "evil fringe" of a thoroughly corrupt department. It is a risky undertaking since its discovery by outsiders almost always creates scandal and forces even a watch department to undertake disciplinary action. Internal payoffs work to the detriment of patrol officers and other subordinate members of a department. They advantage only those few officers in positions to allocate assignments or shifts. It is unlikely that patrol norms or the more general police subculture support either planned theft or internal payoffs. How, then, does the existence of most or all of the other types of corruption give rise to these most serious types?

Two tentative answers suggest themselves. For those officers who engage in planned theft, the existence of other types of misbehavior acts as a kind of insurance for their own activities. Officers involved in other forms of corruption are unlikely to take action against colleagues involved in planned theft for fear of a retaliatory exposure of their own actions. They also may decide not to take action for fear that the resulting investigation by outsiders might not stop at planned theft but instead be expanded to include additional types of corruption.

This is precisely what happened in three cities: Chicago,[61] Newburgh, New York,[62] and New York City.[63] In Chicago and Newburgh, the discovery of police burglary rings resulted in major scandals which ultimately exposed the other forms of corruption also characteristic of these two departments. In New York City, the Knapp Commission investigation had already begun but many remained uncertain of the seriousness of police corruption. In the course of their investigation, Knapp Commission agents inadvertently stumbled upon a police burglary. Agents watched as police broke into a meat warehouse and began carting parts of cows to their cars. The onlookers anonymously called the local precinct station several times to report that the burglary was literally in progress as they observed. No squads were sent to investigate. This incident understandably received extensive publicity. It prompted reform administrator Patrick V. Murphy to take even sterner actions. It also helped convince a sometimes skeptical citizenry of the need to thoroughly investigate the extent of police corruption.

The development of internal payoffs, which benefit only a few officers, also would appear to require the existence of the other types of corruption. When these other types exist, a *department* anomie or sense of normlessness emerges, one which mirrors the anomie of the community "served" by the department. In such a department, distinctions between proper and improper behavior, police officers and criminals, and fair and unfair advantages become blurred and, with time, meaningless. With few norms other than "where's mine?" to guide individual actions, officers in a position to control assignments feel entirely justified in "getting theirs" through internal payoffs. The officers who make these payments also find themselves in an anomic or normless situation, with compliance as the only alternative.

The first point, then, is that officers in watch-style departments take advantage of the extensive opportunities for corruption available to them because of rationalizations and justifications embedded within the police subculture(s) of their departments. Across time there emerges norms protective of *all* types of police corruption.

Also fundamental to the maintenance of patterns of corruption in watch-style departments is the effective socialization of new members. Without complete socialization, corruption is necessarily and precariously confined to particular cohorts of officers. Additionally, unless new members are thoroughly socialized, police corruption ultimately slips to the level of subcultural deviance within an organizational context.

However, all police organizations are effective socializers of new members. This is especially true of corrupt watch-style departments, for three reasons. First, such departments tend to recruit locally. The people who join corrupt watch-style departments are generally well aware of the patterns of corruption characteristic of the department. For example, newspaper journalist Robert H. Williams was born and raised in East St. Louis, Illinois, a city with a thoroughly corrupt watch-style department during Williams' childhood. Growing up in East St. Louis, Williams took police corruption for granted as did many other residents, including those who later became East St. Louis police officers. Williams recalls: "I never really knew until I left there that all cops didn't get paid off by gangsters and ordinary businessmen, or even that they weren't *supposed* to."[64]

A second reason that corrupt watch-style departments are especially effective socializers of new members is that selection procedures tend to be stacked in favor of the maintenance of corruption. Because line officers, administrators, and the segments of the community which benefit from police corruption all stand to lose a great deal should a "do-gooder" somehow manage to slip through, new recruits are selected by reference to the signs they give of their willingness to participate in or at least be silent about corruption.[65]

Lastly although many police adminstrators would prefer to think of policing as a science, it remains a folk art taught and learned on the streets. In all police academies recruits are sent (reluctantly in academies where instructors seek to give at least an initial appearance of integrity) to observe and work with experienced officers. After completion of recruit training, the new police officer generally spends a probationary period under the guidance of a field training officer.

The result is that new officers in corrupt watch-style departments are quickly exposed to the routine corruption characteristic of their department. It is likely that while still at the academy recruits consume the first of many free or discount meals. In addition, they are exposed to the rationalizations and justifications for the corruption characteristic of their department. Finally, they are judged by field and other supervisors by reference to departmental norms, including those supportive of corruption. Although new officers may elect not to engage in these activities, they must at least evidence a willingness to abide by subculture norms emphasizing secrecy.

However, even in corrupt watch-style departments a minority of officers elect to stay straight. Occasionally, this commitment to ethical action leads them to violate the "no rat" rule and alert superiors or outsiders to the existence of police corruption. In Birmingham, Alabama, four young police officers went public about a police burglary ring in their precinct. The officers involved in the ring were ultimately fired, but the consequences for the officers who violated norms emphasizing secrecy were almost as severe:

> Even four months later, the four officers say, half of the [police] in the ... precinct will not speak to them. They work together, in adjacent beats, because they said other officers would not back them up on dangerous calls. . . .[66]

A final element fundamental to an organizational understanding of the origins of police corruption is administrative involvement. This involvement may be active, as when superiors engage in actions essentially similar to those of their subordinates. In Philadelphia, New York, and Chicago, police administrators were found to be actively involved in the widespread corruption characteristic of these departments. The Pennsylvania Crime Commission, for instance, concluded that "patterns of corruption exist within the Philadelphia Police Department ... [that] ... are not random or isolated but systematic and ... citywide ... [and] these patterns are not restricted to low ranking officers."[67] In Chicago, money is "filtered ... from the lowest ranks of the department to the highest levels of command."[68]

Alternatively, involvement of members of the dominant administrative coalition may be passive, as when superiors elect to ignore or tolerate the corrupt activities of their subordinates. James C. Parsons, a reform chief in Birmingham, Alabama, reports "attending a conference with several nationally noted police chiefs and during a dinner discussion the conversation turned to police corruption. . . . [T]he chiefs were reluctant even to discuss the issue."[69] James F. Ahern notes one reason for this:

> Most police chiefs . . . having come up through the ranks of their own departments, alleviate their insecurity—as much as possible—years before they become chiefs. They protect their own, they play politics, and they survive. If they serve in cities where crime machines hold the real power and lubricate police departments with illicit funds, the chiefs function in ways that perpetuate machine power and cut off police from broad democratic controls.[70]

In summary: we have reviewed the various types of police corruption and identified and discussed the external and internal factors productive of this type of police misconduct. The essential conclusion to be drawn is that the opportunities for corruption available in jurisdictions characterized by community anomie, segmentation of interest, and culture conflict are taken advantage of when watch-style departments police these areas. More precisely, opportunities for corruption are seized by watch-style departments because of the presence of rationalizations supportive of corruption; selection, socialization, and evaluation procedures which emphasize involvment in unethical actions; and active or passive support by members of the dominant administrative coalition. In such departments, police corruption is an organizational rather than purely individualistic phenomenon.

Unnecessary Police Force

Two patrol officers had received a call to "check a drunk disturbing." They took their time going to the scene of the reported incident, but an inebriated citizen was still present when they arrived. They got out of their car and told the citizen, "We've heard you've been bothering people." The citizen mumbled that he wanted to be left alone. One officer asked where his bottle was and the citizen refused to answer. Nightstick in hand, the officer spun the citizen around and saw a bottle sticking out of his back pants pocket. The citizen turned to object, and the officer used his night stick to break the bottle in the citizen's pocket. The citizen again turned to object and the officer promptly pushed him down. The citizen landed on the broken bottle and a scream was followed by a small pool of wine and blood. Some of the broken glass in his pocket was now embedded in a buttock. The other officer used the squad's radio to request an ambulance and then said to his colleague, "He's so drunk he won't even remember what happened." The intoxicated and now bloodied citizen was placed in the ambulance when it arrived. He was not seriously hurt, although it did take a physician some time to remove all the glass.

This episode is representative of those situations in which police use force unnecessarily. Force is uncalled for when there is no physical provocation by a citizen or when there are alternatives other than assault available to subdue a citizen. Our analysis of these situations will be directed at the discovery of the circumstances and the frequency of unnecessary police force. We will then develop an organizationally sensitive explanation of needless police force.

Circumstances. In 1949, sociologist William A. Westley asked Gary, Indiana, patrol officers: "When do you think a policeman is justified in roughing a man up?"[71] Their responses to Westley's question are summarized in Table 6–1. As can be seen, the officers described a variety of circumstances in which they would feel justified in assaulting *defiant* or *deviant* citizens.

Some seventeen years, later Albert J. Reiss, Jr., placed observers with police officers in Chicago, Washington, D.C., and Boston.[72] Reiss' observers were attentive to instances of unnecessary force and to the circumstances surrounding these actions. Once again, defiance or deviance precipitated many of the assaults. Specifically, nearly half of the assaults occurred when citizens openly defied police authority, while another third occurred during encounters involving drunken or homosexual citizens or those who used narcotics.[73]

More recent information on the circumstances surrounding excessive police force suggests the continued importance of defiance and deviance as factors precipitating superfluous assaults. In the early 1970s Jonathan Rubinstein observed Philadelphia patrol officers. Rubinstein describes an episode of unessential police force, one directed at a deviant citizen. A woman complained to a sergeant at a station house that a man had molested her four-year-old daughter. The sergeant knew who the man was,

TABLE 6–1. Responses of Gary, Indiana, Police Officers to the Question: "When do you think a policeman is justified in roughing a man up?"*

Basis	Percent as Primary Response
1. Disrespect for police	27
2. When impossible to avoid	17
3. To obtain information	14
4. To make an arrest	6
5. For the hardened criminal	5
6. When you know man is guilty	2
7. For sex criminals	2
Totals	100
	(74)

*Source: William A. Westley, *Violence and the Police.* Cambridge, Mass.: The MIT Press, 1970, p. 122. *These data were collected in 1949.* Adapted and reprinted by permission of author and publisher.

and after talking with the lieutenant it was decided to assign a police wagon to find the man. Several hours later the man was found and brought back to the station house. Here is what happened to him:

> Any squad member who wished was allowed to beat the suspect from the ankles to the armpits with his stick. Men came in off the street to participate in the beating and then returned to patrol. Before he was taken downtown, the suspect had been severely battered, although he had no broken bones. At no time did he utter a complaint, ask for mercy, or curse the police. Without a murmur he absorbed a brutal beating, which caused him to foul himself and drew the admiring comments of several men who admitted he could "really take it."[74]

In 1976, George Kirkham's description of his patrol experiences in Jacksonville, Florida, was published.[75] In his book, *Signal Zero,* Kirkham describes an episode of unneeded police force, directed at a defiant citizen. Kirkham and his partner were called to a stabbing at a bar. They arrested the man allegedly responsible. He was handcuffed, read his rights, and placed in the back seat of the squad car for the trip downtown. From the moment of his arrest, the white alleged violator used racist slurs to verbally abuse Kirkham's black partner. This attack increased as they drove downtown. Kirkham's partner endured it for a considerable period of time, but then instructed Kirkham to pull into a darkened alley. He handed Kirkham his service revolver, uncuffed the alleged violator, and pulled him out of the backseat of the squad. Here is what happened:

> [T]he man protested as the . . . policeman slammed a heavy fist into his face. He fell back against the side of the cruiser with a grunt. Bright red spots splashed against the white door panel. . . . The man started to get up just as another blow drove into his stomach. I heard the rush of air as he doubled up and dropped to his knees. A third blow sent him sprawling noisily into a row of garbage cans. . . . He struck the prisoner again and the man fell sobbing on the ground, crying out in pain as Franklin kicked him once in the side.[76]

The assault attracted the attention of other citizens and the man was quickly placed into the squad car and taken to jail. The jailer refused to accept the alleged violator until he had been seen by an emergency room physician. Kirkham and his partner explained to the jailer, a physician, and later to Internal Affairs Division investigators that the citizen had resisted arrest. The explanation was ultimately accepted.

As this is being written police officers in Houston, Texas[77] and Richland County, Ohio,[78] are under investigation for repeated episodes of unnecessary police violence. In both cases, the circumstances surrounding these episodes include defiance of police authority or deviance on the part of the assaulted citizen. In Richland County, located some one hundred miles southwest of Cleveland, newspaper journalists uncovered a reign of needless violence by county police. In one episode, a young passenger in a car was chased and eventually caught by county police, and was brought to the county jail. During the chase, another man in the car had wounded a police officer. Once at the jail, the young man was assaulted. Here is part of what happened to him:

> "The next thing I knew ... [a police officer] started kicking and hitting me in the head.... I felt my jaw break on one of the first blows." Added one [police] witness: "On about the second kick, I heard the jaw break through the soundproof glass of the dispatch room. When I looked up, blood was splattered on the glass 10 feet away."[79]

Across the 30 years starting with Westley's 1949 research, two factors stand out as descriptive of the circumstances surrounding episodes of excessive police attacks: defiance or deviance on the part of the assaulted citizen.

Frequency.   Most defiant or deviant citizens are *not* assaulted by police. Beyond this vaguely revealing statement, it is difficult to state with any precision what proportion of these types of people experience unnecessary police brutality. Police administrators are reluctant to talk to outsiders about several things, one of which is the frequency of superfluous police force. Data descriptive of the frequency of needless assaults are hard to acquire and they almost always are flawed in some respect. The frequency data we shall rely upon are the best available, but they are old.

In the summer of 1966, Albert J. Reiss, Jr., placed observers with patrol officers in Chicago, Washington, D.C., and Boston. Using a conservative definition of "police brutality,"[80] Reiss' observers reported that *3 percent of the alleged violators involved in encounters with police were victims of uncalled for police violence.* Projecting this figure to the total number of encounters containing violators in a city with a population of half a million, the Reiss data suggest that there are somewhere between 2000 and 4000 instances of unessential police force each year.[81] The proportion of encounters involving unneeded assaults is thus quite low. In absolute terms, however, the total volume is quite large.

But the Reiss data are old and they have not been replicated. We can therefore add only a little to our vaguely revealing opening observation. It is true that most defiant or deviant citizens are not assaulted by police. To this we now can add: it is also true that in absolute terms it appears that many cities contain relatively large numbers of citizens who have experienced needless police force.

Explanations. In the past and to some extent currently, unnecessary police brutality was thought to be caused by a few sadistic police officers —so-called "bad apples."[82] However, the importance of defiance and deviance in precipitating such force and the relatively large number of victims each year suggest that it might be useful to provide an alternative image. Specifically, it would appear useful to attempt to construct an organizationally sensitive explanation of unnecessary police violence.

It can be noted that nearly all of what was said with respect to the origins of police corruption can be applied in the development of an organizationally sensitive explanation of unnecessary assaults. For example, norms emphasizing secrecy and solidarity, a community split along racial and class lines, a watch-style department, and a policy of promotion from within all contribute to needless violence. However, instead of reviewing these issues, it appears more useful to consider three additional factors: 1) police perceptions that citizen acceptance of police authority is fundamental to effective policing; 2) police judgments of the "social value" of certain citizens; and 3) the conservative nature of police decision making.

Police Authority.   It must be recognized that effective policing is dependent upon citizen acceptance of police authority. In order to accomplish the many legitimate tasks a patrol officer is assigned, citizens must accept the commands given them. If rush-hour traffic is to move at all, motorists must accept the directions of the officer assigned that task. If a police officer is to clear a street corner of rowdy juveniles without resorting to arrest, the juveniles involved must comply with the order to disperse. If the ride to jail for an arrested citizen is to be other than a continuous wrestling match, the officer must convince the citizen of police authority to make that arrest. In these and many other situations, citizen acceptance of police authority is fundamental to effective and legitimate policing.

However, not all citizens are willing or able to extend acceptance of police authority. Young, minority, and poor citizens sometimes view police as oppressors rather than servants.[83] They also may view encounters with police as opportunities to validate or acquire valued attributes of self such as masculinity or toughness.[84] The result is that on occasion these citizens challenge police authority.

Other citizens find themselves in proactive encounters with police patrol officers. As the Wiley and Hudik research suggests,[85] if officers approach citizens for information about crimes they consider unimportant or if they fail to explain the reason for their proactivity, then the probability of citizen failure to extend acceptance of police authority is increased.

Still other citizens are situationally unable to extend prompt acceptance of police authority. Citizens who are intoxicated tend to comply with police commands less frequently and promptly than citizens who are not intoxicated. While most inebriated citizens do comply with police orders, a sizeable minority do not.[86]

Because authority is so central to the police role, citizens who question or resist that authority represent a very serious challenge to patrol officers and the organizations they represent. Challenges such as these are not taken lightly because they are seen as threatening an officer's ability to police effectively. As a consequence, intense verbal coercion is used to establish police authority, and if that is not effective, physical force is used to elicit citizen acceptance of authority.

It had been a typical Friday night "back-up" watch for two experienced officers and the recruit the academy had sent to ride with them. They already had handled numerous radio assignments and would later respond to a near-fatal stabbing. For now, though, they were between assignments.

As they drove past a bar, they watched as a man appeared to force a young woman into his car. Without hesitation, they turned on their emergency lights and pulled behind the car. As they prepared to get out of the squad, the citizen drove off at high speed. The officer who was driving put the squad's siren on and told the recruit to hand the microphone to the other experienced officer who was riding the back seat of the squad. The officer then told the dispatcher of the chase, provided a description of the car, and the direction the chase was proceeding.

The radio's emergency tone and the dispatcher's description helped alert other officers to the chase. It was, however, short-lived and, as is true of most chases, it ended in a crash; the citizen being pursued drove his car over a curb and into a tree. But it lasted long enough for officers in several other squads to join the officers who had initiated it. Guns were drawn as the officers approached and the recruit was told to stay out of the way.

The citizens were not injured and the driver was told to get out of the car and to lie, face down, on the ground. He was searched and handcuffed and the officers learned that the woman he had forced into the car was his wife. They had been drinking and arguing and the husband had decided that it was time to go home. The woman had objected and the husband had dragged her out of the bar and forced her into the car.

The man was pushed in the direction of the officer's squad. He asked where he was going. The officers told him: to jail. The man kicked at one officer and attempted to run despite the fact that he was handcuffed. The officers restrained him and after a brief struggle he was once again pushed in the direction of the squad. The citizen said, "You put me in there and I'll kick out a window." An officer responded, "You do that and your ass'll be in a sling."

They did, he did, and his was. The officers pulled him from the squad and despite *the fact that the citizen was no longer verbally or physically resisting,* the officers used their hands, feet, and nightsticks to beat the citizen from the neck down. No blows were landed to the face and the assault lasted less than a minute. A sergeant watched and commented that the "cocksucker deserved it." The citizen was thrown into the back seat of the squad and taken downtown. He later apologized to the officers, who were filling out reports, and suggested that "I had it coming." Although he had not had it coming, he clearly had gotten it.

Use of needless force in this circumstance and others is tolerated, if not encouraged, by the norms characteristic of many police organizations. Actions such as those described are indirectly encouraged during academy training, legitimated by police patrol officers, and tolerated by administrative elites. Albert J. Reiss, Jr., summarizes the nature of the *organizational* norms supportive of unnecessary police violence:

> A striking fact is that in more than one-half of all instances of undue coercion, at least one other . . . [officer] . . . was present who did not participate in the use of force. This shows that, for the most part, the police do not restrain their fellow police. . . . On the contrary, there were times when their very presence encouraged the use of force. One man brought into the lockup for threatening . . . [an officer] . . . with a pistol was so severly beaten . . . that he required hospitalization. During the beating . . . some fellow police . . . propped the man up while others shouted encouragement. Though the official police code does not legitimate this practice, police culture does.[87]

Present within many police organizations are norms supportive of the use of excessive force in situations where citizens resist police authority.

Judgments of Social Value. A second set of factors important in understanding the origins of police brutality are the judgments patrol officers make as to the "social value" of the citizens they encounter. Essentially similar to the members of predatory juvenile gangs, who argue that certain individuals—chronic drunkenness offenders and "crooked" store owners—deserve victimization,[88] officers within many (especially watch-style) police organizations present justifications for acts of violence against certain types of citizens. Public drunkenness offenders, sex offenders, and hardened criminals are among the types of citizens seen as likely candidates. In the view of many patrol officers, these citizens contribute little other than trouble to society. They are not part of society and therefore not protected by more general norms which guide the policing of "normal" citizens. In effect, they are seen as deserving of unnecessary police violence because of what they are or what they do.

One brief example will help illustrate the ways in which judgments of social value prompt police violence. Albert J. Reiss, Jr., describes what two police officers did in response to a radio assignment to check two "drunks" in a cemetery:

> Without questioning the men, the older policeman began to search one of them, ripping his shirt and hitting him in the groin with a nightstick. The younger policemen, as he searched the second, ripped away the seat of his trousers, exposing his buttocks. The policemen then prodded the men toward the cemetery fence and forced them to climb it, laughing at the plight of the drunk with the exposed buttocks. As the drunks went over the fence, one policeman shouted, "I ought to run you fuckers in!" The other remarked to the observer, "Those assholes won't be back; a bunch of shitty winos."[89]

What is important is that what happened to these citizens was not a function of what they had done, being drunk in a cemetery. Instead, their treatment was a function of what they *were* in the eyes of the officers, "shitty winos."

Police Decision Making.   Police work requires that officers make quick decisions on the basis of fragmentary information. Because decisions must be made instantly, police officers and their superiors are quick to defend acts of violence. Their defense is quite straightforward and it is not without appeal to persons not involved in policing. Patrol officers, administrative elites, other members of the criminal justice system, and citizens generally, do not condemn these actions because they cannot be certain that they would not have engaged in these actions had they been in that same situation.

For instance, during the 1968 Chicago Democratic convention, *Chicago Daily News* journalist John O. Linstead observed as police beat three citizens who had done nothing to police. Linstead responded by shouting at police, "Cut that out, you motherfuckers."[90] The police accepted Linstead's suggestion: they turned and assaulted Linstead, causing a minor head wound which required six stitches.

Three police officers were charged with "willful violation" of Linstead's civil rights and the case went to jury trial in federal district court in Chicago. The prosecution introduced nine eyewitnesses and a film of the incident. The presiding judge, Joseph Sam Perry, accused the prosecution of overkill.

The jury returned a "not guilty" verdict. Judge Perry congratulated the jury for its verdict, observing:

> The language that Mr. Linstead used ... was vile and degrading to the officers. He charged some of the officers with committing incest with their mothers in the lowest gutter language, *which I suggest would be provoking in such manner that any red-blooded American would flare-up.*[91]

Despite overwhelming evidence to the contrary, Judge Perry and apparently the jury elected not to convict the three police officers because, to paraphrase Judge Perry, they could not be certain that they would not have done the same thing.

To summarize: unnecessary police force appears traceable to a variety of factors, including in-group solidarity and secrecy. However, three factors appear to be most important: 1) consensually held beliefs about the importance of citizen acceptance of police authority; 2) judgments of the social value of certain citizens; and 3) the conservative nature of police decision making. Although individual patrol officers engage in these needlessly forceful actions, they do so as representatives of deviant organizations.

SUMMARY

In our discussion of routine policing, it was noted that patrol officers do society's dirty work for us. It was also suggested that our minds run from thoughts of dirty work. We would prefer not to know.

There is good reason for believing that our minds also recoil from thoughts of police misconduct. It is hard to study the improper and illegal actions of persons charged with the enforcement of the law. We would perhaps rather not know these things. Perhaps we also deny such knowledge for fear of the label we may earn. To be labeled "antipolice" is to appear to be associated with or supportive of the forces of anarchy.

Ignoring such facts is a serious mistake. Police misconduct is a form of anarchy. Corruption makes policing available only for a price and it makes police criminals. Needless police violence also is a form of anarchy. When it occurs, reason and simple fairness are abandoned in favor of tyranny. These are strong words, intended to overcome our tendency to hide from such thoughts. Police misconduct exists and it frequently has organizational origins. Peer norms support it, police socialization extends it, and administrators tolerate it.

In one sense, the nineteenth-century residents of London and cities in the United States who feared and resisted the creation of modern police were correct. The corrupt and brutal police of Seattle, Houston, "Mid-City," Richland County, Chicago, Philadelphia, New York, and elsewhere confirm their worst fears. In these cities police have promoted anarchy over and against civility. It is a discouraging picture. Out of this discouragement, however, there should emerge a single question. What can be done to control our police? The next chapter addresses and attempts to answer that question.

Notes

1. For a similar argument, see Rodney Stark, *Police Riots* (Belmont, Calif.: Wadsworth, 1972), p. 1.

2. William J. Chambliss, "Vice, Corruption, Bureaucracy, and Power," in William J. Chambliss and Milton Mankoff (eds.), *Whose Law, What Order?* (New York: Wiley, 1976), pp. 173ff.

3. Herbert Beigel and Alan Beigel, *Beneath the Badge: A Story of Police Corruption* (New York: Harper & Row, 1977).

4. Jonathan Rubinstein, *City Police* (New York: Ballantine, 1973), pp. 341–434.

5. David Blum, "Houston's Illness," *The New Republic* (July 8 and 15, 1978): 12–14.

6. See, for example, William K. Muir, *Police: Streetcorner Politicians* (Chicago: University of Chicago Press, 1977), pp. 1–36.

7. Muir, *Police,* p. 7.

8. The section which follows is an expanded version of M. David Ermann and Richard J. Lundman, *Organizational Deviance* (New York: Holt, Rinehart and Winston, 1981, forthcoming). For a similar discussion, see Lawrence W. Sherman, *Scandal and Reform: Controlling Police Corruption* (Berkeley, Calif.: University of California Press, 1978), pp. 3–26.

9. For a general discussion of this point, see John Kenneth Galbraith, *The New Industrial State* (New York: New American Library, 1967), Chapter 6.

10. For a general discussion of this point, see Marvin E. Olsen, *The Process of Social Organization* (New York: Holt, Rinehart and Winston, 1968), p. 103ff.

11. Olsen, *The Process,* p. 103.

12. This is an expansion of M. David Ermann and Richard J. Lundman (eds.), *Corporate and Governmental Deviance* (New York: Oxford University Press, 1978), pp. 7–9. Also see Sherman, *Scandal and Reform,* pp. 3–26.

13. Sherman, *Scandal and Reform,* p. 4.

14. See Clifton Bryant (ed.), *Deviance: Occupational and Organizational Bases* (Chicago: Rand McNally, 1974).

15. Based upon Lawrence W. Sherman (ed.), *Police Corruption: A Sociological Perspective* (Garden City, N.Y.: Doubleday/Anchor Books, 1974), p. 6.

16. Thomas Barker and Julian Roebuck, *An Empirical Typology of Police Corruption: A Study in Organizational Deviance* (Springfield, Ill.: Charles C. Thomas, 1973), pp. 26–27.

17. See Beigel and Beigel, *Beneath the Badge,* pp. 277–278.

18. Barker and Roebuck, *An Empirical Typology,* pp. 21–41.

19. Based upon Rubinstein, *City Police,* pp. 405–406; and personal observation.

20. Sherman, *Scandal and Reform,* p. 138.

21. Edward F. Droge, Jr., *The Patrolman: A Cop's Story* (New York: Signet, 1973), p. 110.

22. Mike Royko, *Boss: Richard J. Daley of Chicago* (New York: Signet, 1971), p. 111.

23. James P. Spradley, *You Owe Yourself a Drunk* (Boston: Little, Brown, 1969), p. 286.

24. This is a paraphrase of Albert J. Reiss, Jr.'s statement: "of such evenings is much police work made." See Albert J. Reiss, Jr., *The Police and the Public* (New Haven, Conn.: Yale University Press, 1971), p. 21.

25. Beigel and Beigel, *Beneath the Badge,* p. 32; also, see Royko, *Boss,* p. 113.

26. See Robert H. Williams, *Vice Squad* (New York: Crowell, 1973) for a description of special function units.

27. Reiss, *The Police and the Public,* p. 86.

28, *The Knapp Commission Report on Police Corruption* (New York: Braziller, 1972), p. 1.

29. *Knapp Commission Report,* p. 2.

30. Chambliss, "Vice," p. 173.

31. John A. Gardiner, "Ticket Fixing," in John A. Gardiner and David J. Olson (eds.) *Theft of the City* (Bloomington Ind.: Indiana University Press, 1974), p. 160.

32. Nicholas Gage, "Organized Crime in Court," in Gardiner and Olson, *Theft of the City,* p. 165.

33. Rubinstein, *City Police,* p. 375.

34. Barker and Roebuck, *An Empirical Typology,* p. 36.

35. Ellwyn R. Stoddard, "The Informal 'Code' of Police Deviancy: A Group Approach to 'Blue-Coat Crime,'" *Journal of Criminal Law, Criminology and Police Science, 59* (1968): 201–213.

36. Williams, *Vice Squad,* passim.

37. Sherman, *Scandal and Reform,* pp. 74–75. Also see Fred J. Cook, *The Corrupted Land: The Social Morality of Modern America* (New York: Macmillan, 1966), p. 243.

38. See Beigel and Beigel, *Beneath the Badge,* p. 277.

39. Barker and Roebuck, *An Empirical Typology,* p. 36.

40. Barker and Roebuck, *An Empirical Typology,* p. 37.

41. *Knapp Commission,* pp. 61ff.

42. Jerome Skolnick, *Justice Without Trial* (New York: Wiley, 1966), p. 28. Peter K. Manning identified "Westville" as Oakland. See Peter K. Manning, "The Researcher: An Alien in the Police World," in Arthur Niederhoffer and Abraham S. Blumberg (eds.), *The Ambivalent Force* (Hinsdale, Ill.: The Dryden Press, 1976), p. 105.

43. Jerome Skolnick, *Justice Without Trial,* 2d ed. (New York: Wiley, 1975), p. 269; and Sherman, *Scandal and Reform,* pp. xxx–xxxiv.

44. Sherman, *Police Corruption;* and Sherman, *Scandal and Reform.*

45. Sherman, *Police Corruption,* p. 31. Sherman also lists several additional factors, pp. 31ff.

46. See Émile Durkheim, *Suicide,* John A. Spalding and George Simpson, (trans.) (New York: Free Press, 1951).

47. Durkheim, *Suicide,* p. 258.

48. Robert K. Merton, "Social Structure and Anomie," *American Sociological Review, 2* (October 1938): 672–682.

49. Royko, *Boss,* p. 73.

50. See George Lee Haskins, *Law and Authority in Early Massachusetts* (New York: Macmillan, 1960).

51. See Norman K. Denzin, "Notes on the Criminogenic Hypothesis: A Case Study of the American Liquor Industry," *American Sociological Review, 42* (December 1977): 905–920.

52. See Charles H. McCaghy, *Deviant Behavior: Crime, Conflict and Interest Groups* (New York: Macmillan, 1976), pp. 345–381.

53. See James Q. Wilson, *Varieties of Police Behavior* (Cambridge, Mass.: Harvard University Press, 1968), pp. 140–199, for a discussion of watch and legalistic departments.

54. Sherman, *Police Corruption,* p. 115.

55. I am grateful to William B. Sanders for alerting me to this point and for convincing me that it needed to be covered.

56. Sherman, *Scandal and Reform,* passim.

57. Sherman, *Scandal and Reform,* p. 41; and Rubinstein, *City Police,* pp. 407–409.

58. Personal observations.

59. Skolnick, *Justice Without Trial,* p. 208.

60. *Knapp Commission Report,* p. 7.

61. Royko, *Boss,* pp. 116–120.

62. Sherman, *Scandal and Reform,* pp. 74–75.

63. Sherman, *Scandal and Reform,* pp. 123, 222, and 225.

64. Williams, *Vice Squad,* p. 6.

65. See Stoddard, "The Informal Code"; and Beigel and Beigel, *Beneath the Badge,* p. 272.

66. Steve Gettinger, "Profile: Birmingham Police," *Police Magazine* (Prototype Issue, April 1977): 42.

67. Williams, *Vice Squad,* p. 55.

68. Beigel and Beigel, *Beneath the Badge,* p. x.

69. James C. Parsons. "A Candid Analysis of Police Corruption," in Jerome H. Skolnick and Thomas C. Gray (eds.), *Police in America* (Boston: Little, Brown, 1975), p. 255.

70. James F. Ahern, *Police in Trouble* (New York: Hawthorn Books, 1972), p. 96.

71. William A. Westley, *Violence and the Police* (Cambridge, Mass.: The M.I.T. Press, 1970), p. 121.

72. Albert J. Reiss, Jr., "Police Brutality—Answers to Key Questions," in Niederhoffer and Blumberg (eds.), *The Ambivalent Force,* pp. 333–342.

73. Reiss, "Police Brutality," p. 341.

74. Rubinstein, *City Police,* p. 183.

75. George Kirkham, *Signal Zero* (New York: Ballantine, 1976).

76. Kirkham, *Signal Zero,* p. 141.

77. See Jerrold K. Footlick, "The Wild Bunch," *Newsweek* (June 6, 1977): 80–81; and Blum, "Houston's Illness."

78. See Bob Hiles and Ron Rutti, "Hurler Victim of Circumstance, Brutality," *News Journal,* Mansfield, Ohio (Sunday, May 7, 1978), p. 6A.

79. Hiles and Rutti, "Hurler Victim," p. 6A.

80. Reiss, "Police Brutality," pp. 335–336.

81. This as follows: in a city of 500,000 there are approximately 400,000 potential police–citizen encounters each year. One-third of these are GOA's (remaining n = 268,000) and two-thirds of these do not contain violators (remaining n = 91,200). Using the Reiss estimate (91,200 x .03), there would be approximately 2700 assaults each year. This is a very crude estimate.

82. See Richard W. Harding and Richard P. Fahey, "Killings by Chicago Police, 1969–1970; An Empirical Study," *Southern California Law Review* (1973): 284–315.

83. See, for example Richard E. Sykes and John P. Clark, "Deference Exchange in Police–Civilian Encounters," *American Journal of Sociology, 81* (November 1975): 589–590.

84. See Walter B. Miller, "Lower Class Culture as a Generating Milieu of Gang Delinquency," *Social Issues, 14* (1958): 5–19.

85. Mary Glen Wiley and Terry L. Hudik, "Police–Citizen Encounters: A Field Test of Exchange Theory," *Social Problems, 22* (October 1974): 119–127.

86. See Richard J. Lundman, "Routine Police Arrest Practices: A Commonweal Perspective," *Social Problems, 22* (October 1974): 135; and Paul A. Pastor, Jr., "Mobilization in Public Drunkenness Control: A Comparison of Legal and Medical Approaches," *Social Problems, 25* (April 1978): 377.

87. Reiss, "Police Brutality," p. 341.

88. For a discussion of this, see Gresham Sykes and David Matza, "Techniques of Neutralization: A Theory of Delinquency," *American Sociological Review, 22* (December 1957): 664–670.

89. Reiss, "Police Brutality," p. 336.

90. See: "Verdict in Chicago," *Newsweek* (June 23, 1969): 92.

91. "Verdict in Chicago," p. 92.

CHAPTER 7

Controlling Police and Policing

INTRODUCTION

One of the major problems associated with all public-serving organizations is external control. In a democratic society, the actions of public-serving organizations are to be monitored and controlled so as to insure that the persons being served are those intended by reference to the commonweal mandate of the organization.[1] In the absence of democratic monitoring and control, there is present the possibility of organizational actions contrary to commonweal interests.[2]

Urban policing is rich in opportunities to act in ways contrary to public interests. Patrol officers work alone or with trusted partners and supervision is minimal. Officers are therefore free to make discriminatory arrests and to accept money, goods, or services for special favors or for ignoring illegal actions. They are also free to assault verbally defiant or behaviorally deviant citizens.

Study of the available evidence suggests that police officers routinely act in ways contrary to commonweal interests. They make arrests on the basis of factors which benefit polite and affluent citizens at the expense of less fortunate citizens. Patrol officers also frequently take advantage of improper and illegal offers of money, goods, and services. And unnecessary police force is common in contemporary society. In New York,[3] Philadelphia,[4] Chicago,[5] Houston,[6] Seattle,[7] and elsewhere,[8] patrol officers bring prejudice, corruption, and violence to their work and our lives. As citizens it is clear that we have failed to master[9] our police.

Purpose of the Chapter

The final chapter seeks to determine whether it is possible for citizens in a democratic society to regulate their police. The chapter begins by identifying the unique control problems posed by police organizations. Then attention is given to proposed solutions to the problems of controlling police and policing, principally those involving "professionalism." Third, alternative solutions are advanced and described. We will focus throughout the chapter on the prospects for effective mastery of police by citizens.

PROBLEMS OF CONTROLLING POLICE AND POLICING

Police organizations pose a minimum of four unique monitoring and control problems. First, they have been granted the privilege to exercize force and this privilege is essentially unrestricted. Second, many of the origins of police misconduct are external to police organizations. Third, police misbehavior is frequently an organizational rather than purely individualistic phenomenon. Fourth, police organizations are opposed to external control by citizens. Effective control of police and policing requires that these problems be recognized and overcome.

Coercive Force[10]

One indicator or sign of an organically solidary society is a proliferation of governmental agencies intended to administer the interdependent segments of an industrialized or "advanced" society. As compared to mechanically solidary societies wherein activities are integrated by reason of a collective conscience, organically solidary societies require external administration and integration. Police organizations, health boards, zoning committees, and the other administrative and enforcement agencies of contemporary government operate interdependently to sustain modern society.

What distinguishes police organizations from other governmental agencies is the societal delegated privilege to exercise coercive force. Instead of relying upon self-defense or each other for protection from disorder, we have given to police the privilege to use coercion in our name and on our behalf. Our calls to police reflect awareness of the power we have given them. Police are called to deal with barking dogs, automobile accidents, rowdy juveniles, husband–wife disputes, noisy parties, and the criminally belligerent. In each of these situations police use the power that we as citizens have given them: they warn owners, reroute traffic, disperse juveniles, tell obstreperous husbands to leave, and arrest people.

What lends unity to the infinite variety of police actions is their exercise of coercive force.

The problem this privilege poses for restraint of police is that we have failed to control its use. With the exceptions of restrictions on the use of deadly force, the use of force for personal rather than public interests, and the requirement that force not be used maliciously, few legal rules govern police coercion.[11]

Additionally, citizens in most communities find that bureaucratic indifference and cumbersome procedures make it difficult and time consuming to complain about police misuse of force.[12] For instance, if we are assaulted by a citizen, a simple phone call will produce a responding officer.[13] If we wish, the officer will write a report of the incident. If, however, we are assaulted by a police officer, we must make a special trip to police headquarters to file a complaint. We may have to make a second trip to sign the complaint. Throughout this process, our complaint frequently is met with skepticism and occasional hostility. In the case of "normal" assaults, police came to us and they appear willing to believe us. In the context of police assaults, we must go to the police and confront their doubts.

Finally, the nature of police work and court processing combine to further limit review of police use of force. The majority of police–citizen encounters do not end in arrest[14] and most police actions are not scrutinized by outsiders. What happens during these encounters is known only to the police and citizens involved in them. If an arrest does occur, mass "trials"[15] and plea bargaining[16] limit court examination of police arrest practices.

The position of the police therefore emerges as logically and empirically contradictory: on the one hand, police departments are commonweal organizations ostensibly subject to external democratic control, while on the other they possess an essentially unrestricted privilege to exercise coercive force. This contradiction poses a clear and fundamental threat to citizens in democratic society. It is therefore one of the problems which must be overcome if citizens are to dominate their police.

External Opportunities for Misconduct[17]

The problem of effectively controlling police and policing is further complicated by the fact that many of the forces which give rise to police misconduct are external to police organizations. Police in all communities are charged with attempting to enforce laws intended to define and control public morality—heroin addiction, use of soft drugs such as marijuana, gambling, prostitution, and distribution of sexually explicit ("pornographic") materials. Community sentiments regarding these laws are mixed, as evidenced by the large numbers of persons willing to sell and buy these goods and services. Because these actions are currently illegal, buyers and sellers take special precautions to avoid entanglement with police.

One of the more effective ways of avoiding such involvement is for sellers to pay police to ignore both buyers and sellers. However, it is not particularly efficient to purchase arrest immunity from one officer or even a small group of officers since disruption by the unpaid is a constant threat. It is more efficient for sellers to buy an entire department by filtering money, goods, or services to officers at all levels. If sellers are successful in their efforts to buy a department, then the entire organization is corrupt: a deviant department.

All police departments in large urban areas are capable of becoming deviant. This is because all are charged with the task of attempting to enforce laws people are willing to pay police not to enforce. Certain of the forces which give rise to police misconduct are therefore external to police organizations. Effective control of police and policing requires that these external opportunities be recognized and eliminated.

Police Misconduct as Organizational Deviance[18]

Sellers of illegal goods (heroin) and services (gambling) have successfully purchased immunity from arrest in several cities. At the very least this has occurred in the past in New York City; Oakland; Newburgh, New York; "Central City";[19] "Mid-City";[20] Philadelphia;[21] Chicago;[22] and Seattle.[23] Recent evidence suggests that sellers of illegal goods and services currently enjoy immunity in Philadelphia;[24] Chicago;[25] Seattle;[26] "Central City";[27] and perhaps New York City.[28] In each of these cities, past or current police departments have become deviant organizations with officers at all levels accepting money, goods, and services for not enforcing the law.

In other cities, excessive police violence has become so common as to suggest that it too has largely organizational origins. Police routinely assault large numbers of verbally defiant or behaviorally deviant citizens. They do so in an effort to teach respect and propriety. Occasionally their efforts at curbstone education result in the death of their unwilling students. When these actions are common, they reflect involvement in deviant departments. Officers use force unnecessarily on a regular basis and do not attempt to hide their actions from most colleagues or administrators. They lack fear because of their membership in deviant departments.

The actions of Houston police suggest membership in a deviant department. Across the last three years they have killed a large number of citizens in suspicious circumstances. David Blum provides a description of one such death:

> A suspect armed with a pair of scissors lost a gun battle with a police officer ... inside a store late one night. It wasn't even close; when the officer finished shooting his first round of bullets he paused, reloaded his gun and began shooting his gun. The policeman's gun fired 13 shots, while the suspect's scissors fired none.[29]

In this case and others, Houston police have either not been punished or have received only mild sanctions. They have been protected by their deviant department.

Police misconduct therefore has organizational origins. Patrol officers support these actions and socialization practices prepare new officers to engage in them. Administrators are, of necessity, aware of the actions of their subordinates and routinely protect them. This is the third problem which must be solved if citizens are to supervise their police.

Police Opposition to Citizen Control

Police departments are commonweal organizations mandated to serve the best interests of the public-at-large. As part of this mandate, citizens have granted to police the privilege to exercise coercive force. Given departments' commonweal obligations and their unique privilege, it does not seem unreasonable to suggest that citizens have the right and obligation to monitor and control police organizations. This would seem to be true especially when a community is policed by a deviant department.

These may well be reasonable suggestions, but patrol officers and administrators do not see them as such. They are vigorously opposed to civilian review. The list of cities where police fraternal groups and unions have successfully opposed creation (or eventually forced abolishment) of civilian review boards is quite long: Philadelphia; New York City; Rochester, New York; Los Angeles; Denver; Cincinnati; Seattle; Detroit; Newark, New Jersey; Hartford, Connecticut; Baltimore; and San Francisco.[30] It is interesting that police opposition has succeeded even in cities with deviant departments—Philadelphia, New York City, and Seattle.

The reasons police give for opposing civilian review are several. A common one is that effective policing requires secrecy.[31] Routine civilian penetration of police organizations for purposes of monitoring and control is said to compromise secrecy and thus threaten effective policing.

A second commonly advanced reason for opposing civilian control is the argument that citizens cannot properly and fairly evaluate police actions. This argument is based on the belief that unless a person has been in a police uniform and been cursed; spit at; assaulted; compelled to arrest a urine-, vomit-, or feces-stained chronic public drunkenness offender; or forced to decide, *quickly,* whether the hand coming out of a pocket contains a pack of cigarettes or a gun, then he or she cannot possibly evaluate, much less attempt to control, police and policing.[32] Since most citizens have not done these things, they obviously cannot pass judgment on police who have.

Police are opposed to civilian control, and they have been very successful in their opposition. This is the final problem which must be resolved if citizens are to oversee their police.

Control of police and policing is thus made difficult by a minimum of four unique problems. *Unless a control strategy overcomes most or all of these problems, there is little reason to believe that it will succeed.*

PREVIOUS SOLUTIONS

Police misconduct is not a recent problem. Prior to 1900, investigative commissions in most of our large cities reported extensive corruption of police. This was true of police in New York City; Philadelphia; Atlanta; Kansas City; Baltimore; Chicago; Los Angeles; San Francisco; Washington, D.C.; Milwaukee; and Boston.[33]

Unnecessary police force is also not new. Writing in 1903, a former commissioner of police in New York City, Frank Moss, observed:

> There has been through the courts and the streets a dreary procession of citizens with broken heads and bruised bodies against few of whom was violence needed to effect an arrest. Many of them had done nothing to deserve an arrest. In a majority of such cases, no complaint was made. If the victim complains, his charge is generally dismissed. The police are practically above the law.[34]

Because police organizations have long been involved in misconduct, many people have been attempting to control it for a long time. In the past, primary attention has been directed at the *individuals* who enact the police role. Police misconduct generally has been viewed as a problem involving a few corrupt or brutal officers—"bad apples"[35] in otherwise good departments. Ellwyn R. Stoddard nicely summarizes the essential thrust of this approach:

> It has been asserted by various writers of criminology, deviant behavior, and police science that unlawful activity by ... police ... is a manifestation of personal moral weakness, a symptom of personality defects, or a result of recruitment of individuals unqualified for police work.[36]

As a consequence of this individualistic approach to the causes of troublesome police actions, strategies for the control of police also have been individualistic in orientation. The single most frequently advanced solution is that policing must be made into a profession.

The Police Professionalism Movement[37]

Police professionalism is a movement based upon three fundamental principles. The first is the recruitment of better-educated police officers, with a college degree being established as a requirement. The second is the creation of a bureaucratically efficient central police administration headed by persons skilled in modern management techniques. The third principle follows from the first two: once police are better educated and administered, they have the same right to autonomy as members of other professions, the law and medicine being favored examples. A number of people have championed these ideas and we now will examine the ideas of two of them: August Vollmer and O. W. Wilson.[38]

August Vollmer (1876–1955). [39] Vollmer was a leading advocate of professionalism as a solution to the problem of controlling police. Vollmer started his police career in 1905 as an elected town marshall in Berkeley, California. He became chief of the Berkeley department in 1909 and, except for one year when he was chief in Los Angeles, he served in that position until 1932. During Vollmer's long tenure as chief, Berkeley was a model professional police organization and it served as a proving ground for many of his ideas.

However, the effects of Vollmer's ideas were not limited to the Berkeley department. Vollmer travelled extensively, conducted surveys of numerous police organizations, taught at the University of Chicago, helped establish the Berkeley School of Criminology, and wrote for both academic and popular audiences. Vollmer's ideas had a profound impact on police and policing. He was a leading spokesperson for police professionalism and his ideas continue to form the core of the professional movement.

At the very center of Vollmer's notion of the professional police officer was the college-educated person. Vollmer believed that all police officers should be exposed to a liberal education, given technical police academy training, and then sent out to police in a responsible, humane, and professional manner. Each officer was to be "chief" of their beat. Biographers Gene F. Carte and Elaine H. Carte provide a concise summary of Vollmer's ideas:

Vollmer believed that "society needs and must somehow obtain truly exceptional men to discharge police duties." They must be of "superior intellectual endowment, physically sound, and free from mental and nervous disorders; they must have character traits which will insure integrity, honesty, and efficiency; their personality must command the respect and liking of their associates and of the general public."[46]

For Vollmer, the fundamental solution to the problems of controlling police was to make policing into a profession. Vollmer's primary method was to attract college-trained personnel.

The college-educated officer, however, was only the core of Vollmer's ideas about professionalism. Vollmer advocated creation of an efficient central bureaucracy administered by persons skilled in modern management techniques. Vollmer was also in favor of vigorous internal control of police and policing.

O. W. Wilson (1900–1972).[41] Along with Vollmer, the name of Orlando Winfield Wilson is most frequently associated with the police professionalism movement. Wilson began his police career as a patrol officer and protegé of August Vollmer in Berkeley in 1921. He was chief of police in Fullerton, California, in 1925 and 1926, and in Wichita, Kansas, from 1928 to 1939. His Doctor of Laws (LL.D.) degree permitted entry into the academic world, and in 1939 he became a professor of public administration at the University of California, Berkeley. In 1950, he was appointed dean of the school of criminology at Berkeley. During his long tenure at Berkeley, Wilson travelled and lectured extensively and authored several books on police professionalism. In 1960, he left the academic world to become superintendent of the scandal-ridden Chicago Police Department.

Wilson's conception of professionalism was essentially similar to that of his mentor and friend August Vollmer. Wilson believed that a college education was the "best hope"[42] for improving police services. Wilson also championed the development of efficient central police bureaucracies administered by college-educated officers skilled in modern management techniques. And he was predictably firm about police autonomy. In his widely recognized text on *Police Administration,* Wilson argued:

> Ideally, any chief of police or executive head of the department should have enough independence, courage, and integrity to consider himself to be bigger than the job. . . . If he is asked by the city manager or mayor to carry out an unethical order or if he is placed in an untenable position, the chief should be prepared to resign if he is unable to effect a change in the direction of events.[43]

August Vollmer and O. W. Wilson were thus leaders of the police professionalism movement. They championed three fundamental principles: better-educated police, a more efficient central bureaucracy, and police independence. And their ideas continue to attract the approving attention of people concerned with control of police and policing: "the professional model . . . has been upheld until recently as the solution to all the problems of the police."[44]

Shortcomings of Professionalism

The greatest shortcoming of the professionalism movement is that its fundamental principles have not been widely implemented.[45] Despite the sometimes persuasive arguments of Vollmer and Wilson, only a handful of local police departments require a college degree for patrol officers.[46] Police administration has improved, but it cannot be said that most departments are run by persons skilled in modern management techniques.[47] And despite Wilson's strong admonitions, many departments remain mired in partisan politics.[48] It is obviously difficult to assess the controlling effects of a movement whose ideas have not been widely implemented.

However, if we assume that the fundamental principles of professionalism will soon be realized, then we can use the scattered evidence that is available to assess the control prospects of professionalism. This is the strategy we will follow and the criteria to be applied are those previously identified as requiring recognition and elimination.

When judged by these criteria, professionalism does not appear to be a promising mechanism for the control of police and policing. Professionalism: 1) *implies insularity* and thus fails to overcome the uncontrolled nature of police exercise of coercion; 2) is *environmentally misdirected* and thus does not eliminate the external opportunities for police impropriety; 3) is *organizationally insensitive* and thus overlooks the organizational origins of police misconduct; and 4) is *opposed to citizen control* and thus fails to abolish traditional police opposition.

Insularity. Professionalism increases rather than decreases restrictions on police use of coercive force. Professionalism is an argument and assumption that police know best how to police and use force. Professionalism excludes citizen restraints on police power. There is no better description of the insulating effects of professionalism than William A. Westley's:

> Professionalism, which has been a major goal of modern police administrators during the past two decades, has the effect of insulating the police from public pressures. In addition, it is presumably accompanied by higher standards and better training. ... That we want better trained, more competent police ... insulated from political influence and graft, is evident. Yet we must be wary, since insulation ... without other methods of integration ... can mean insulation from all of us, and if the goals of the police should vary from those of the citizens, it can become a very serious problem.[49]

Therefore, professionalism is insular and it reduces external control over police. *Effective control of police and policing requires external control. Professionalism is contrary to external control.*

Environmental Misdirection. Professionalism recognizes that outside forces corrupt police and policing. Its proposed solution is to advocate independence and autonomy for police, principally by withdrawing the department from active political involvement. To create this independence, proponents of professionalism erect barriers between a department and its environment. Once these barriers are in place, professionals believe they can get on with the task of creating an efficient, nondeviant department.

Withdrawal is an environmentally misdirected solution. It ensures that a department's environment will remain unchanged. Police still have the responsibility for attempting to enforce laws intended to control public morality. Police still confront countless sellers of illegal goods and services willing to buy arrest immunity. Opportunities for corruption are still extensive, and withdrawal ensures that they will continue to be available. The constant presence of such temptations makes reform difficult. August Vollmer's experiences help suggest the nature of this problem.

In 1923, Vollmer took a leave of absence from the Berkeley department to accept a one-year appointment as chief of police in Los Angeles.[50] The city was experiencing a level of property crime which threatened businesses with the loss of theft coverage by insurance companies. Additionally, organized gambling was entrenched in Los Angeles and police corruption was a major problem. Vollmer was brought in to "clean up" the Los Angeles Police Department by making it into a professional organization.

Vollmer concentrated his attention on isolating the department from the political machine controlling Los Angeles. Patrol officers were warned not to take advantage of extensive opportunities for corruption. Better-educated officers were placed in managerial positions, and accountability to the central police administration was increased. His efforts were not successful. Vollmer encountered a powerful political machine with strong connections to organized crime. His limited isolating efforts did little to dissuade officers from taking advantage of widespread corruption opportunities.

Therefore, professionalism is environmentally misdirected. It advocates police independence and autonomy, principally in the form of withdrawal. *Effective control of police and policing requires change in the external environment of police organizations. Professionalism is not concerned with environmental change.*

Organizational Insensitivity. Police misconduct has largely organizational origins when the internal operating norms of a department support it, socialization procedures perpetuate it, and when administrators ignore, tolerate, or encourage it. In such a department individual officers act as members of a deviant organization.

In addition to its thrust towards independence, two ideas are at the center of the professionalism movement. One is that college-trained personnel make more efficient and less deviant police officers. The second is that policing can be improved by creating an efficient bureaucratic structure administered by persons skilled in modern management techniques. To the extent that these two ideas are part of the professionalism movement, it is insensitive to the organizational origins of police misconduct. The experiences of George Kirkham illustrate the problem with the first idea, while O. W. Wilson's ordeals suggest the difficulty with the second.

George Kirkham's actions show that extensive education does not make a person any less susceptible to the pressures associated with being a member of a deviant department. Kirkham teaches criminology at Florida State University. In addition to his instructional duties, Kirkham became a police officer in a large Florida City. Prior to entering this field, Kirkham reports that he was critical of police and as best as he could determine, was not racially prejudiced or inclined to resolve interpersonal problems in a violent manner. Yet, Kirkham reports in a series of vivid articles and in his book *Signal Zero*[51] the process whereby he acquired negative images of black citizens and became willing to use aggression and violence to resolve problematic situations. For instance:

> My tour of duty had been a long, hard one—one that had ended with a high-speed chase of a stolen car in which we had narrowly escaped serious injury.... As we checked off duty, I was vaguely aware of feeling tired and tense. My partner and I were headed for ... breakfast when we heard the ... sound of breaking glass, and ... spotted two ... boys running. We confronted them and ... one ... sneered at me, cursed, turned, and started to walk away. The next thing I knew I had grabbed the youth by his shirt and spun him around, shouting, "I'm talking to you punk!" I felt my partner's arm on my shoulder and heard his reassuring voice ... "Take it easy, Doc!" ... My mind flashed back to a lecture during which I had told my students, "Any man who is not able to maintain absolute control of his emotions at all times has no business being a police officer."[52]

Despite extensive education and a personal commitment to less deviant policing, Kirkham was unable to resist personal involvement in police misconduct.

Therefore, professionalism is organizationally insensitive to the extent that it emphasizes recruitment of college-trained personnel. *Effective control of police and policing requires sensitivity to the organizational origins of police misconduct. A college education does not preclude involvement in police misconduct.*

O. W. Wilson's experiences in Chicago suggest that bureaucratic efficiency does not prevent police wrongdoing. In 1960, the city of Chicago was experiencing another of its periodic police scandals. Residents of Chicago were used to police corruption and literally took it for granted.

In 1957, for instance, *Life* magazine confirmed what most residents of Chicago already knew: "Chicago's police were the most corrupt in the nation."[53] There was something different, however, about the "Summerdale Scandal."

In January of 1960, a professional burglar was arrested by Chicago police.[54] In an attempt to reduce his own sentence, he told the public defender that the other members of his burglary gang were Chicago police officers stationed in the Summerdale police district. A minimum of eight "burglars in blue" were involved. Chicago newspapers reacted indignantly. It was one thing for police to shake down tavern owners and traffic law violators. It was quite another when police also were burglars.

Mayor Richard J. Daley appointed a committee to search for a replacement for police commissioner Timothy J. O'Connor. O. W. Wilson chaired the search committee for Daley, and after interviewing over 100 candidates, the committee recommended that its chair, Orlando W. Wilson, be appointed commissioner. Wilson accepted the appointment after he was promised a salary twice his university income and a free hand to reform Chicago police. On March 2, 1960, Wilson became superintendent of the Chicago Police Department.

Wilson did many things one would expect from a proponent of police professionalism. He obviously could not immediately require a college education for Chicago police. But he spoke with all 10,000 Chicago patrol officers during two mass meetings and sternly warned them that ethical conduct was now expected and required.[55] He also dropped all of the old civil service promotion lists and held competitive examinations. Many police officers were rapidly promoted to positions of power and responsibility.[56] Some of Wilson's efforts were thus directed at improving the quality of the people policing Chicago.

However, Wilson gave his greatest attention to the creation of an efficient central police bureaucracy administered by the officers who had scored well on the competitive promotion examinations he had initiated.[57] He closed 17 of 38 police district stations to increase accountability to the central police administration. Civilians replaced police doing clerical work, releasing approximately 1000 officers for patrol work. Over $2 million was spent to build and equip a central communications and dispatch center. In all, Wilson generally is credited with creating a more modern and efficient police organization in Chicago.

However, he is *not* credited with eliminating or even reducing police corruption in Chicago.[58] Despite his stern warnings to patrol officers, they continued to shake down tavern owners and motorists. Police burglaries also continued. The officers who experienced rapid promotion by reason of Wilson's competitive examinations were among those indicted and jailed for corrupt activities in the 1970s. In the words of two recent researchers:

In reality, many of Wilson's reforms had nothing to do with eliminating corruption (for example, the new and much heralded communications center). Some may even have contributed to the spread of police abuses.... Corruption ... managed to live comfortably under Wilson's aegis.[59]

Despite extensive modernization and improved efficiency, Chicago police remained corrupt during Wilson's tenure as police superintendent.

Therefore, professionalism is organizationally insensitive to the extent that it emphasizes bureaucratic efficiency. *Effective control of police and policing requires sensitivity to the organizational origins of police misconduct. Bureaucratic efficiency does not prevent police misconduct.*

Opposition to Citizen Control.   Effective control of police and policing requires review of police actions by citizens. Police, however, have long and successfully resisted attempts to create effective civilian review. For instance, in the mid-1960s, Mayor John Lindsay of New York City added four civilians to the police department's three officer Civilian Complaint Review Board.[60] The Police Benevolent Association objected to the introduction of civilians and eventually convinced New York voters to abandon this attempt to control their police. By the early 1970s, the situation was similar in most other cities: "all ... civilian review boards were defunct."[61]

Professionalism helps legitimate traditional police opposition to civilian control. It is a movement which suggests that college-trained police are more capable and less deviant. It emphasizes that bureaucratically efficient and centrally controlled departments are less capable of becoming or remaining deviant. Professionalism stresses the need to free police from local partisan politics and promises vigorous and internal control of police and policing. It suggests there is no need for civilian control.

Regretably, none of this is even close to being accurate. Neither a college education nor effective management precludes police misconduct. And police have not proven themselves capable of internal control.[62] Cumbersome and time-consuming procedures discourage complaints. If a complaint is filed, complainants and witnesses generally are poorly treated by police. And most complaints are not upheld: in most departments less than 5 percent of the complaints filed by citizens are declared valid by police.[63] Self-policing has not worked and there is a clear and continuing need for civilian control.

Therefore, police have long been opposed to civilian control. *Effective control of police and policing requires external regulation by citizens. Professionalism suggests there is no need for civilian control.*

In sum: previous solutions to the problems of controlling police and policing have emphasized professionalism, the recruitment of college-

educated personnel into bureaucratically efficient and autonomous organizations. These principles have not been widely implemented, but it is
possible to assess the control prospects of professionalism. When judged
by the criteria advanced earlier, it appears that even if executed, professionalism would not result in effective control of police and policing.
Although the available data are not extensive, the prospects for control of
police and policing via professionalism do not appear promising. It therefore appears necessary to look elsewhere for alternative solutions.

ALTERNATIVE SOLUTIONS

The task at hand is to identify control mechanisms which simultaneously restrict police use of violence and direct attention to external
opportunities for police misdeeds. These means also must be sensitive to
the organizational origins of police misconduct and must open police
organizations to external control by citizens.

In light of these requirements, four control mechanisms will be advanced. They are: 1) honest description of the capacities of contemporary
police and policing; 2) decriminalization of laws intended to control public
morality; 3) appointment of top level administrators committed to change;
and 4) creation of citizen monitoring organizations.

Honest Description of Police Capacities

Modern police departments are involved in an awkward but resolvable
situation. This awkwardness is the result of a gap between public perceptions of police abilities and the actual capacities of contemporary police
and policing. The public has been encouraged to view police as law enforcers and crime preventers. The problem is that police do not accomplish
the first all that often or the second all that well.

Contrary to public perception, law enforcement is not the primary activity of patrol officers. Instead, recent research tells us that they spend more
time providing services and writing reports than arresting alleged violators.[64] Patrol officers are not primarily or even frequently law enforcers.

Also, the available data suggest that routine patrol activities do not
prevent crime. During an experiment in Kansas City,[65] one group of police
districts received routine patrol while a second group of districts received
double the usual number of patrols. In a third group of police districts,
patrol cars entered only when called in by citizens or to make an arrest.
All three areas were compared for a year, using measures ranging from
police response times to levels of crime. The essential conclusion advanced was that there were no significant differences between the three
areas despite variation in levels of patrol. Although replicative data would

clearly be beneficial, it must be recognized that the available evidence suggests that routine patrol is not an effective deterrent to crime.

The evidence also suggests that detectives can do little to prevent crime. A Rand Corporation study[66] of detectives revealed that most of the detective's time is spent in unproductive questioning of victims. It was found that most clearances are the result of information contained in the original report of the incident. It was also found that most additional clearances are the result of routine clerical tasks. Detectives are limited in what they can accomplish and these limits are evidenced by the clearance rate information published each year in the *Uniform Crime Reports.* Crimes against property (burglary, larceny, and auto theft) generally involve victims unable to provide detectives with useful information. Detectives therefore clear (by arrest) less than 20 percent of all crimes against property.[67] If would-be criminals were to consult these figures, there is precious little reason to believe that they would come away deterred.

The traditional method for closing the gap between public perceptions and police capacities has been for police organizations to lie. Many of the "little lies" we examined in earlier chapters - unfounding and defounding crimes to improve clearance rates, use of silent cars to generate moving and parking citations, sharing of felony arrests, and quota systems - are advanced by police organizations to give the public the *appearance* of being law-enforcing and crime-preventing agencies. In Peter K. Manning's words:

> If lying is endemic in police operations, it is not an isolated commentary on either the moral status of police ... as individuals or even police organizations; it is a commentary on the society in which the activity is rooted.[68]

In this instance, police lying is indicative of the public's ignorance of the capacities of contemporary police and policing.

Some of you, however, might want to argue that these little lies are a minor problem as compared to police corruption or excessive police force. This is true. But it also is necessary to consider one additional point. Little lies help create an environment which is productive of the more serious forms of police misconduct. They foster the development of a departmental anomie in which "police see the world as infinitely manipulable - paper can be written to justify an enormous range of phenomenon."[69] Little lies contribute to bigger and more serious lies and are thus an important starting point for any overall strategy for controlling police and policing.

The solution to reducing police lies is simple honesty. Police organizations are limited in what they can accomplish. Members of the general public must learn that police organizations:

1. *cannot* prevent most crimes, especially those that currently attract the greatest public attention - homicide, rape, aggravated assault, and armed robbery,
2. *do not* solve most crimes and of those which are solved, citizen cooperation and blind luck are the major facilitating factors,
3. and therefore have *little or nothing* to do with the overall incidence of criminality. [70]

Public knowledge of these limitations would appreciably reduce the frequency with which police organizations and officers feel compelled to lie to citizens.

What, then, are the capacities of contemporary police and policing? A brief review of the experiences of two patrol officers will help anticipate an answer to this question.

It was a bitterly cold night and the heater in the patrol car did not work well. During eight cold hours the two officers were assigned a total of three calls. The first was to "check the welfare of" a citizen living in an apartment in a decaying residential section. The officers drove to the apartment, knocked, and were invited in. An elderly man was softly crying on the floor next to his bed. He explained that he had fallen out of bed and that the person who took care of him would not be back until the next morning. He was unhurt save for his pride as he asked to be lifted back into bed. One officer lifted the man back into bed and, perhaps out of a habit acquired as a parent, gently tucked him in. They talked briefly as the man stopped crying and finally made eye contact as he thanked the officers. The officers then returned to an even colder patrol car.

The next call was to "check some kids throwing snowballs at cars." They took their time driving to the location given them by the dispatcher. They found some youngsters who could have been the ones involved and told them to stop - "a windshield might get busted and cause an accident."

The officers then patrolled for a considerable period of time. With about an hour left in their watch, they called the dispatcher and said they were going downtown to fill up on gas. When they were well out of their patrol district, a call came out to "check a stabbing" at a bar. The officers were only two blocks from the scene and they informed the dispatcher that they would respond. They put on their emergency lights, but not their siren, and proceeded cautiously on the icy streets. They literally arrived within seconds and the alleged violator was still present. He was handcuffed, read his rights, placed in the back seat of the patrol car, taken to the county hospital for a blood alcohol test, and then downtown to be booked.

The two officers clearly had been very lucky to make this felony arrest. A citizen had called the police dispatch room about the incident and the call had been quickly dispatched. Because the two officers had been on their way downtown, they were able to respond within seconds. The result was an arrest, not because of extraordinary police effort but rather because of citizen cooperation and blind luck.

The experiences of the two officers help indentify the capacities of contemporary police and policing. They suggest that police organizations can:

1. provide services not available or not constantly available from other sources;
2. assist citizens in attempting to maintain a level of order which citizens by their calls to police deem appropriate; and
3. assist citizens in attempting to prevent and control the types of crimes which citizens, by their calls to police, deem appropriate.

Each of these activities are within the capacities of contemporary police and policing, and many others have advanced similar conclusions.[71] Unless contradictory evidence becomes available, it seems prudent to conclude that there is not much that police can do about crime except to respond to citizen reports of it.

Simple honesty would appear to be an effective tool for reducing police lies. Police lie in order to give members of the general public the appearance of being law enforcers and crime preventers. If members of the general public knew that police are not primarily or frequently either of these, then police would have no reason to lie. Honesty would therefore appear to be an inoffensive and viable control mechanism since there is seemingly little reason for believing that we as citizens cannot learn of and accept the truth. The issue thus shifts from whether our police should be honest to whether they will be.

The Prospects for Honesty   The prospects are not good. Patrol officers, detectives, and police administrators have long been aware of the fact that police are not law enforcers or crime preventers. Patrol officers complain that too much of their work involves providing service and maintaining order.[72] Officers, detectives, and administrators know that most arrests are the result of citizen assistance and luck.[73] Police do not need to be told these things by researchers. On the basis of their own experience, they know that the Kansas City and Rand Corporation conclusions are essentially correct. After all, that is the reason they lie.

Even though their work experiences suggest the accuracy of the Kansas City and Rand findings, police have been quick to condemn the results of these two studies. Edward Davis, former chief of police in Los Angeles, has been an especially outspoken critic. Davis, speaking as president of the International Association of Chiefs of Police (IACP) and as a leader of the Major City Police Chiefs, observed:

The Major City Police Chiefs are so sick and tired of . . . Police Foundation [sponsors of the Kansas City experiment] hokey research findings and Rand-type research projects. They come and use you and then they start making false claims. . . . It isn't that we're against research; it's that we're against this terrible trend of real trashy types of research, real harmful types of research.[74]

When confronted by evidence confirming what most police already know, police have responded by criticizing it.

The reason police have castigated these findings is not difficult to discover. Police traditionally have legitimated their share of municipal resources by arguing that they are the "thin blue line" standing between anarchy and civility. Police correctly fear that the Kansas City and Rand findings will make it more difficult to secure increasingly scarce municipal resources. Bruce R. Baker, chief of police in Portland, Oregon, has taken precisely this position:

This can be very destructive. Almost every major city in the United States faces a true budget constraint. They'll wave . . . [these findings] . . . in your face.[75]

The prospects for honesty are not good. Police denounce the Kansas City and Rand evidence which they know to be correct. The reason is simple: police correctly fear that these findings will make municipal funding more difficult. There is consequently little room for optimism regarding the elimination of the little lies police advance to give citizens the appearance of being law enforcers and crime preventers.

Decriminalization

American police have long been unfavorably compared with police of other nations. In 1915, Raymond P. Fosdick argued that European police were uniformly more capable and less corrupt than American police. Fosdick observed:

The point to be emphasized is that in the European police organization there is no "system", to use the word in its evil association. No organized connection exists between the police department and the underworld. No official collects for another or shares his plunder with a group. There is no passing of money to "men higher up". Dishonesty, where it occurs, is an individual matter. . . .[76]

Contemporary research suggests that European police misconduct remains an individual matter.[77]

More recently, David Bayley compared American police with those of Japan.[78] Once again the comparison was unfavorable. Bayley reported that the mini-police stations, or *Kobans,* scattered throughout Japanese neighborhoods encourage direct community involvement in and control over routine policing. Bayley also reported that organized police misconduct was extremely infrequent in Japan:

> Ask a senior police officer anywhere in Japan . . . what kind of misconduct by subordinate officers causes him the greatest concern and he will invariably cite *off-duty* traffic accidents, drunkenness, and indiscretions with women . . . One listens in vain for concern about disciplinary problems that trouble commanders in the United States - brutality, rudeness, corruption.[79]

Bayley went on to note that newspaper journalists, defense attorneys, and members of the general public confirm that police wrongdoing is rare. When it does occur, it is similar to the individual misbehavior characteristic of European police.

When police and policing are examined cross-culturally, there emerges some interesting data. Police everywhere do not escape civilian control or display high levels of misconduct. Why do police of other nations display these valued characteristics?

The reasons are several. Police in Europe and Japan work in societies that are more homogeneous. There is less ethnic, racial, and religious diversity. They also are under more direct and strict supervision. Police report more strictly and frequently to their superiors. And there exists a more vigorous tradition of civilian control. In many European countries, administrative positions are filled by persons who have no police training or background. Lawyers, judges, and even teachers supervise police in other countries.[80]

One factor, however, is of prime importance, especially insofar as the incidence of police corruption is concerned. Police in other nations are less involved in the policing of public morality since there are fewer laws intended to control morality. *Opportunities* for police misconduct are therefore considerably less frequent.

In 1915, Raymond Fosdick isolated this reduced involvement as a major reason that European police were less corrupt than their American counterparts.[81] Bayley reached the same conclusion on the basis of his more recent research in Japan. Writing in 1976, he observed:

> Stepping back and looking at victimless crime as a whole, it is apparent that the Japanese have avoided many of the problems that strain law enforcement in the United States. The police have not been corrupted or demoralized by having to enforce laws against victimless crime.[82]

These observations suggest a second means for more effectively controlling police and policing: *American police must also become less involved in attempting to control public morality.* To reduce police misconduct, the illegitimate opportunities available to our police must be reduced or eliminated. The principal way to accomplish this is to decriminalize certain actions.

The number of laws which should be eliminated is quite large. At the very least, the following actions should be decriminalized: public drunkenness, use of soft drugs such as marijuana, gambling, prostitution, homosexuality, traffic in sexually explicit ("pornographic") materials, and heroin addiction.

The Decriminalization Logic.   It is very important to recognize that control of police misconduct is not the only or even the most important reason that these and perhaps other actions should be decriminalized. The decriminalization logic is richer and more complete.[83] The complete theory behind decriminalization is as follows:

1. Police can do little to control the social forces thought to give rise to these actions.
2. Laws making these actions illegal are for all practical purposes unenforceable.
3. Police attempts to enforce these laws often worsen the problem.
4. Continued criminalization of these actions invites continued police misconduct.
5. Alternatives to criminalization exist and they are more humane and possibly more effective.

This complete logic will now be illustrated by briefly examining two of these currently illegal actions: public drunkenness and heroin addiction.

Public drunkenness.   Alcohol addiction is a serious problem in our society. The best estimate is that there are between 6 and 12 million alcohol addicts nationwide.[84] Theories of the causes of alcoholism abound but no single theory has repeatedly or even regularly escaped empirical rejection. Social scientists are currently unable to state with any precision what causes alcohol addiction. They are also unable to state with any precision what might be done to prevent or control alcoholism. There is no widely accepted or successful treatment strategy.[85] In the absence of reliable causal or treatment information, police cannot prevent or control the unknown social forces which give rise to alcohol addiction.

The most that police can do is partially control the visibility of the least frequent type of alcohol addiction: chronic public drunkenness. Police respond to our complaints of unsightly public drunkenness offenders by telling them to move to less visible locations. If offenders can not or will not move, they are arrested.

In arresting chronic public drunkenness offenders, police contribute to a system which does more harm than good. Arrest is a degrading experience and it helps reinforce a chronic alcohol addict's negative sense of self.[86] Time spent in a drunk tank, court, and in jail also is demeaning and can hardly be said to promote cure. Indeed, those arrested and processed come out feeling they "owe themselves a drunk."[87]

Policing public drunkenness offenders is productive of police misconduct. Jails cannot hold all who could be arrested, and police arrests are influenced by factors such as demeanor, social class, and race.[88] Additionally, nearly all chronic public drunkenness offenders have not bathed recently and some are covered with filth. A minority are disrespectful in their interaction with police. Since deviance and defiance are the usual precipitants to police violence, policing public drunkenness offenders often leads to police brutality.[89]

Alternatives to the continued criminalization of public drunkenness exist.[90] Massachusetts has decriminalized public drunkenness and established medically supervised detoxification facilities for chronic alcohol addicts. In Boston, detoxification center personnel patrol the skid-row areas frequented by public inebriates. They offer publicly intoxicated citizens transport to the detoxification center. Citizens who accept their offer receive medical attention as they dry out for five days. For those who wish, follow-up and referral services are available. Because the Massachusetts system is voluntary, it is more humane. And it is at least as effective as the involuntary drying out associated with arrest.

In sum: by making public drunkenness illegal we give police responsibility for an action they can do little to prevent or control. Police attempts to enforce these laws damage the already fragile self-esteem of chronic alcohol addicts. Continued criminalization invites continued discrimination and excessive police force. Alternatives to criminalization exist and they are more humane and just as effective. For these reasons, it is suggested that public drunkenness be decriminalized.

Heroin addiction.   We know more about the incidence and origins of heroin addiction. Heroin addiction is much less frequent than alcohol addiction. Nationwide, there are approximately 500,000 heroin addicts.[91]

Novice users appear attracted to heroin by experimenting friends,[92] curiosity about the effects of a drug reputed to be so powerful it should not even be tried once,[93] and by the fact that its use is illegal. Continued use and eventual addiction appear to be the results of positive initial experiences with heroin and the frequently mistaken belief that increasing recreational use will not result in addiction. Police do not appear to be in a position to legally interrupt these processes.

There are three major harms associated with heroin addiction and all are a function of the fact that heroin addiction is illegal. The first is heroin-related criminality.[94] Few heroin addicts can support their habit from legitimate sources. Most addicts therefore engage in a wide variety of illegal "hustles" to secure money to buy heroin.

A second detriment is the frequently debilitating lifestyle of the heroin addict.[95] Unlike alcoholism, heroin addiction causes no permanent physiological damage. While addicted, however, heroin addicts run considerable risks. Deaths due to "overdose" are common. They occur because addicts obtain their heroin from illicit sources where cutting agents and strengths are unknown. Hepatitis is also common. We know, and addicts know, that it is not a good idea to us a hypodermic syringe that someone else has just used.[96] Heroin addicts, however, cannot obtain hypodermic syringes legally and simple possession of a syringe increases the likelihood of being arrested. Addicts therefore use other people's "works" and contract hepatitis.

The third deleterious effect is police misconduct. There are enormous profits associated with the importation, distribution, and sale of heroin. The persons involved in these activities protect their profits by corrupting our police.[97] For those officers who choose to avoid opportunities for corruption, attempts to enforce heroin laws provoke other forms of police misconduct.[98] Attempted enforcement is possible only if informants are cultivated and given a license for their own dealing or addiction and if extralegal means of securing evidence are employed. Even these frequently illegal methods generally affect the visibility but not the incidence of heroin addiction.

Addiction does not have to considered criminal.[99] Public policy in Great Britain emphasizes that heroin addiction is incurable. Physicians are permitted to prescribe heroin for registered addicts, and many users are employed while under the influence of their maintenance doses. Addicts do not resort to crime because heroin is inexpensive; they also do not die from overdose or become ill from hepatitis. There apparently is no large and profitable market for illicit drugs, police are not corrupted, and rates of heroin addiction are much lower than in the United States. The controlled-substance approach to heroin is more humane and effective.

In sum: by making heroin addiction illegal we cause heroin-related crime, expose addicts to avoidable illnesses and deaths, and provide opportunities for police misconduct. It is suggested that heroin addiction be decriminalized. Heroin should be a controlled substance as is currently the case in Great Britain.

As illustrated by our brief examination of public drunkenness and heroin laws, there are sound reasons for advocating decriminalization of most, if not all, crimes with willing victims. These reasons range from police inability to control the social forces which give rise to these actions, to the availability of more humane and possibly more effective alternatives. This logic compels decriminalization and elimination of these laws and promises to reduce the incidence and seriousness of police misconduct. The issue thus shifts from the logic of decriminalization to the probability of eliminating such laws.

The Prospects for Decriminalization.   The chances for decriminalization, like those for honesty, are slim. Many citizens and quite a number of police support state attempts to control crimes with willing victims. They view these actions as sins and believe in state punishment of the sinful.[100] Their position is strongly and emotionally held and they are not swayed by logic. They oppose decriminalization and support the traditional view of these actions. Examination of the criminal codes of all 50 states reveals that their beliefs are our laws. There is little reason to believe that their resistance to decriminalization will be quickly overcome.

Additionally, the inability of police to prevent or control these actions and the harmful consequences of their attempts have long been recognized. Police have long arrested chronic public drunkenness offenders; our courts and jails are literally full of chronic inebriates.[101] Police-based prevention and control strategies have been given every effort to succeed. Chronic offenders recidivate despite police efforts, and many do life sentences on the installment plan.[102] The same is true of heroin addiction. There is no known cure and certainly no police-based or initiated cure.[103]

The fact that laws intended to control public morality invite police misconduct also has long been acknowledged. Laws in New York City in the 1880s required that saloons be closed on Sundays.[104] Many citizens wanted to drink and socialize in saloons on Sundays, and because there was money to make, saloonkeepers were more than willing to accommodate. Their solution was as simple then as it is now: they paid police for the privilege of violating the law.

Lastly, alternatives to criminalization have been long available. As early as 1926, physicians in Great Britian were dispensing heroin to registered addicts. For over 50 years that system has proven more humane and effective than our own.[105]

The outlook for decriminalization is pessimistic. All of the arguments supportive of decriminalization have long been available. These actions continue to be illegal and there is no reliable indicator of impending decriminalization. Consequently, there is no sign that opportunities for police misconduct will be reduced.

Top-Level Administrators Committed to Change

There exists considerable consensus that one of the most important determinants of the quality of the policing characteristic of a community is the person who occupies the top-level administrative position. Representative of this consensus is Lawrence W. Sherman's argument that the "primary condition for doing anything about police ... [misconduct] ... is that the top police administration view it as ... [a] ... number one priority.[106]

There is reason to believe that Sherman's representative argument is correct but incomplete. August Vollmer was committed to change in Los Angeles and he failed miserably. Orlando Wilson tried to reform the police in Chicago and failed too, although less miserably. Richard Hongisto, whom we will discuss later in the chapter, attempted the same thing in Cleveland and was unsuccessful. Appointment of top-level administrators committed to change clearly is necessary if police misconduct is to be reduced. It is not, however, sufficient.

The Importance of Political Support.   What Vollmer, Wilson, and Hongisto had in common was a failure to receive support from the political structures of their respective communities. In each case they were brought in to give an appearance of change and then were essentially abandoned. They did their best to improving police and policing. The municipal officials who attracted and appointed them did not.

The experiences of Vollmer, Wilson, and Hongisto suggest expansion of Sherman's argument. Specifically, *the primary condition for doing anything about police misconduct is that the top-level administrator's attempts at change receive the support of municipal officials.* The data supportive of this expanded argument are not extensive but they are sufficiently provocative to make illustration worthwhile. Consider four brief examples.

"Westville."   Jerome Skolnick's fine book, *Justice Without Trial,* was first published in 1966.[107] In it, Skolnick reported the results of his study of the "Westville" police department, commonly thought to be Oakland, California.[108] The single most pressing problem confronting the Westville department was its relations with black citizens. Police-black relations were mutually suspicious, and violent clashes were frequent.

Some ten years later Skolnick returned to Westville in the context of updating the second edition of *Justice Without Trial.*[109] He found that a new top-level administrator, "Chief James," had been appointed. Chief James was dedicated to improving the department, including its relations with black citizens, and the steps he took were several.

James dealt with the subcultural solidarity characteristic of the patrol division by giving Internal Affairs investigators more power. Patrol officers were told they had to cooperate with Internal Affairs and that if they lied or were less than truthful, they would be fired. In six years, 38 officers were fired for their failure to fully cooperate with Internal Affairs, and others resigned.

Chief James also dealt with the racism within the department. Westville police frequently used racial slurs and advanced negative stereotypes of minority citizens in their conversation with one another. When unchallenged, such verbalizations contribute to an appearance of a prejudicial consensus among officers and encourage discriminatory policing. One way of reducing this seeming consensus is to forbid racial slurs. That is precisely what Chief James did:

> ... [i]t was strictly forbidden that any police ... at any time, under any circumstances, including the telling of a joke, employ the word "nigger" while in uniform or in the confines of the police department. Penalties on the order of five, ten, and fifteen day suspensions were in fact imposed for this sort of violation.[110]

James also was troubled by police shootings of fleeing felons. For instance, patrol officers responding to a burglary in progress call would see an alleged violator, give chase, and then fire, wounding or killing the person. Although entirely legal, Chief James was disturbed by the fact that people were being shot and sometimes killed for offenses otherwise punishable by only a few years in prison. James' response was to order Westville police to shoot only "in defense of life." Police were no longer permitted to shoot fleeing felons.

The results of Chief James' efforts were positive. Police–black relations improved significantly and there was a decline in police shootings. The extent of improvement is best suggested by the retirement dinner held for James in the fall of 1973. Skolnick describes part of what happened:

> [It was] attended by more than 800 persons representing every segment of the community. Accolades were the most fulsome from representatives of minority groups and perfunctorily polite from the police association representative, who at least made an appearance, however faint his praise of the outgoing chief.[11]

We find strong evidence in Westville that a single upper-level administrator can make a considerable difference. It is crucial to recognize that Chief James did these things without the support of patrol officers or other higher police administrators. In the context of the rule prohibiting the shooting of fleeing felons, Chief James relates that he "wasn't getting any counsel or support from any of my subordinates, none of them. I was alone with the damn thing and had been with everything else and I was for years after that."[112] However, *Chief James did receive the support of the political structure of the community.* In Westville, it was the city manager who provided that support and without it, "I could never have made it.... he backed me all the way all the time."[113]

Birmingham.   During the civil rights movement of the early 1960s, Birmingham, Alabama, was the "Johannesburg of America."[14] Under the
racist and brutal leadership of Bull Connor, Birmingham police used
clubs, dogs, and fire hoses on Dr. Martin Luther King, Jr., and the hundreds of others who had the temerity to protest the racism in the United
States by demonstrating in Birmingham.

By 1977, however, the Birmingham Police Department had been
dramatically changed:

> At one national workshop ... a[n] official said, "The Birmingham Police
> Department has moved faster and further than any police department in the
> nation." An academic ... declared, "The Birmingham Police Department has
> been transformed into one of the most open, progressive and approachable
> police forces in the nation."[115]

Most of the credit for these changes goes to an administrator who was
devoted to reforming the department in Birmingham: Chief James Parsons.

Parsons began as a patrol officer in Birmingham in 1954 and worked his
way to the chief's position in 1972.[116] In changing the Birmingham department, Parsons used many of the same techniques employed by Chief
James in Westville. Parsons also received the support of the political
community in his successful efforts to change the image and practice of
policing in Birmingham.

Parsons discouraged the use of racial slurs and sanctioned officers for
doing so in public situations. He instituted new weapons regulations and
established a vigorous Internal Affairs Unit. He also acted against corruption by dismissing 14 officers for involvement in or knowledge of a police
burglary ring. In this latter situation, officers were also fired for refusing
to take polygraph tests. Parsons did these things without the support of
most patrol officers and many administrators. However, he consistently
received the support of the Birmingham political community.

"Laconia."   The efforts of the new chief of the "Laconia" Police Department studied by William K. Muir appear to have had effects similar to
those reported in Westville and Birmingham.[117] A new chief changed the
department from a hard-nosed, watch-style organization with a reputation for racism and violence, to a service-oriented department with an
image of civility and restraint. The new chief accomplished these positive
changes even though many patrol officers loathed and resented their new
chief. But the chief received support from Laconia's political community:

> There was an almost total absence of illegitimate political influence applied
> to the department. Elected politicians in Laconia accepted the widely under-

stood taboo against seeking favors and interfering in the administration of the department. No Laconia police ... I met ever suggested that someone other than ... uniformed superiors would affect ... promotion or duties.... The police chief, the city manager, and the civil service director ... agreed on "merit" as the sole basis for employment and promotion; each insisted that no citizen should get covert special favors.[118]

Cleveland.   The experiences of Richard Hongisto in Cleveland suggest that in order for reformers to be effective, they must have the support of the political community.[119] Hongisto began his police career as a patrol officer in San Francisco in 1960, and then moved to the Sheriff's Department of San Francisco County. In 1970, he ran for county sheriff and was elected by putting together a coalition of "liberals, radicals, minorities, homosexuals, and the young."[120] During six controversial years, he created significant change in San Francisco County, once refusing to serve eviction papers on low-income residents. He served five days in jail for his refusal.

In December of 1977, Hongisto was appointed Police Chief in Cleveland by Mayor Dennis Kucinich. Chief Hongisto immediately undertook some of the same activities that had won him support in San Francisco County, ..."roaming the streets in his squad car ... stopping to visit precinct houses and occasionally collaring suspects himself." He also sought to free Cleveland police from political control. He quickly learned that Cleveland is not San Francisco. In February of 1978, Mayor Kucinich dismissed Chief Hongisto, sparking a recall vote for Mayor Kucinich and earning Hongisto a temporary new job: Commissioner of New York State's Correctional Services. Much like August Vollmer in Los Angeles and Orlando Wilson in Chicago, Richard Hongisto failed in Cleveland because he did not receive support from the political leaders.[121]

Although these data are limited, they do suggest an important tool for the control of police and policing. They indicate that top administrators devoted to change can improve police departments, even in the face of strong opposition by patrol officers and other administrators. This is possible, however, only when the political structure of a community is supportive of the administrator's efforts or at least willing to give an administrator a free hand, as in Laconia.

The major implication of these limited data is that the political leaders of a community also must see reform of police and policing as being in their best interests. And although this topic alone could fill an entire book, one point requires brief mention.

The Prospects for the Appointment of Change-Oriented Administrations.

There are several reasons that the privatized political structure of a community remains unconcerned about change in its watch-style department. One important reason is that political leaders also profit from the same illegal services which corrupt police.[122] If the actions mentioned earlier are decriminalized, political leaders have less of a vested interest in maintaining existing patterns of policing. Change becomes possible because there are fewer reasons for preventing it. If no decriminalization takes place, political leaders prefer to keep things the way they are, for their own benefit. It again is clear that decriminalization of laws intended to control public morality is fundamental to effective control of police and policing.

This leads to a depressing but inescapable conclusion. The chances for the decriminalization of actions which corrupt both municipal authorities and police, as well as those for the widespread appointment of top level administrators committed to change, are very slight.

Citizen Monitoring Organizations

Thus far, three mechanisms for controlling police and policing have been suggested: honest description of the capacities of contemporary police and policing, decriminalization of crimes with willing victims, and appointment of top-level administrators dedicated to reform. A final task remains: provision of a mechanism for insuring effective external democratic control over police and policing. This job is critical since without effective monitoring and control, the possibility of organizational abuse of commonweal privileges continues to exist. The mechanism to be suggested is the Citizen Monitoring Organization (CMO).

It is necessary to begin our discussion of Citizen Monitoring Organizations by noting that there is considerable opposition to the concept of civilian control. Police officers and their superiors have long and successfully resisted civilian control.[123] Their essential argument has been that civilians do not possess the knowledge or motivation to fairly review, evaluate, or sanction police actions. If systematic discussion of police misconduct is one red herring, then the Civilian Review Board, even when renamed a Citizen Monitoring Organization, is surely a second.

Additionally, there are academics who are generally opposed to the idea of Citizen Monitoring Organizations. Radical criminologists at the University of California, Berkeley, argue that civilian review only serves to give the *appearance* of external control. Civilian review also is said to result in superficial change. In their words, Civilian Review Boards:

> have not been able to significantly alter police practices; and it's clear that, even if such boards did have the power to enforce changes in police performance or regulations, they could only soften, but not really challenge, the fundamentally *oppressive* function of the police in U.S. society.[124]

Why trouble most police and some academics by raising the issue of citizen control over police and policing? There are at least two reasons.

First, in a society which is ostensibly democratic, there is no alternative to civilian control. As has repeatedly been argued, police departments are commonweal organizations. Citizens have both the right and obligation to control their police. Police officers and organizations in a democratic society have neither the right or prerogative to object to civilian control. When they do object, their objections are without foundation.

Consider a brief analogy. Public schools also have something of a commonweal mandate. Public schools are obligated to serve a precious collective resource, our young people. Because children are so important and because public schools do have commonweal obligations, civilians routinely penetrate and control our schools, to the occasional dismay of educators. Parent–Teacher Organizations (PTOs) and Associations (PTAs), School Boards, Boards of Trustees, and a host of local, state, and federal governmental committees consisting of both elected and appointed officials occupy their time with our educational system. Attempts by professional educators to exclude civilians are rejected as being without foundation. Imagine the public's response to a local school principal who announced that the PTO was to be disbanded, the School Board ignored, and parents barred from the school so that professional educators could get on with the task of educating. It would not be allowed to happen.

There is no good reason that it should be condoned with police organizations. In a democratic society, police departments are similar to schools in that both have commonweal obligations. If we will not allow our schools to escape civilian control, there is no reason that our police should be allowed to do so. Attempts by police to exclude citizens should be rejected.

Second, police misconduct frequently has largely organizational origins. Misbehavior is organizational in origin when internal norms support it, socialization practices perpetuate it, and administrators tolerate it. These conditions have been met in a variety of cities including New York, Philadelphia, Chicago, Houston, and Seattle. In these cities citizens are policed by deviant departments.

Individuals are not in a position to control organizations generally or deviant departments specifically.[125] Individuals do not have the resources, persistence, or power to control organizational deviance. Organizations are thus able to resist attempts at control by individuals.

In contemporary society, only organizations have the resources, persistence, and power to control other organizations. Organizational deviance requires organizational control. Deviant police organizations therefore require organizational control.[126] CMOs represent a countervailing organizational response to deviant departments.

There are two reasons for raising the issue of civilian control. CMOs are logical, given the commonweal mandate of police departments, and necessary, given the frequently organizational nature of police misconduct. This issue thus shifts from whether there should be CMOs to their composition and power, and to the prospects for their creation.

The Composition of CMOs.   Examination of the available evidence suggests that CMOs should be *local, representative* of the community served by the department, and *permanent.* Citizen Monitoring Organizations must be local since police misconduct varies depending upon the area. In certain departments organizational norms emphasize the differential treatment of Native Americans, while the norms of other departments stress discrimination against black citizens.[127] Local CMOs are inevitably more responsive to the problems of particular departments than state or federal organizations.

CMOs also must be representative of the entire community served by a local police department. In the past, similar organizations were dominated by powerful community members who were ferquently least critical of police misbehavior.[128] This was because these persons were least likely to be the victims of police misconduct. CMOs must include clear and forceful representation of all segments of the community.

CMOs also must be permanent, even in the face of police opposition. In the past, civilian control groups have emerged in the face of particular episodes of misconduct and then disbanded when the appearance of a problem has been eliminated or when police forced their dismissal.[129] The long-run effects were minimal since impropriety varied with the periodicity of citizen involvement. Permanent organizations insure constant monitoring and control. Permanence also would discourage repeated attempts by police to eliminate Citizen Monitoring Organizations.

The Power of CMOs.   Citizen control groups have been formed and then disbanded by police in many cities, including New York, Philadelphia, and Los Angeles.[130] They generally have been eliminated because they lacked the resources and power to oppose police efforts to destroy them. In the words of the radical criminologists opposed to CMOs:

> These boards ... [have not had] ... significant legal, investigative, or sanctioning powers, so that whether they focus on general departmental procedures or action against individual officers, they ... [have not had a] ... way of enforcing their recommendation.[131]

To be effective, then, the power of future CMOs must be increased.

The lifeblood of all public agencies, including police organizations, is municipal funding. Although local police organizations can and do receive state and federal funding,[132] it is generally for new and frequently exotic equipment. Day-to-day operation is dependent upon local money.

One way of insuring effective CMOs is to give them budgetary control over local police departments. In the past, similar groups have relied on publicity and good will as the primary control mechanisms. These tools have not been effective. Budgetary control, similar to that exercised by a local school board, places a meaningful control mechanism in the hands of civilians.

Another method of increasing the power of CMOs is to provide them with an independent investigative staff, one with subpoena power. Police departments clearly have large numbers of investigative personnel. It is only logical that CMOs charged with controlling police and policing have similar investigative resources.

A final method of increasing the power of local CMOs is to give them hiring, tenure, and promotion responsibilities. Currently, these are internal decisions and they reflect the operation of organizational norms, including those supportive of police misconduct. CMOs should review and be responsible for providing final decisions on hiring, incumbency, and promotion for all officers, including the top-level administrator. External review by CMOs would help insure that these decisions do not reflect adherence to organizational norms supportive of misconduct as a condition for being hired, tenured, or promoted.

In sum: the reasons for insisting upon CMOs are the commonweal mandate of police organizations and the need for an organizational countervailing force. It also has been suggested that CMOs be local, representative, and permanent and that they be given budgetary and investigative along with hiring, tenure, and promotion responsibilities. It is believed that CMOs with these characteristics can help control police and policing. The final issue is whether CMOs will actually emerge.

The Prospects for CMOs. The likelihood that citizen control will be established is small. As was noted in our discussion of the origins of organized police, the power to bring about change in organically solidary societies is not uniformly distributed across all class levels.[133] Instead, power is concentrated in the hands of a relatively small number of elites. When necessary, elites use their power to protect and promote their vested interests.

It does not appear that CMOs would function to favor elite interests. Elites and their interests are generally not harmed by discriminatory arrest practices or by acts of excessive police force. Additionally, elites frequently benefit from police corruption, especially that which concerns gambling and narcotics, because they are involved in providing these currently illegal services. Police misconduct either fails to touch elites or, in the case of certain forms of corruption, actually benefits elites. It does not appear likely, therefore, that CMOs will be formed in the future.

This prediction receives additional support when we recall that police officers and organizations are opposed to CMOs. Where they have existed in the past, as in Philadelphia, Newark, and New York, police lobbying has forced their elimination.[134] Lack of elite interest, when coupled with police opposition, makes the chances for the creation of CMOs highly remote.

CMOs, in sum, are both logical, given the commonweal mandate of police organizations, and necessary, given the organizational nature of police misconduct. Lack of elite interest and police opposition combine to suggest that the probability of strong and effective CMOs is low.

SUMMARY

We have failed to master our police. This is partially because police organizations pose unique monitoring and control problems. These problems range from the essentially unrestricted nature of police exercise of force to the simple but important fact that police are opposed to civilian mastery.

We also have failed to dominate our police because previous solutions have emphasized professionalism. Belief in the positive effects of professionalism has led to attempts to recruit college-educated personnel and to create bureaucratically efficient and autonomous organizations. Professionalism, however, is an unsatisfactory solution to the problem of controlling police and policing. It fails to overcome any of the monitoring and control problems posed by police organizations.

Regulation of police requires alternative solutions, ones which open police organizations to democratic control. The first of these is honesty. Police organizations are extremely limited in what they can accomplish. Honesty regarding the capacities of police and policing is an important first step in eliminating or reducing more serious forms of police misconduct.

The prospects for police honesty are slim. Police correctly fear that honesty will make it more difficult to secure increasingly scarce municipal resources. Little lies and the bigger lies they encourage will likely continue to be characteristic of police and policing.

Effective control of police and policing also requires elimination or reduction in external opportunities for police misconduct. This is admittedly a more difficult task, but it is crucial since it also is fundamental to the third control mechanism: appointment of top-level administrators committed to change.

The chances for the second and third control mechanisms are also slight. We have long recognized that laws intended to govern public morality are essentially unenforceable. We also have learned through bitter experience that the existence of such laws corrupt our police and the politicians who might otherwise appoint administrators dedicated to reform.

Citizen Monitoring Organizations are fundamental to democratic control of police and policing. CMOs represent a method of democratically mastering our police. They also are a countervailing organizational force to deviant departments. However, the probability of their creation is very low. Elites who have the power to create them are not interested and police are opposed to civilian control.

It appears likely that we will continue to fail to govern our police, although there are scattered signs of change. Some laws, such as those affecting marijuana use, private sexuality between consenting adults, and public drunkenness, are being modified. Reform-minded administrators are sometimes appointed and given support. Moreover, demographically heterogenous police recruits, less stressful training academies, and softer field training experience all promise to increase the number of patrol officers who bring compassion and civility to their work and our lives.

But we must not allow these indications of improvement to blind us to the fact that we have not mastered our police. Seattle police continue to make discriminatory arrest decisions, just as they did in the past.[135] Police in Chicago and Philadelphia are as corrupt now as they were previously.[136] And the brutally racist murders of citizens by Houston police[137] remind us that superfluous police brutality remains "far from rare."[138] Thousands of police in hundreds of cities bring discrimination, corruption, and violence to their work and our lives. We are obligated to continue to attempt to better understand and control our police.'

Notes

1. The commonweal characterization of police organization is from Peter M. Blau and W. Richard Scott, *Formal Organizations* (San Francisco: Chandler, 1962), pp. 45ff.

2. For a general discussion, see Frank J. Remington and Victor G. Rosenblum, "The Criminal Law and the Legislative Process," *Current Problems in Criminal Law* (Winter 1960): 481–499.

3. Syd Cooper, former New York City narcotics officer, asserts that police corruption involving narcotics "hasn't changed." "For Your Information: Drugs in America," Public Broadcasting Service, November 29, 1978. For a contrary position, see Lawrence W. Sherman, *Scandal and Reform: Controlling Police Corruption* (Berkeley, Calif.: University of California Press, 1978), p. xxix.

4. Jonathan Rubinstein, *City Police* (New York: Ballantine, 1973), pp. 341–434.

5. Herbert Beigel and Alan Beigel, *Beneath the Badge: A Story of Police Corruption* (New York: Harper & Row, 1977).

6. David Blum, "Houston's Illness," *The New Republic* (July 8 and 15, 1978): 12–14.

7. Paul A. Pastor, Jr., "Mobilization in Public Drunkenness Control: A Comparison of Legal and Medical Approaches," *Social Problems, 25* (April 1978): 373–384.

8. See Sherman, *Scandal and Reform.*

9. The choice of words, especially the use of the word "master," is from Egon Bittner, "Die

Polizie: Soziologische Studien und Forschungsberichte" (book review), *American Journal of Sociology, 79* (July 1973): 223.

10. For a discussion of this police privilege, see Egon Bittner, *The Functions of the Police in Modern Society* (Chevy Chase, Md.: National Institute of Mental Health, Center for Studies of Crime and Delinquency, 1970), pp. 36–47.

11. Bitner, *The Functions,* p. 37.

12. See, for example, David H. Bayley and Harold Mendelsohn, *Minorities and the Police* (New York: Free Press, 1969), pp. 129ff.

13. This example is based upon Sherman, *Scandal and Reform,* p. 154.

14. See, for example, Donald J. Black, *Police Encounters and Social Organization: An Observation Study* (unpublished Ph.D. dissertation, University of Michigan, 1968).

15. See, for example, Maureen Mileski, "Courtroom Encounters: An Observation Study of a Lower Criminal Court," *Law and Society Review, 5* (May 1971): 473–538.

16. Arthur Rosett and Donald R. Cressey, *Justice by Consent: Plea Bargains in the American Courthouse* (Philadelphia: Lippincott, 1976).

17. For a discussion of this general point, see Thomas Barker and Julian Roebuck, *An Empirical Typology of Police Corruption: A Study of Organizational Deviance* (Springfield, Ill.: Charles C. Thomas, 1973).

18. For a discussion of this general point, see Sherman, *Scandal and Reform;* Barker and Roebuck, *An Empirical Typology;* and M. David Ermann and Richard J. Lundman, *Organizational Deviance* (New York: Holt, Rinehart and Winston, 1981, forthcoming).

19. Sherman, *Scandal and Reform.*

20. Ellwyn R. Stoddard, "The Informal 'Code' of Police Deviancy: A Group Approach to 'Blue Coat Crime'," *Journal of Criminal Law, Criminology and Police Science, 59* (1968): 201–213.

21. Rubinstein, *City Police,* pp. 341–342.

22. Mike Royko, *Boss: Richard J. Daley of Chicago* (New York: Signet, 1971), passim.

23. William J. Chambliss, "Vice, Corruption, Bureaucracy, and Power," in William J. Chambliss and Milton Mankoff (eds.), *Whose Law, What Order?* (New York: Wiley, 1976), pp. 173ff.

24. State of Pennsylvania, *Report on Police Corruption and the Quality of Law Enforcement in Philadelphia* (Saint Davids, Pa.: Pennsylvania Crime Commission, 1974).

25. Beigel and Beigel, *Beneath the Badge.*

26. Chambliss, "Vice."

27. Sherman, *Scandal and Reform,* p. xxxviii and passim.

28. Cooper, "Drugs in America." Also see Sherman, *Scandal and Reform,* p. xxix and passim.

29. Blum, "Houston's Illness," p. 12.

30. Robert Fogelson, *Big-City Police* (Cambridge, Mass.: Harvard University Press, 1977), pp. 285–286.

31. William A. Westley, "Secrecy and the Police," *Social Forces, 34* (1956): 254–257.

32. See Richard Harris, *The Police Academy: An Inside View* (New York: Wiley, 1974), p. 78.

33. Fogelson, *Big-City Police,* pp. 1–12.

34. Cited in Albert J. Reiss, Jr., "Police Brutality—Answers to Key Questions," in Arthur Niederhoffer and Abraham S. Blumberg (eds.), *The Ambivalent Force* (Hinsdale, Ill.: The Dryden Press, 1976), p. 333.

35. Rubinstein, *City Police,* pp. 403ff.

36. Stoddard, "The Informal 'Code'," p. 201.

37. See O. W. Wilson and Roy Clinton McLaren, *Police Administration,* 3d ed. (New York: McGraw-Hill, 1972), passim.

38. Vollmer and Wilson are the best-known of the police professionalism advocates. See Herman Goldstein, *Policing a Free Society* (Cambridge, Mass.: Ballinger, 1977), p. 2.

39. The material on Vollmer is from Gene E. Carte and Elaine H. Carte, *Police Reform in the United States: The Era of August Vollmer, 1905–1932* (Berkeley, Calif.: University of California Press, 1975).

40. Carte and Carte, *Police Reform*, p. 84.

41. The biographical material on Wilson is from "Wilson, Orlando Winfield," *Who's Who in America: Volume 36, 1970–1971* (Chicago: Marquis Who's Who Incorporated, 1970–1971), p. 2474; and Charles Moritz (ed.), "Wilson, O.W.," *Current Biography, 1966 Yearbook* (Bronx, N. Y.: H. W. Wilson, 1966), pp. 452–454.

42. Wilson and McLaren, *Police Administration*, p. 310.

43. Wilson and McLaren, *Police Administration*, p. 24.

44. Goldstein, *Policing*, pp. 228–229.

45. I am grateful to Kenneth W. Eckhardt for emphasizing this point.

46. There is no list of departments that *require* a college degree for entrance. I am aware of three: Burnsville, Minnesota; Lakewood, Colorado; and Multnomah (County), Oregon. I am certain there are others, but not many.

47. See Goldstein, *Policing*, pp. 225–256.

48. See Beigel and Beigel, *Beneath the Badge*, pp. 149–162.

49. William A. Westley, *Violence and the Police: A Sociological Study of Law, Custom, and Morality* (Cambridge, Mass.: The M.I.T. Press, 1970), pp. xv–xvi.

50. Carte and Carte, *Police Reform*.

51. George Kirkham, *Signal Zero* (New York: Ballantine, 1976).

52. George Kirkham, "From Professor to Patrolman: A Fresh Perspective on the Police," *Journal of Police Science and Administration, 2* (1974): 136.

53. Cited in Mike Royko, *Boss: Richard J. Daley of Chicago* (New York: Signet, 1971), p. 113.

54. See Royko, *Boss*, pp. 116–123; Moritz, "Wilson," p. 453; and Beigel and Beigel, *Beneath the Badge*, p. 10.

55. Moritz, "Wilson," p. 453.

56. Beigel and Beigel, *Beneath the Badge*, p. 6.

57. Moritz, "Wilson."

58. Beigel and Beigel, *Beneath the Badge*, pp. 6, 19, 29–30, 130–132, 149–151, 251; and Sherman, *Scandal and Reform*, pp. 253–255.

59. Beigel and Beigel, *Beneath the Badge*, p. 29 and p. 131.

60. Fogelson, *Big-City Police*, pp. 285–286.

61. Fogelson, *Big-City Police*, p. 286.

62. Sherman, *Scandal and Reform*, p. 154.

63. Fogelson, *Big-City Police*, p. 284. In 1975, the Columbus, Ohio, Division of Police validated four of the 93 complaints of "undue force" received.

64. See John Webster, *The Realities of Police Work* (Dubuque, Iowa: William C. Brown, 1973).

65. George Kelling, Tony Pate, Duane Dieckman, and Charles E. Brown, *The Kansas City Preventive Patrol Experiment—A Summary Report* (Washington, D. C.: Police Foundation, 1974).

66. Peter W. Greenwood, Jan M. Chaken, Joan Petersilia, and Linda Prusoff, *The Criminal Investigation Process, Rand Corporation* (Washington, D. C.: U.S. Department of Justice, 1975). Also see William B. Sanders, *Detective Work: A Study of Criminal Investigations* (New York: Free Press, 1977). For a study of federal investigators, see James Q. Wilson, *The Investigators: Managing FBI and Narcotics Agents* (New York: Basic Books, 1978). For a fictionalized account of detective work, see Joseph Wambaugh, *The Black Marble* (New York: Dell, 1979).

67. *Crime in the United States, 1977.* (Washington, D. C.: U. S. Government Printing Office, 1978), p. 161.

68. Peter K. Manning, "Police Lying," *Urban Life and Culture, 3* (October 1974): 301.

69. Letter from Peter K. Manning, November 9, 1976.

70. Goldstein, *Policing,* p. 9.

71. Goldstein, *Policing,* p. 9; Peter K. Manning, *Police Work* (Cambridge, Mass.: The M.I.T. Press, 1977), p. 116; and Kelling et al., *Kansas City.*

72. See John Van Maanen, "Kinsmen in Response: Occupational Perspectives of Patrolmen," in Peter K. Manning and John Van Maanen, *Policing: A View From The Street* (Santa Monica, Calif.: Goodyear, 1978), p. 118.

73. Manning, *Police Work,* p. 300.

74. Steven Keeney, "Research Becomes a New Battleground for Police," *Police Magazine* (Prototype Issue, Summer 1977): 54. Prototype published by Correctional Information Service Inc., 801 Second Avenue, New York, N. Y. 10017.

75. Keeney, "Research," p. 54.

76. Raymond P. Fosdick, "The Integrity of the European Police in 1914," in Lawrence W. Sherman (ed.), *Police Corruption: A Sociological Perspective* (Garden City, N.Y: Doubleday Anchor Books, 1974), p. 63.

77. Lawrence W. Sherman (ed.), *Police Corruption: A Sociological Perspective* (Garden City, N.Y.: Doubleday Anchor Books, 1974), p. 7.

78. David H. Bayley, *Forces of Order: Police Behavior in Japan and the United States* (Berkeley, Calif.: University of California Press, 1976).

79. Bayley, *Forces of Order,* p. 1.

80. Rodney Stark, *Police Riots* (Belmont, Calif.: Wadsworth, 1972), p. 227.

81. Fosdick, "The Integrity of the European Police," p. 67.

82. Bayley, *Forces of Order,* p. 131.

83. For a similar argument, see Jeffrey H. Reiman, *The Rich Get Richer and the Poor Get Prison: Ideology, Class, and Criminal Justice* (New York: Wiley, 1979), pp. 196–198.

84. Earl Rubington, *Alcohol Problems and Social Control* (Columbus, Ohio: Merrill, 1973), p. 11.

85. Edward W. Saden. "The Need for a Realistic Treatment of Alcohol and Drug Addiction," *Federal Probation, 37* (March 1973): 40.

86. James Spradley, *You Owe Yourself a Drunk* (Boston: Little, Brown, 1970). passim.

87. Spradley, *You Owe Yourself a Drunk.*

88. See Richard J. Lundman, "Routine Police Arrest Practices: A Commonweal Perspective," *Social Problems, 22* (October 1974): 127–141; and Pastor, "Mobilization in Public Drunkenness Control."

89. Reiss, "Police Brutality," p. 336.

90. Pastor, "Mobilization in Public Drunkenness Control."

91. Dan Waldorf, *Careers in Dope* (Englewood Cliffs, N. J.: Prentice-Hall, 1973).

92. Waldorf, *Careers in Dope,* pp. 31ff.

93. David E. Smith and George R. Gay (eds.), *"It's So Good, Don't Even Try It Once": Heroin in Perspective* (Englewood Cliffs, N. J.: Prentice-Hall, 1972).

94. See Leroy Gould, Andrew L. Walker, Lansing E. Crane, and Charles W. Lidz, *Connections: Notes from the Heroin World* (New Haven, Conn.: Yale University Press, 1974), pp. 47ff.

95. See Richard R. Lingman, *Drugs From A To Z,* revised and updated 2d ed. (New York: McGraw-Hill, 1974), pp. 101–112.

96. Jan Howard and Philip Borges, "Needle Sharing in the Haight: Some Social and Psychological Functions," in Smith and Gay, *It's So Good,* p. 126.

97. See William Knapp, *The Knapp Report on Police Corruption in New York* (New York: Brazillier, 1972).

98. See Gould et al., *Connections,* pp. 52ff.

99. John Barbara and June Morrison, "If Addiction is Incurable, Why Do We Try to Cure It?: A Comparison of Control Methods in the U. K. and the U. S.," *Crime and Delinquency,*

20 (January 1975): 28–33; Alfred R. Lindesmith, *The Addict and the Law* (New York: Vintage, 1967), pp. 162–179.

100. For a sociological discussion of sin, see Stanford M. Lyman, *The Seven Deadly Sins: Society and Evil* (New York: St. Martin's, Inc., 1978).

101. Spradley, *You Owe Yourself a Drunk;* Lundman, "Routine Police Arrest Practices" and Pastor, "Mobilization in Public Drunkenness."

102. Spradley, *You Owe Yourself a Drunk,* p. 11.

103. Barbara and Morrison, "If Addiction is Incurable," p. 33; and Soden, "The Need for a Realistic," p. 40.

104. James F. Richardson, "Corruption in the New York Police, 1870–1900," in Sherman (ed.), *Police Corruption,* p. 53.

105. Barbara and Morrison, "If Addiction is Incurable"; and Lindesmith, *The Addict and the Law.*

106. Sherman, *Police Corruption,* p. 275.

107. Jerome Skolnick, *Justice Without Trial* (New York: Wiley, 1966).

108. See Peter K. Manning, "The Researcher: An Alien in the Police World," in Arthur Niederhoffer and Abraham S. Blumberg (eds.), *The Ambivalent Force: Perspectives on the Police* (Hinsdale, Ill.: The Dryden Press, 1976), p. 105.

109. Jerome Skolnick, *Justice Without Trial,* 2d ed. (New York: Wiley, 1975). All of the material which follows is from pp. 246–273 of the *second* edition.

110. Skolnick, *Justice Without Trial,* p. 257.

111. Skolnick, *Justice Without Trial, p. 271.*

112. Skolnick, *Justice Without Trial,* p. 260.

113. Skolnick, *Justice Without Trial,* p. 261.

114. The material on Birmingham is from Steve Gettinger, "Profile: Birmingham Police," *Police Magazine* (Prototype Issue, Summer 1977): 27–44.

115. Gettinger, "Profile: Birmingham," p. 28.

116. Gettinger, "Profile: Birmingham," p. 28.

117. See William K. Muir, *Police: Streetcorner Politicians* (Chicago: University of Chicago Press, 1977).

118. Muir, *Police,* p. 7. It should be noted that when one compares Skolnick's description of "Westville" with Muir's description of "Laconia," there exists a close resemblance. Sherman, who studied and *identified* Oakland, provides a description which is similar to those of Skolnick and Muir. It is possible, therefore, that Westville and Laconia are both Oakland. Skolnick, however, has asserted that most identifications of Westville, presumably including Manning's labeling of it as Oakland, are incorrect. If Westville and Laconia are in fact Oakland, then we need to be even more cautious in our assessment of the evidence suporting the assertion under examination. For the sources for all of this, see Skolnick, *Justice Without Trial,* pp. 23–25; Muir, *Police,* pp. 1–7; Sherman, *Scandal and Reform,* pp. xxx–xxxiv; Manning, "The Researcher," p. 105; Skolnick, *Justice Without Trial,* 2d ed., p. 251.

119. See E. J. Dionne, Jr., "Cleveland's Dismissed Police Chief Named Corrections Head by Carey," *The New York Times,* July 18, 1978, pp. A1 and B4; and Sheila Rule, "New State Prison Appointee: Richard Duane Hongisto," *The New York Times,* July 18, 1978, p. B4.

120. Rule, "New State Prison," p. B4.

121. "CBS Evening News," June 18, 1979.

122. For a discussion of this, see John A. Gardiner and David J. Olson (eds.), *Theft of the City: Readings on Corruption in Urban America* (Bloomington, Ind.: Indiana University Press, 1974).

123. Fogelson, *Big-City Police,* pp. 283–286.

124. Center for Research on Criminal Justice, *The Iron Fist and the Velvet Glove* (Berkeley, Calif.: Center for Research on Criminal Justice, 1975), p. 140.

125. James S. Coleman, *Power and the Structure of Society* (Philadelphia: University of Pennsylvania Press, 1974), p. 37.

126. Sherman, *Scandal and Reform,* p. 246.

127. Irving Piliavin and Scott Briar, "Police Encounters with Juveniles," *American Journal of Sociology, 70* (September 1964): 206–214; and Lundman, "Routine Police Arrest Practices."

128. Fogelson, *Big-City Police,* pp. 283–286.

129. For an example of this, see George Washnis, *Citizen Involvement in Crime Prevention* (Lexington, Mass.: Lexington Books, 1976).

130. Center for Research, *The Iron Fist,* pp. 139–140.

131. Center for Research, *The Iron Fist,* p. 140.

132. See Center for Research, *The Iron Fist,* pp. 83–86.

133. Richard Quinney, *Criminology: Analysis and Critique of Crime in America* (Boston: Little, Brown, 1975), pp. 37–41.

134. Fogelson, *Big-City Police,* pp. 283–286.

135. Compare Spradley, *You Owe Yourself a Drunk,* with Pastor, "Mobilization in Public Drunkenness Control."

136. Compare Royko, *Boss,* with Beigel and Beigel, *Beneath the Badge;* and compare Rubinstein, *City Police,* with Pennsylvania Crime Commission, *Report on Police Corruption and the Quality of Law Enforcement in Philadelphia* (Saint Davids, Pa.: Pennsylvania Crime Commission, 1974).

137. Blum, "Houston's Illness."

138. Reiss, "Police Brutality," p. 339.

Index

Communications, 61–62
Community, anomie in (*see* Anomie, community)
  and styles of policing, 45–51
Community relations division, 46, 47, 83
Connor, Bull, 194
Conservatism, as attribute of working personality, 73
  in decision making, 164–165
Constable, office of, 19
Control, of police and policing, 4–5, 9–10, 169–201
Convictions, illegally securing, 44
Coolidge, Calvin, 40
Corruption, police, 4, 9, 140, 142–157
  factors related to incidence and seriousness of, 148–157
    rationalizations and justifications for, 153, 155, 156
  and styles of policing, 46, 47–48, 49, 50
  types of, 143–148
  See also Control, of police and policing; Misconduct, police
Couzens, Michael, 65
Crime, absence of, during police strike, 41–42
  and "dangerous classes" (*see* "Dangerous classes")
  inability of police to control or prevent, 42, 182–186
  prevention of, 21, 22, 32
  rising levels of, 14, 22–23, 24–25, 31
  statistics, alteration of, 42–43
  as threat to civility, 22–23
  as threat to liberty, 25
  See also Clearance rates
Crime clock, 13
Criminal justice programs, 92–93
Crisis intervention, 49
Critchley, T. A., 18, 24
Cross-cultural studies, 186–187
Culture conflict, 151–152
Cumming, Elaine, 109
Cumming, Ian, 109
Cynicism, as attribute of working personality, 73
  of Field Training Officer, 87
  level of, in recruits, 77, 86

Daley, Richard J., 45, 151, 180
Dallas, Texas, blacks in police department of, 76

"Dangerous classes," 14, 28, 29–30, 44, 84, 137
Davis, Edward, 46, 185
Dead people, and routine policing, 82, 84, 103
Decision making, police, based on technical knowledge, 54
  conservative nature of, 164–165
  See also Discretion, police
Decriminalization, 186–191
Defensiveness, theme of, 55, 82, 83–84, 87, 88
Defounding, 64, 65, 66, 183
Denver, Colorado, opposition to civilian review board in, 173
  police corruption in, 148
  police salaries in, 58
  transitional policing in, 20
Depersonalization, theme of, 82, 83, 84–85, 87, 88–89
Des Moines, Iowa, police corruption in, 148
Detectives, 63–66, 183
Detroit, Michigan, opposition to civilian review board in, 173
Deviance (*see* Organizational deviance)
Discipline, 57–58
Discretion, police, 113, 114, 124–133, 132–133
  See also Decision making, police
Discrimination, and education, 93
  and hiring practices, 93
  and screening procedures, 56–57, 75, 77, 91–92
  See also Arrests, discriminatory; Racism
Dispatch room, 7, 59–60, 61
Division of labor, 51–52
Domestic disputes, 46, 47, 48–49, 88, 112
Droge, Edward F., Jr., 144
Due process protections, 43–44, 50, 59
Durkheim, Émile, 17, 150

East St. Louis, Illinois, police corruption in, 155
Edell, Laura, 109
Educational background of recruits, 7, 76, 92–93, 94
  and professionalism, 175, 176, 179, 181
Efficiency, 104
Elected officials, 50–51, 150–151
  See also Political support
Eligibility lists, 91

About the Author

Richard J. Lundman, Associate Professor of Sociology at The Ohio State University, received his B.A. from Beloit College (1966), M.A. from the University of Illinois (1968), and Ph.D. from the University of Minnesota (1972). Prior to his affiliation with Ohio State, he taught at the University of Delaware. His teaching and research interests include police and policing, deviance, criminology, and organizational deviance. He has presented papers at numerous national meetings, authored chapters for *The Police in Society, Police Roles in the Seventies: Volume II,* and *Critical Issues in Criminal Justice,* co-authored *Corporate and Governmental Deviance* (Oxford University Press, 1978) and *Organizational Deviance* (Holt, Rinehart and Winston, 1981), authored *Police Behavior* (Oxford University Press, 1980), and contributed articles to *Journal of Police Science and Administration, Criminology, Social Problems, Crime and Delinquency, The Sociological Quarterly, The Journal of Research in Crime and Delinquency, The Journal of Criminal Law and Criminology,* and *Law and Policy Quarterly.* He also has taught at the New Castle County, Delaware, Police Academy, and now teaches a section on unnecessary police force at the Columbus Police Academy.